Experience and Experimental Writing

EXPERIENCE AND EXPERIMENTAL WRITING

Literary Pragmatism from Emerson to the Jameses

Paul Grimstad

OXFORD
UNIVERSITY PRESS

UNIVERSITY PRESS

Oxford University Press is a department of the University of Oxford.
It furthers the University's objective of excellence in research, scholarship,
and education by publishing worldwide.

Oxford   New York
Auckland   Cape Town   Dar es Salaam   Hong Kong   Karachi
Kuala Lumpur   Madrid   Melbourne   Mexico City   Nairobi
New Delhi   Shanghai   Taipei   Toronto

With offices in
Argentina   Austria   Brazil   Chile   Czech Republic   France   Greece
Guatemala   Hungary   Italy   Japan   Poland   Portugal   Singapore
South Korea   Switzerland   Thailand   Turkey   Ukraine   Vietnam

Published in the United States of America by
Oxford University Press
198 Madison Avenue, New York, NY 10016

Library of Congress Cataloging-in-Publication Data
Grimstad, Paul
Experience and experimental writing : literary pragmatism from
Emerson to the Jameses / Paul Grimstad.
pages cm
Includes bibliographical references and index.
ISBN 978-0-19-987407-1 (acid-free paper)   1. American literature—History and criticism.
2. Pragmatism in literature.   3. Literature, Experimental—United States—History and criticism.
4. Experience in literature.   5. Literary form.   I. Title.
PS169.P68G75 2013
810.9'384—dc23
2012047344

9 8 7 6 5 4 3 2 1
Printed in the United States of America
on acid-free paper

CONTENTS

This book is dedicated to the memory of my father, Paul Hayden Grimstad.

ACKNOWLEDGMENTS

I have benefitted in many ways from the guidance, generosity and friendship of Ross Posnock who got me reading Emerson and the Jameses. Ross's books and seminars were the perfect stimulus for a graduate student wanting to fuse philosophically informed close reading with intellectual history. Emily Apter and Richard Sieburth made a refugee from the English Department feel at home in French and Comp Lit. It gladdens me to find that hospitality, which has fundamentally shaped my understanding of American literature, continuing into the present. David Bromwich and Paul Fry have been, in different ways, uniquely generous and stimulating colleagues at Yale. I thank both of them for their intellectual companionship, encouragement, and for the great conversation. For companionship intellectual and otherwise I also wish to thank: Branka Arsić, Howard Bloch, Harold Bloom, Eduardo Cadava, Stanley Cavell, Rob Chodat, Tom Cohen, Thomas Constantinesco, Ian Cornelius, William Day, Richard Deming, Richard Eldridge, Mark Ford, Mason Golden, Dave Gorin, Martin Hägglund, Lanny Hammer, Jim Hepokoski, Amy Hungerford, Oren Izenberg, Brian Kane, Tony Kronman, David Lapoujade, Jane Levin, Pericles Lewis, J.D. McClatchy, Maria Rosa Menocal, Walter Benn Michaels, Paul North, Siobhan Phillips, Robert Pippin, David Possen, Jessica Pressman, Anthony Reed, Bernie Rhei, Joan Richardson, Lisi Schoenbach, Adi Shamir, Nigel Smith, Steven Smith, Norma Thompson, Gary Tomlinson, Alan Trachtenberg, Joseph Urbas, John Williams, Ken Winkler and Christopher Wood. A late stage reading of the Introduction by Michael Fried was totally clarifying, and I thank him for that.

My editor at Oxford, Brendan O'Neill, has been a voice of reason at every step, from readers' reports to jacket design. I feel lucky to have been able to work with him. Gwen Colvin has been a sharp-eyed production editor and heroically patient with my revisions. I thank them both for their good sense. The comments of three anonymous readers led to a manuscript rather different from the one I'd submitted, and I thank them for the acuity of their criticisms.

Pami, I would be lost if not for you and you know its true. I hope this book plays some small role in kindling in our son August Amiram that love of learning my dad gave to me. And thanks again, mom, for the summer psych course.

Parts of the Introduction originally appeared in *Stanley Cavell and Literary Studies: Consequences of Skepticism* (New York: Continuum, 2011). I am grateful to Bernie Rhie and Richard Eldridge for permission reprint that material here. Other parts of the Introduction appeared in *nonsite.org*, and I thank Oren Izenberg for permission to print it here. An early version of chapter 2 appeared as "Antebellum AI: 'Maelzel's Chess-Player' and Poe's Reverse Constraints" in *Poetics Today*, Vol. 31, issue. 1, pp. 107–125; Copyright, 2010, Porter Institute for Poetics and Semiotics, Tel Aviv University. All rights reserved, Duke University Press. I thank Meir Sternberg and Sharon Himmelfarb for permission to reprint that material. Parts of chapter 2 also appeared, in very different form, as "C. Auguste Dupin and Charles S. Peirce: An Abductive Affinity," in *The Edgar Allan Poe Review*, Fall 2005, Volume VI, Number 2. 22–30. Parts of chapter 4 first appeared as "*Pym*, Poe and 'the golden bowl' " in *The Henry James Review* 29.3 (2008), 229–235. Copyright © 2008 The Johns Hopkins University Press. I thank Susan M. Griffin for permission to reprint that material here.

This book could not have been completed without a Morse Fellowship leave from Yale University and a Frederick W. Hilles publication grant from the Whitney Humanities Center at Yale.

Experience and Experimental Writing

Introduction

In the last of the prefaces he added to the New York edition of his fiction, Henry James poses an ambitious thought experiment. What "would be really interesting, and I dare say admirably difficult to go into," James writes

> would be the history of [an] effect of experience; the history, in other words, of the growth of the immense array of terms, perceptional and expressional that... in sentence, passage and page, simply looked over the heads of the standing terms... or perhaps rather like alert winged creatures, perched on those diminished summits and aspired to clearer air. What [such an interest would] come back to is the how and the whence and the why these intenser lights of experience come into being and insist on shining.[1]

What does James mean by experience here? Is he referring to events undergone between the 1892 notebook sketches for the plot of *The Golden Bowl* and the final revisions to it in 1908? Or does he rather refer directly to the "growth of an immense array of terms," as if experience named an impersonal fecundity latent in the very doing of composition? Would the "history of an effect of experience" then be a story about how the new terms—those "alert winged creatures"—had appeared from out of the accidents and surprises of rewriting, and the "admirable difficulty" that of giving an account of how and whence and why such experience had come into being at all? What would you have to take experience to be to think you could arrive at an "intenser" version of it through the process of revision?

In what follows I take James up on his invitation to go into these questions, finding in what he calls a "history of an effect of experience," not only a way of thinking about composition, but the prehistory of the pragmatist insight that experience is not a matter of correspondence but of process and experiment. When the classical pragmatists talk about experience they do not mean getting inner representations to correspond with outer phenomena, nor of securing conditions of possibility for rationally justified knowledge, but an experimental loop of perception, action, consequences, further perception of consequences, further action, further consequences, and so forth. Richard Poirier, for one, links this understanding of experience to composition, such that for "poet-pragmatists" like Ralph Waldo Emerson, the Jameses, Robert Frost, Wallace Stevens, and Gertrude Stein, experience is not so much a matter of securing correspondence between mind and world as it is modeled on "writing itself as an activity ... as a dramatization of how life may be created out of words."[2] If the preface to *The Golden Bowl* invites us to imagine an "effect of experience" that is one with the process of composition, I follow Poirier in finding a version of that idea beginning in Emerson, and in his description of the writers he discusses as Emersonian pragmatists.[3] But rather than moving to writers more typically thought of as "modernist" (Stevens and Stein), I turn here to two of Emerson's contemporaries, Edgar Allan Poe and Herman Melville.[4] In treating all three of them—along with James—as exemplifying in their poetry and prose an experimentation typically associated with modernism, I want not only to identify an arc of influence in American literary history—roughly from Emerson's leaving the Unitarian ministry to Henry James's late style—but to offer an account of the relation of literature to pragmatism as a function of the relation of experience to experiment.[5]

To make concrete the transition from thinking of experience as the squaring of inner and outer matters to thinking of experience as a process continued in composition, each chapter is organized around a particular scene or encounter: Emerson, in the middle of a crisis of vocation, arrives at a method for treating his journal entries as material for building up lectures and essays after seeing George Cuvier's cabinets of comparative anatomy in Paris; Poe, precariously launched on a career as a work-a-day magazinist, invents the analytic detective story after witnessing and devoting an editorial to Bavarian inventor Johann Maelzel's traveling exhibition of a mechanical chess-player; the impacted style of Melville's *Pierre* emerges out of his agon with the literary-critical dogmas of New York literati, specifically some less than favorable reviews of *Moby-Dick*. These three different ways of dramatizing in prose the replacement of experience as correspondence with experience as composition is made most explicit in the relation between Henry and William James. Despite William's complaint that his brother's late style was "all perfume and simulacrum," Henry's 1903 novel *The Ambassadors* takes as its formal organizing principle precisely the central claim of his brother's radical empiricism: that relations are external to, and as real as, their terms. In building a novel around the multiple ambassadorial relations between New England and Paris, Henry enacts at the level of style William's most ambitious and encompassing account of experience, despite William's professed impatience with the indirection of that style. The "encounter" described in the final chapter is then between the Jameses themselves.

Other figures play a role in the span of time I am calling "Emerson to the Jameses." Most immediately, there are the three representatives of classical pragmatism: Besides William James and John Dewey (whose naturalist account of experience I take up in detail in the remainder of this introduction), there is Charles Peirce, often considered to be the founder of pragmatism. Usually remembered for his magazine articles of the 1870s on truth and verification, and for his work on semeiotic, Peirce enters the picture here as the author of some little-known essays on reasoning machines and for a specific innovation in the theory of inference. Also discussed are Georges Cuvier, whose work on taxonomy and comparative anatomy were not only a decisive influence on Emerson at a crucial moment in his search for a vocation, but factors centrally in the dénouement of Poe's "The Murders in the Rue Morgue"; Evert Duyckinck, whose role as publisher and critic in New York City in the 1840s and 1850s in part made careers (however precarious) like Poe's and Melville's possible; Friedrich Nietzsche, who turned to making some of his most experimental books just after re-reading and re-annotating German translations of all of Emerson's *Essays* in 1881 and 1882; Henri Bergson, whose ongoing friendship and correspondence with William James was decisive for the development of James's radical empiricism; and George Santayana, who said that the James brothers were unique for their way of breaking with what he called the "Genteel Tradition"; a claim that could be made for all the writers to whom I have devoted chapters here (even if Santayana himself believed Emerson and Poe were still in that tradition's grip).[6]

No treatment of Emerson as anticipating pragmatism's account of experience can ignore Stanley Cavell's formidable challenge to the idea that Emerson is any kind of pragmatist. Asking whether the phrase "Emersonian pragmatism" is "intended [as] the idea that there was a particular brand of pragmatism called Emersonian, or rather that Emersonianism was always a kind of pragmatism," Cavell finds in this identification "one more form in which the distinctiveness of Emerson's prose is repressed."[7] This worry over the repression of Emerson's distinctiveness as a writer continues a conversation—conducted mostly in remarks made *en passant* and in footnotes—begun in Poirier's *Poetry and Pragmatism*. There Poirier acknowledges at the outset an affinity with Cavell, saying that he feels some "exasperation" at the way Emerson's achievement as a prose stylist has been overlooked in the literary culture he helped to found.[8] And while Poirier is concerned to treat pragmatism as a "form of linguistic skepticism" (a claim that places him squarely in dialogue with Cavell's specific concerns), he also says that part of the distinctiveness of Emerson's writing is the way it is "to be experienced as it is written, and not in any clarifying translation into some other syntax."[9] The description is echoed later in *Poetry and Pragmatism* in a footnote addressed explicitly to Cavell, in which Poirier says that in Emerson's sentences experience is to be found in "the actual accomplishments *in* the writing, word by word."[10] Cavell's reservations about seeing Emerson as any kind of pragmatist are also voiced in relation to prose style; what Cavell calls Emerson's "difficulty."

The simultaneous convergence and conflict between Poirier and Cavell around the distinctiveness of Emerson's style might be considered in light of questions Cavell raises in his *Senses of Walden*: "Why has America never expressed itself philosophically? Or has it, in the metaphysical riot of its greatest literature?"[11] The questions seem both to signal Cavell's attraction to great nineteenth-century American prose—not only Emerson's, but Thoreau's, Poe's, and Henry James's—and to profess a commitment to working through aspects of the metaphysics pragmatism set out to reject. The tension between metaphysics and pragmatism, though, conceals a deeper one, between skepticism and naturalism; a difference that depends on differing construals of the meaning of experience. That Poirier finds in Emerson the beginnings of pragmatism and that Cavell distrusts this idea—conflicting convictions held for the same reason: the *way* Emerson writes—invites us to unpack the distinction between skepticism and naturalism in relation both to Emerson's style and to different understandings of experience.

Cavell says that in the essay "Experience" Emerson "explicitly challenges the...idea of experience to be found in Kant and in the classical empiricists."[12] Both of these models of experience—on the one hand, the way the making of determinate judgments functions as the condition of possibility for objects to become intelligible at all; on the other, the mechanism by which sense impressions come to furnish the mind with ideas—are representationalist. That is, both descriptions of experience come down to giving an account of how "outer" phenomena can be made to square with "inner" representations.[13] Consider this, then, in relation to what Cavell takes to be Emerson's challenge to such models of experience, particularly his line, "but far be it from me the despair which prejudges the law by a paltry empiricism."[14] Cavell takes the line to say that what is wrong with empiricism is "not its reliance on experience but its paltry idea of experience"; a reading that leads him to consider a "little argument" he takes Emerson to be having with Kant about "the nature of experience in its relation to, or revelation of, the natural world."[15] Cavell sees this argument at work in Emerson's saying that "the secret of the illusoriness [of life] is in the necessity of a succession of moods or objects. Gladly we would anchor, but the anchorage is quicksand. This onward trick of nature is too strong for us. *Pero si muove.*"[16] Finding in these lines an engagement with Kant's second Analogy of Experience, Cavell hears in the word "anchorage" an allusion to Kant's well-known example of a boat moving down a river: if an anchorage in *outer* succession were to turn out to be quicksand, then our inner representations would be set adrift. Since the point of the boat analogy for Kant is to give a proof for the objectivity of outer succession (and thus avoid what he calls "dogmatic" idealism), the melting away of *this* anchorage would indeed lead to an extreme form of external world skepticism.[17]

But matters are not so simple as this. Cavell rather tells us that for Emerson "the succession of moods is *not tractable* by the distinction between subjectivity and objectivity Kant proposed for experience," and that it is "*this* onward trick of nature that is too much for us; the given bases for the self are quicksand. The fact that we are given over by this succession...means that you can think of it as at once a succession of moods (inner matters) and a succession of objects (outer matters). This very evanescence of the world proves its existence to me; it is what vanishes from me."[18] On Cavell's account, Emerson is saying that the "secret of the illusoriness of life" is our inability to gauge the one order of succession by the other, because you can think of succession as at once a series of moods or objects. And if neither is tractable by the other taken as fixed, then the "given bases of the self are quicksand," since for Kant one of the conditions of the self's unity—"unity of apperception" as the necessary ground for the synthesis of experience—requires and implies an isomorphism between inner and outer matters. Cavell's recognition of Emerson's "bringing to mind the characteristics of skepticism's mood"[19] thus leads him to hear in these lines from "Experience" both an acknowledgment of one of the more sophisticated efforts at heading off at the pass the threat of the world's becoming alien to us, and a resistance to the idea that the skeptical mood either arises out of or is properly addressed in relation to a problem of inner representation of outer objects. This wariness about the effort to provide an answer to the skeptic is an instance of what Cavell elsewhere calls the "truth of skepticism"; as if Emerson's disappointment in the proof Kant offers as a way of dealing with skepticism were not a failure to be persuaded by Kant's arguments but a part of skepticism's mood.[20]

While Cavell finds in Emerson a skeptical mood not so much characterized by a doubt about knowledge of the external world, but by an inability to feel satisfied with Kant's effort at "answering" the skeptic, he does so by pointing precisely to that feature of Kant's empirical realism—the boat as an emblem for the objectivity of outer succession—that brings Emerson's lines back to the epistemological problem of representation. If our moods succeed each other (even if, as Emerson has it elsewhere, they "do not believe in each other"[21]) then the "logic of moods" remains expressible in the kind of argument that would ground the fact of their succession in something outside us. And that last *Pero si mouve*—an allusion to Galileo's tactful response to his persecutors that, while he did not mean to suggest that the Earth moves around the Sun, nevertheless added "and yet it does move"— while pointing to Copernican turns both astronomical and epistemological, might then be read as a sort of *sotto voce* reminder of the nagging pull on us of Kant's understanding of experience as (in part) premised on the gauging of inner by outer succession. Changing course from riverboats to celestial bodies, we might say that Cavell's effort to show Emerson both feeling the gravitational pull (or getting out of the orbit) of skepticism, nevertheless depends on the intelligibility of its threat for a finding in "Experience" a little argument with Kant.

Despite this rendering of the role of succession in Emerson, and despite Cavell's own disappointment with the Kantian "settlement with skepticism"—for all the glory of transcendental idealism, it still requires that things in themselves drop out of the picture (to this gift from Kant Cavell has replied: "thanks for nothing"[22])— Cavell's reading of Emerson's lines returns experience to the problem of aligning "inner [with] outer matters"; that is, to the problem of representation, or at any rate a successor of this problem.[23] We might push this further and say that to get off the ground as a genuine problem skepticism *must* understand experience as some form of (however failed) representation. If we are worried about our access to the external world, or to other minds, or whether we can have a firm grasp on what it means to follow a rule, or whether we can have our selves reflected back to us in another's recognition; or if it is just that we have begun to wonder how a simultaneous respect for, and doubt about, efforts to answer the skeptic might stand for some deep truth about us: in each case, what we are worried or wondering about is the correspondence of some set of representations with a condition of life.

But consider some of the steps that led to the making of Emerson's essay "Experience." A journal entry of January 1841 says "the method of advance in nature is perpetual transformation," and on September 11, 1841, Emerson says: "It is much to write sentences; it is more to add method & write out the spirit of your life symmetrically... to arrange many reflections in their natural order so that I shall have one homogeneous piece... this continuity is for the great."[24] Here, the role of "succession" seems not to be bound up with the problem of representation, but of arriving at a practicable method of composition. The move from the "perpetual transformations" of nature to what Emerson calls "writing out the spirit of your life" is made more explicit in the lecture "The Method of Nature," given at Waterville College in Maine, also in 1841. In that lecture Emerson says to his audience that they (and he) will "celebrate this hour by exploring the method of nature. Let us see that, as nearly as we can, and try how far it is transferable to the literary life."[25] Some months later in his lecture called "The Poet," Emerson describes what the poet does as "vehicular," "fluxional," and "transitive," such that the poet's lines "flow with the flowing of nature."[26] Rather than think of outer succession as lost to us, because of a veil or an imbalance between inner and outer matters, Emerson wants to find a continuity running from nature to composition.

Given Cavell's assertion that Emerson's idea of experience is a challenge to both transcendental idealism and classical empiricism (a claim with which I agree), I want to treat that challenge as the way he replaces a worry over the vicissitudes of representation with what he simply calls "method." And given that Cavell is as concerned as Poirier with the distinctiveness of Emerson's way of writing (yet is reluctant to find in Emerson any form of pragmatism) we ought to consider how the method by which Emerson got his sentences to sound the way they do informed John Dewey's description of experience as the "continuity between natural events... and the origin and development of meanings [as a] naturalistic link which does away with the often alleged necessity of dividing the objects of experience into two worlds."[27] Dewey's naturalist rejection of correspondence epistemology, and the way it informs his aesthetics, encourages us to stop puzzling over how to connect the chasm between mind and world and imagine rather a course or continuum of experience moving from one to the other. In his 1925 Paul Carus lectures, *Experience and Nature*, Dewey offered a naturalist account of experience premised on what he called a "shift of emphasis from the experienced (the *what*) to the experiencing, the *how*, the method of its course." He later describes this move from the "what" to the "how" of experience as a desire to eliminate the "division of everything into nature *and* experience," encouraging us rather to think of experience as the "direction of natural events to meanings"; what John Murphy has called "opposing the spirit of Cartesianism with what might be called the spirit of experimentalism."[28]

All of this sounds like a belated reformulation of Emerson's "Method of Nature." Indeed, in his 1903 essay on Emerson, Dewey challenges the view of Emerson as a mere amasser of charming aphorisms, or of having a "lack of method."[29] Instead, Dewey praises Emerson's "movement of thought"; a thinking that happens through "art" not "metaphysics"; the way he "set out to be a maker rather than a reflector."[30] More attuned to the "surprises of reception than any fixed goal," Emerson's prose arises as a "following the unfolding of perception," of the "*way* of things"; a form of making that "takes the *way* of truth...for truth."[31] Summarizing the importance of method for Emerson, Dewey quotes from "Spiritual Laws," that a man is "a method, a plan of arrangement" and, taking literally the etymology of the word "method" (μέθοδος; road), quotes Emerson's line from "Experience," "everything good is on the highway."[32]

Despite the differences between Dewey's naturalist inheritance of Emerson and Cavell's finding in his writing a grappling with the problem of skepticism, Cavell too sees composition as linked to method and to experimentation. In an essay written before he'd found a model pitch for his own prose in Emerson and Thoreau, Cavell asks, in "Music Discomposed": "What is composition, and what is it to compose?"[33] The question for Cavell amounts to asking—in keeping with his concern, in all his work, with the notion of criteria—What is to *count* as an example of composition? Answering his own question, he calls composition the "search for an object worthy of our attention"; a process he describes as an "experimental problem."[34] By "experimentation" Cavell seems to mean an activity taking the form of a search; one which does not know where it is going ahead of time, fashions provisional goals as part of the unfolding of the process, and remains open to the surprises that emerge from an attention to work as it is being made.[35] When Cavell extends this idea to a discussion of Emerson's and Thoreau's practice of working up from journal entries into lectures, essays, and books, it is just this kind of experimentation he has in mind. What the earlier essay calls "attention" is now called "interest":

> Emerson [and Thoreau's] relation to poetry is inherently their interest in their own writing...their interest in the fact that what they are building is writing, that their writing is, as it realizes itself daily under their hands, sentence by shunning sentence...the making of it happen, the poetry of it.[36]

If we put together some of his different claims, we might say that for Cavell the words "composition," "experiment," "attention," "search," "interest," and "poetry" are related in the way they each contribute to a description of experience. And this would then be one that bears some affinity with Dewey's description of Emerson's open-ended, experimental method.[37]

If both Dewey and Cavell can be said to find in Emerson a notion of experience as experiment, there is still the fundamental difference between Cavell's staying within the problem of skepticism and Dewey's naturalism. Cavell acknowledges this in a recent book, *Philosophy the Day After Tomorrow*, saying of Dewey's work that it "sometimes…demonstrates how a mass of experience can go philosophically almost nowhere (for Dewey into a hundred abstract rejections of some patently unintelligible thesis together with its obviously undesirable antithesis)."[38] An entire philosophic position is squeezed into that parenthetic aside, and it is worth unpacking a bit. The "hundred abstract rejections" are presumably the relentless critique of representationalism that is the backbone of *Experience and Nature*, and the "patently unintelligible thesis" must be that experience can (or should) be understood as a continuum running from nature to meaning. But given Cavell's claim that Emerson offers a challenge to the models of experience found in classical empiricsm and Kant, we are left to wonder if Cavell has still a different idea of how such accounts of experience might be challenged, and in a way that would be both attuned to Emerson's literary method, and yet not fall into line with Dewey's "abstract rejections."

Here, then, we ought to turn to Cavell's essay "What's the Use of Calling Emerson a Pragmatist?," which both develops the idea of composition as a form of experimentation and offers a new set of arguments for why Emerson should not be thought of as a precursor to pragmatism. Cavell describes Emerson's writing as an appeal to "the words we are given in common," and the way the "proposals for what we say…require something like experimentation…trials that inherently run the risk of exasperation [and so leads to a] writing which is *difficult* in a way no other American philosopher's (save Thoreau's) has been, certainly not that of James and Dewey. Are these different responses to language not philosophically fundamental? They seem so to me."[39] Here the relation of philosophy to style—the claim that the doing of philosophy is inseparable from a way of writing—is used to buttress Cavell's annoyance at how pragmatism seems "designed to refuse to take skepticism seriously, as it refuses [in Dewey's case] to take metaphysical distinctions seriously."[40] But in linking the issue of prose style to the accusation that Dewey refuses to recognize the problem of skepticism, Cavell implicitly suspends aspects of his earlier account of composition as experiment. If, for Cavell, "the sound [of prose] makes all the difference," and Emerson and Dewey sound just too different for there to be a substantive link between them, it should be remembered that Dewey treated Emerson's method—his "movement of thought"—as the basis for his naturalist account of experience. Rather than treat Emerson's difficulty as forming a difference in kind from Dewey's way of doing philosophy (for Cavell presumably too drably scientistic), we should see Dewey as belatedly formalizing, in his account of the relation of nature to meaning, what Emerson had all along been doing at the level of the sentence.[41] In this sense at least, we can counter Cavell's assertion that Dewey "never took up [Emerson] philosophically."[42]

I want to turn now to two thinkers who, while taking themselves to be inheritors of the pragmatist tradition, nevertheless, raise a different set of objections to Dewey's naturalism.[43] While a self-identifying pragmatist like Robert Brandom entirely rejects the word "experience" (it is "not one of his words" as he puts it), he nevertheless offers one of the best descriptions we have of what Dewey means by experience. Brandom tells us that for Dewey experience is

> transactional and structured as learning; a process rather than a state or episode. Its slogan might be "No experience without experiment."[Dewey] conceives experience as *Erfahrung* [such that] the unit of experience is a Test-Operate-Test cycle of perception, action and further perception of the results of the action. On this model, experience is not an *input* to the process of learning. Experience *is* the process of learning.[44]

Brandom's characterization of Dewey's replacement of a "state" or "episode" with "process"—what he has more recently described as "processual, developmental *Erfahrung* rather than episodic, self-intimating *Erlebnis*... a feedback loop of perception, responsive performance, and perception of the results of performance"[45]— imagines experience as developmental learning over time rather than encounters with discrete bundles of impressions. To say that experience *is* the process of learning is to get out of habit of thinking of experience as a matter of leaping the chasm between mind and world, and to start thinking of it as a process running from perception to meaning.

While Richard Rorty, Brandom's *Doktorvater*, thought of Dewey as one of his philosophical heroes and inherits from him and the other classical pragmatists the desire to abandon representation in favor of process and practice (what he sometimes simply calls "conversation") he, like Brandom, rejects the term "experience."[46] Specifically, he rejects Dewey's notion of experience as a continuum bridging the causal order of nature to the normative order of linguistic meaning.[47] Taking Dewey to task in his essay "Dewey's Metaphysics," Rorty says Dewey makes the mistake of "cross[ing] the line... between causal [relations] and the self-conscious beliefs and inferences they make possible," cautioning that "nothing is to be gained for an understanding of human knowledge by running together the vocabularies in which we describe the causal antecedents of knowledge with those in which we offer justifications of our claims to knowledge."[48] In a later essay, "Dewey Between Hegel and Darwin," Rorty makes more explicit his criticism of what he calls Dewey's "running together sentences with experiences," which he says amounts to a blurring of the "distinction between cognitive and non-cognitive states... between sensations and beliefs... the distinction between the question 'What causes our beliefs?' and the question 'What justifies our beliefs?'"[49] Presuming pre–Linguistic Turn forms of pragmatism have not entirely expunged the false problem of representationalism, Rorty goes on to critique the radically empiricist aspect of classical pragmatism, saying that "the blurring of cause and justification of belief is characteristic of both British empiricism and of British idealism [and] all that the 'radical empiricism' side of pragmatism did was to qualify this blurring by denying that relations among ideas are 'contributed by the mind' rather than 'given.'"

Rorty singles out as evidence of this qualification Dewey's claim that "unless there is a breach of historic and natural continuity, cognitive experience must originate within that of a non-cognitive sort."[50]

James Kloppenberg describes Rorty's hard-and-fast distinction between the cognitive (linguistic) and the non-cognitive (causal) as part of his treating the Linguistic Turn as "as a step forward rather than a dead end [and so Rorty] dogmatically refused to accept any philosophy in which something other than language, namely experience...plays an important part."[51] Brandom inherits this apprehension about the blurring of experience and language, saying that what separates late-twentieth-century analytic philosophers from classical pragmatists is that "they do not share the distinctively twentieth century philosophical concern with...the *discontinuities* with nature that it establishes and enforces [since the classical pragmatists] emphasize the *continuity* between concept users and organic nature."[52] In short, for analytic neopragmatists like Rorty and Brandom, it is not so simple to move from causal mechanism to linguistic meaning simply by intoning the word "experience." You cannot set up, as Dewey puts it, a "continuity between natural events...and the origin and development of meanings," without accounting for the fundamental discrepancy between nature as the order of causes and the linguistic as the normative order of reason giving and justification.[53]

The analytic critique of classical pragmatism thus hinges on the idea that language is bound up with justification, and so is something qualitatively different from experience understood as the causal impingements of the senses: you can't move from the cause to the justification of a belief because to be able to say something at all is to be in what Wilfrid Sellars called the "space of reasons." A thinker of immense importance for both Rorty and Brandom, Sellars is best known for his critique of what he called the "myth of the given"; the myth that causal determinations—what the classical empiricist might call "impressions"—could serve as a foundation for discourse in the space of reasons. The critique of givenness follows from the view that the deliverances of the senses alone are not enough to get a language game going; indeed, that the capacity even to make non-inferential observation reports already *depends* on the normative ability to subsume experienced particulars under general concepts.[54] Mere reliably differential responses to stimuli are not enough for an autonomous discourse, since bare causal transactions cannot stand as reasons for holding a belief. While, say, parrots can be trained to be reliable differential responders, parrots (or ravens, to use Edgar Allan Poe's example, about which I will have more to say below) do not then go on to keep playing the game of giving and asking for reasons. Parrots are in this sense like a piece of iron that "responds" to rain by rusting, or a photo-electric cell wired up to a tape recorder that "says" "red" when we shine red light on it.[55]

With the analytic pragmatists' sensitivity to the myth of the given in mind, I want to return to Cavell's description of composition as an experimental search, with the aim of finding in it an account of meaning that would be sensitive to the tension between the "given" and linguistic meaning, yet not reduce meaning simply to a matter of justification. Cavell says that in those objects we call compositions, "the concept of intention does not function as a term of...justification," such that "we follow the progress of a [composition] the way we follow what someone is saying or doing. Not however to...learn something specific, but to see what *it* says, to see what someone has been able to make out of these materials."[56] We might hear in this description a partial resemblance to the analytic pragmatists' critique of classical pragmatism, which we could imagine rephrased in the question: What does one have to be able to *do* in order to count as *saying* something? But to claim, as Cavell does, that composition is a matter of following what someone is saying or doing is not to treat it as bound up with giving and asking for reasons (or, for that matter, with inferences of material implication that can in principle be made explicit in logical vocabulary), but to be involved in what is for Cavell the specifically modernist predicament of needing to *find* the criteria by which the work becomes intelligible.[57] On this account, composition is the process of "trying to find the limits or essence of [its] own procedures" since it is "not clear a priori what counts, or will count" as a work.[58] Thus for Cavell the "task of the modernist artist...is to find what it is his art finally depends on [such that] the criteria are something we must *discover*... in the continuity of [the work] itself."[59] It is as if each individual work has to discover anew the criteria by which its particular forms of saying become sharable.

Like the analytic pragmatists, Walter Benn Michaels warns against confusing merely causal matters with meaning. It is a mistake, to use one of Michaels's examples, to think that part of what counts as an Emily Dickinson poem is the shape of the letters as she wrote them: how she crossed her "t"s, say, or the sort of ink or paper she used, or a blank space left between poems or words. To be concerned with the physical features of writing in this way is, for Michaels, to "turn the text...into a drawing" and so to blur the distinction between seeing letters and reading them. And for Michaels, the word that encapsulates this whole falsifying relation to the literary work is "experience," leading to his claim that when experience is allowed to replace meaning in our relation to the work, we no longer "have different interpretations but different experiences."[60]

Michaels's argument about the relation of meaning to experience is a fairly direct elaboration of Michael Fried's polemic against minimalism in his essay "Art and Objecthood."[61] What Fried calls "minimalist theatricality" is epitomized for him in an anecdote sculptor Tony Smith tells about a drive along the New Jersey turnpike. Because the drive on the turnpike offered a "reality that had not had any expression in art"—that "there was no way you could frame it, you just have to experience it"—this meant for Smith that the whole immersive, situated encounter in the car on the turnpike was both the "end of art" and a revelatory vision of "artificial landscape[s] without cultural precedent," leading to his own minimalist sculptures. While Fried agrees with Smith that the epiphany on the turnpike amounts to a direct affront to art as such, he makes a strong case against the sort of work Smith thought had to follow from that insight. What Fried calls "modernist" are works whose formal procedures, in seeking to "defeat or suspend theatre," would accordingly seek to defeat their mere objecthood as works. So while minimalist (what Fried calls "literalist") theatricality dissolves the work into a lived situation—your "just having to experience" the New Jersey turnpike in a car at night—modernist aesthetics center around the work's integrity as a composed network of intentions.[62] Ruth Leys captures this distinction when she writes of an aesthetic that "emphasizes the reader's or viewer's *experience* of a text or image to the extent that that experience might be said to stand in for the text or image in question. An opposing position would insist that although a work of art might make us feel happy or sad or envious or ashamed, what matters is the meaning of the work itself, which is to say the structure of intentional relationships built into it by the artist."[63]

It is not that experience plays *no* role in Fried's account of the relation between the modernist work and the beholder.[64] What Fried attacks in "Art and Objecthood" is the extreme case when the beholder's embodied immersion in a lived scenario *becomes* the work. The minimalist-literalist aesthetic is, you might say, one of *under-composition*, so as to elicit the maximum amount of stray affect. In his book, *Four Honest Outlaws*, Fried describes this as an "esthetic [of] inbuilt indeterminacy with respect to subjective response: since what mattered [for minimalism] was the embodied subject's ongoing perception of his or her negotiation of the total situation (that is, the gallery space including the lighting plus the object plus the embodied subject himself or herself), there could be no sense given to any claim as to the 'rightness' of any particular understanding of a given work, for each subject's 'experience' was unique and in a sense incommensurable with every other subject's. (Each subject's experience *was* the work, in a manner of speaking.)"[65] In "modernist" works, by contrast, "the viewer's 'experience' matters as a channel of insight into the overall structure of intentions that make the work what it is [and such that] the viewer's merely subjective response cannot stand in for the work itself."[66]

While I agree that it is wrong to equate a work's meaning with its physical features (poems shouldn't turn into drawings, as Michaels has it), or dissolve it into a lived situation (a situation Michaels, Fried, and Leys tend to generalize under the label "experience"), I want to avoid descriptions of the relation between work and beholder that would pit experience *against* intention. In other words, what Fried sees going on in the minimalist-literalist work—some version of Smith's turnpike—isn't experience at all; it is a field of unorganized affects. And here is where I look to the experience-experiment relation as a way of showing *how* intentional structures get built into artworks; and how beholders (or readers) come into conceptual possession of those structures. As Cavell puts it at the end of "Music Discomposed," in a discussion geared to "how [modernist] works are made" (and the possibility of an audience for such works): the "task of the modern artist is to find something he can mean."[67] We might say that on this account, the work is a *source* of experience; not in the minimalist sense, where a structure of intentions dissolves into a situation in which everything counts, but in the sense that both artist and beholder find the conditions for the work's meaning becoming shareable *in* the set of experiments that have led to the work.[68] Dewey captures this very precisely when he writes, in *Art as Experience,*

> Until the artist is satisfied in perception with what he is doing, he continues shaping and reshaping...the artist embodies in himself the attitude of the perceiver while he works [and] because the artist operates experimentally [in this way] does he open new fields of experience.[69]

What is Dewey's "operating experimentally" but the way a process of composition becomes a search for the criteria by which the work begins to mean? And what are "new fields of experience" but the way those meanings depend on the discovery in composition of the conditions by which they become publically intelligible? Far from "standing in" for the work *tout court*, experience is what is *found* in the work. And rather than a discrete "channel" through which intention moves as a kind of cargo transmitted from work to beholder, experience names the conditions under which intentions become sharable in and as the work (and always with the possibility that this will fail; that the work will *not* arrive at those conditions).

The difference between Fried's account of the role of experience, and my account of the role of experience, in the relation of work to beholder becomes more vivid when we look at another of the claims of "Art and Objecthood." If in the minimalist-literalist work time plays a crucial role, it is because the real-time unfolding of immersion in a situation just *is* the work; what Fried calls a "present-ment of endless or indefinite duration of the experience." Conversely, Fried suggests that with modernist art "at every moment the work itself is wholly manifest [in a] continuous and entire presentness" such that "a single infinitely brief instance would be long enough to see everything, to experience the work in all its depth and fullness, to be forever convinced by it."[70] More recently, Fried has described this complete presentness as the way the modernist work's formal "claim" on the beholder is renewed at every moment, as if "nothing less than that is the condition of [the work's] expressiveness."[71] If Fried wants to replace experience understood as continuousness or duration with experience understood as a channel through which one accesses something at every moment "wholly manifest," I want to *equate* experience with the work's "conditions of expressiveness." Again, the idea is to prevent "experience" from becoming either a synonym for affect, or a mere conveyer along which intention travels (even if that intention comes in a single flash of convincingness). Rather, a given work's condition of expressiveness just is the specific experience searched out and made shareable through the amassed decisions of composition. Something like this is, I think, close to what Cavell means by "modernism": an experimental search for "an object worthy of our attention," such that composition becomes a search for what is going to count as a work of art at all (for both artist and audience).[72] This is also a way of understanding what Henry James meant in describing the process of revision as the "history of an effect of experience."[73]

My effort to fuse Cavell's account of modernism, understood as the search in composition for an object worthy of our attention, with Dewey's account of composition as an experiment in opening up "new fields of experience," is made explicit when Cavell says of Emerson's prose that in it can be found a "deduction of every word in the language."[74] Transposing Kant's transcendental deduction of the conditions for possible experience, Cavell imagines a deduction resulting not in twelve categories of the understanding but in a prose that would be continually deducing the meaning of "every word." Cavell finds a description—and, presumably, an example—of this sort of deduction at work in a line from "Self-Reliance": "primary wisdom is intuition whilst all later teachings are tuitions," hearing that line as saying that "the occurrence to us of intuition places a demand upon us, namely for tuition; call this wording, the willingness to subject oneself to words, to make oneself intelligible." In an earlier essay on *King Lear* Cavell describes this as being in "straits of mind in which only those words said in that order will suffice," and in a later interview he speaks of the conviction a piece of writing can elicit as a matter of "nothing other than this prose here, as its passing before our eyes."[75] These last examples, in their different ways, offer both the clearest alternative to thinking of language as bound up with justification—as if just *these* words in *this* order, as if style itself, amounted to a kind of claiming—and the moment where Cavell's (however qualified and embedded) affinity with pragmatism becomes most vivid. When Poirier says that Emerson's prose is to be "experienced as it is written" (its accuracy is such that it cannot be translated into paraphrase) he echoes precisely Cavell's claim about Emerson's deduction of every word in the language; the tuition by which, in composition, intuitions turn into shareable meanings. Thought of as exemplified in Emerson's distinctively difficult prose—a difficulty about which Poirier and Cavell thought they were disagreeing but were illuminating from different angles—this sort of search is what the classical pragmatists call "experience."

In taking up the thought experiment posed in the preface to *The Golden Bowl*— that of looking into the "history of an effect of experience"—I aim to show how certain writers exemplify, in different ways, the move from earlier accounts of experience (classical empiricism; transcendental idealism) to pragmatism's idea of experience as experiment. Since I want to make vivid the transition away from an idea of experience as bound up with correspondence—getting the person's private affects to line up with worldly phenomena—I ground my readings in particulars of intellectual and literary history. Far from wanting to reduce literary works to epiphenomenal aftereffects of sociohistorical formations, I try to provide enough historical context to make concrete where and how compositional methods take shape, and always as part of a larger concern to show a shift from one way of thinking about experience—the affective encounter—to another: the process by which literary works become through composition conditioned experiences; the way experimental writing involves the wording of the world into something shareable and meaningful.

The first chapter, "The Method of Nature," argues that Emerson's 1833 epiphany in Georges Cuvier's *Jardin des plantes* led him to treat his journal entries as specimens for the building up of lyceum lectures, essays, and addresses. At a moment of vocational crisis, Emerson saw in Cuvier's taxonomic displays a way of converting Kant's "conditions of possibility for experience" into a method of composition; one he goes on to explain in his first lyceum lecture "The Uses of Natural History" (1834), the philosophy of language outlined in his first book, *Nature* (1836), and in the essay "The Method of Nature" (1841). Looking closely at one of the more controversial products of this new method—his "Divinity School Address" (1838)—I show how Emerson came to see the process of composition as carrying forward the causal series of nature; a conviction that led him to challenge the Unitarian understanding of miracles as anomalous suspensions of the natural order. I conclude the chapter by looking at the way Emerson's theopolitical agon with Unitarian Cambridge led him to what he called, in a journal entry composed shortly after the "Divinity School Address," "the joyous science." Finally, I turn to a consideration of Emerson's influence on Friedrich Nietzsche; specifically how Emerson's idea of "joyous science," as elabortated in the essays "Experience" (1844) and "Fate" (1860), can be read in relation to Nietzsche's *Die Fröhliche Wissenshaft* (1886), in what I identify as their shared compatibilism.

In chapter 2, "Nonreasoning Creatures," I show how Edgar Allan Poe treated the spectacle of Johann Maelzel's mechanical chess-player—which antebellum audiences believed to be a thinking machine—as the basis for the first detective story, "The Murders in the Rue Morgue" (1841). From the witnessing of the performance of the machine, to Poe's editorial "Maelzel's Chess-Player" (1835), which attempts to debunk the illusion, to the invention of a genre that stages the problem of knowing as leaps from sensory observation to guesses at hypotheses to correct inference, Poe's experiments strikingly anticipate Charles Peirce's papers on logical machines and his notion of "abductive" inference. From the machine, which only appears to play chess, to the motiveless murders of the Ourang-Outang, which serves as the dénouement of the first detective story, to the talking bird in "The Raven" (1845), to Poe's algorithmlike explanation of how he arrived at the idea for a "non-reasoning creature" to utter the poem's refrain, Poe's literary experiments—and Peirce's invention of a new type of inference—repeatedly imagine the move from sensory affection to discursive meaning as paralleled in processes of composition.

Chapter 3, "Unearthing *Pierre*," shows how Herman Melville found in the emergent literary criticism in the United States both a target for parody and a provocation to experiment with the form of the novel. Looking closely at the chapter Melville hastily added to *Pierre* (1852)—"Young America in Literature," directed explicitly at the *Literary World*, and composed just after he read his friend Evert Duyckinck's luke-warm review of *Moby-Dick* (1851)—I show how the novel's prose amounts to a rejection of the magazine's dogma of "unity and verisimilitude." Further, I claim *Pierre's* rejection of verisimilitude is given form in the novel's obsessive concern with rocks and stone. From its title and titular character, to its opening dedication to Mt. Greylock, to the "Memnon Stone" of Saddle Meadows, to Pierre's "Enceladus" dream, I show how experience in *Pierre* is a matter of replacing "Young American" literary aesthetics with an allegory of Melville's precarious career.

In the final chapter, "The Ambassador Effect," I show how the figure of "ambassadorship" works as a coordinating term for understanding both Henry James's *The Ambassadors* (1903) and his brother William's ongoing friendship and correspondence with French philosopher Henri Bergson (1904–10). Placing William's and Bergson's distrust of the verbal (as falsely conceptualizing the flux of experience), in counterpoint with the hyper-verbosity of Henry's late style, I extend that discussion to close readings of *The Ambassadors*'concern with life outside the confines of the local (in its emblem of American parochialism, "Woollett, Mass"). Finally, I turn to the question of cosmopolitanism, arguing that the James brothers confront the problem of the "genteel tradition," through both the indirections of the late style and a radically empirical understanding of experience (embodied in William's phrase "relations are external to their terms"). William and Henry, in their different ways, each enact a version of cosmopolitanism as an ambassadorlike shuttling between provincial locality and provisional universal.

In a brief conclusion I identify four of these provisional universals—compatibilism, genre, allegory, and cosmopolitanism—as they have arisen in each of the four chapters. The cosmopolitan concern to find the universal embedded in the particular, and the move from experience understood as private affect to experience as had on condition, are each captured in the way artworks discover and acknowledge the criteria under which their specific ways of saying become provisionally universal. I call these "provisional" universals because they too are arrived through experiment, are in the making, and are revisable.

CHAPTER 1
The Method of Nature

To what end is nature?

Ralph Waldo Emerson

THE UNITARIAN SCHISM

The first use of the word "transcendentalism" to designate an emergent radical wing within liberal Unitarianism appeared in a review essay by Frederick Henry Hedge in the March 1833 issue of *The Christian Examiner*. Commenting on the transmission, via Samuel Coleridge, of Kant's *Critique of Pure Reason* into the New England milieu, Hedge writes that he is aware "that a mere translation [of the *Critique*], however perfect, would be inadequate to convey a definite notion of transcendentalism to one who has not the metaphysical talent necessary to conceive and reproduce in himself [its] system."[1] To say that in order to understand the Kantian philosophy one must already possess a talent for metaphysics is like saying that if you found it unintelligible—as many established Unitarians did—you must be somehow deficient. Aware of the incomprehension (and distrust) surrounding the influx of German thought, Hedge noted that explications of transcendental idealism tended to have an "effect upon the uninitiated [of] being in the company of one who has inhaled an exhilarating gas. We witness the inspiration, and are astounded at the effects, but we can form no conception of the feeling until we ourselves have experienced it."[2] The tension between Unitarians and incipient transcendentalists thus comes down to different ways of thinking about the meaning of experience: what Hedge describes, later in the essay, as "reducing all things to impressions, ideas and sensations," versus beginning from a "fixed point" within consciousness and then "deducing from that point the whole world of intelligences, with the whole system of their representations."[3] The distinction neatly spells out the difference between Locke's sensationalist empiricism and what Kant called his "critical" philosophy of arriving at the conditions of possibility for experience to occur at all.

The occasion for Hedge's review was James Marsh's 1831 edition of Coleridge's *The Friend* and his 1829 edition of Coleridge's *Aids to Reflection*. In the long preliminary essay he added to his edition of the *Aids to Reflection*, Marsh wrote that he refused "to accept the divorce empiricism seemed to mandate between matters of philosophy and matters of faith," and sees the possibility for arriving at a synthesis designed to reconcile Christianity with Kantian idealism. For Marsh, an Andover graduate and Calvinist, the appeal of German idealism was the way it fueled his conviction that the "age demanded a renewed understanding of how religious experience could be discussed."[4] Specifically, Coleridge's discussion of Kant made vivid how the empiricism that underwrote Unitarianism seemed untenable as a basis for divinity. Perry Miller says of the way Marsh's Calvinism informed his introduction to the *Aids* that Unitarianism was for Marsh "reprehensible [since] in the middle of the eighteenth century, Jonathan Edwards rephrased Calvinism in the language of Locke; by the end of the century, his version generally triumphed [and] the debate between orthodox and Unitarians was conducted upon the common acceptance of Lockean premises."[5] In his preliminary essay, Marsh makes explicit what he found inadequate in the Lockean premises:

> In the minds of our religious community especially some of [Locke's] most important doctrines have become … so connected with our theoretical views of religion, that one can hardly hope to question their validity without hazarding his reputation, not only for orthodoxy, but even for common sense. To controvert, for example, the prevailing doctrines with regard to the freedom of the will, the sources of our knowledge, the nature of the understanding … and the universality of the law of cause and effect … may even now be worse than in vain.[6]

Calling for a basic shift in intellectual approach, Marsh was drawn particularly to Coleridge's explanation of the distinction between reason and understanding; terms, Marsh complained, "the Unitarians used interchangeably."[7] Aware that his own interpretation might be deemed incompatible with accepted uses, he wrote in his essay of having "used several words, especially *understanding* and *reason*, in a sense somewhat diverse from their present application."[8] Marsh wanted to highlight the distinction Coleridge made between the faculties, so that reason would not be conflated with the mere receptivity to sensory impingements we share with animals. For Marsh,

> many confusions have arisen from the habit of using, since the time of Locke, the terms understanding and reason indiscriminately [such that] the powers of understanding and reason have not merely been blended and confounded in the view of our philosophy [but] the higher and far more characteristic [power of reason] as an essential constituent of our proper humanity, has been as it were obscured and hidden from our observation in the inferior power, which belongs to us in common with the brutes. … But understanding these [terms] in their strict and proper sense and according to the true *ideas* of them,

as contemplated by the older metaphysicians, we have literally, if the system of Locke and the popular philosophy of the day be true, neither the one or the other....What [these older metaphysicians] esteemed, the image of God in the soul...distinguishing us...each and all of the irrational animals, is found, according to [Locke's] system, to have in fact no real existence.[9]

Marsh wants to undo the "blending" of Reason with Understanding, so that the "image of God in the Soul" will not be confused with an inferior capacity. The Unitarian schism as Marsh confronts it thus entails a specific understanding of the relation of nature to rationality. If what we have in common with animals is, for Marsh, a capacity for passive sensory affection then, he concludes, there must be something more to experience than mere receptivity. Marsh thus sought to "intensify the moral dimension of natural law by relocating its power from external force to [something] internal...acted on not by exercising legislative command from without but by organizing irresistibly from within [and] not by crude mechanisms of force but by innermost conviction of the right and true."[10] The partitioning of mental function into discrete faculties was a way of arriving at conditions for experience outside the flux of the sensory manifold, and so secure a freedom of the will not determined by mere causal occurrences. At stake for Marsh was nothing less than the preservation of the moral dimension of human being as an "absolute self-determination" outside the order of natural processes alone.[11]

But there was more to Coleridge's *Aids to Reflection* than a run-through (and distortion of) the Kantian faculties. Less under Marsh's curatorial control were Coleridge's extravagant descriptions of the emergence of mind from *out* of natural processes. Due in part to the influence of William Paley's *Natural Theology*, and certainly playing a role in Marsh's worry over the blurring of reason and understanding, theological and philosophical discussion was at the time concerned with the question of whether mental processes had a material basis.[12] Taking up the idea of a graduated scale running from matter to mind, Coleridge glosses a passage from Robert Leighton's *Practical Commentary upon the First Epistle General of St. Peter*: "Your blessedness is not,—no believe it, it is not where most of you seek it, in things below you. How can that be? It must be in a higher good to make you happy."[13] Coleridge writes:

Every rank of Creatures...ascends in the scale of creation...the Metal at its height of Being seems a mute Prophecy of the coming Vegetation, into a mimic semblance of which it crystallizes. The Blossom and Flower, the Acmè of Vegetable Life, divides into correspondent Organs with reciprocal functions, and by instinctive motions and approximations seems impatient of that fixture, by which it is differentiated in kind from the flower-shaped Psyche, that flutters with free wing above it. And wonderfully in the insect realm doth the Irritability, the proper seat of Instinct, while yet the nascent Sensibility is subordinated thereto—most wonderfully, I say, doth the muscular Life in the Insect and musculo-arterial in the Bird, imitate and typically rehearse the adaptive

Understanding…All things strive to ascend and ascend in their striving. And shall man alone stoop?[14]

For all of its imagining man's ascent toward the higher order of the Spirit, Coleridge's description delights in the puzzle pieces of nature's material particularity, and the combinatory possibilities of a prose that would imitate its patterns. Alongside the telos implicit in the description of the emergence of human rationality from out of natural processes—like metal and vegetables and birds man must also strive and ascend—we have Coleridge's embellishments of the Kantian faculties: the "muscular Life in the Insect and musculo-arterial in the Bird," for example, is seen as "rehearsing the Understanding," with man at the end of the chain presumably left to mutate further upward in accord with Reason. In seeing Reason as aligned with a priori principles cordoned off from Locke's empiricism, Coleridge had, in Marsh's estimate, "provided rational grounds for believing in the supernatural agency of Jesus Christ." But he also inadvertently bequeathed to enthusiastic American readers like Emerson and Hedge an alluring rhetorical pyrotechnics, however idiosyncratic his rendering of the Kantian epistemology.[15]

If Coleridge's gloss on Leighton's aphorism is as much about a *way* of writing as it is about his account of the relation of nature to reason, a concern with expression as such becomes the focus of his "Essays on the Principle of Method." Written first as a contribution to the *Encyclopaedia Metropolitana* in 1817, Coleridge added revised versions of the essays to issues of *The Friend* in 1818. These essays, Coleridge says, are to be a "discussion of Method as employed in the formation of the understanding and in the construction of science and literature," and as such attempt to explain the "germinal power" of organizing particulars into "progressive arrangement."[16] As he put it in the earlier encyclopedia entry, method for him is a matter of a "transition from one step in any course to another"[17]; and in the *Table Talk* we are told that method extends to include his definition of poetry (and literary composition in general) as "the best words in the best order."[18] In the version that appeared in *The Friend*, Coleridge tells us that the "Greek, μέθοδος, literally a *way* or *path of transit*"[19] amounts to a "union and interpenetration of the universal and the particular"; a union he finds exemplified in Shakespeare. "The great Dramatist," Coleridge wrote, "possessed a Science of Method [which was] his power to enumerate and analyze the relations by which the mind classified things."[20] In another of the essays Coleridge links this principle to "methodical arrangements [in] botany," such that beyond the mere artificial classifications of that science, "some *antecedent* must have been contributed by the mind itself."[21] One sees how Coleridge's notion of method buttressed Marsh's appeal to the distinction between reason and understanding. If the understanding is a mere classifier or arranger, then reason—the ordering principle—is the method. However idiosyncratic his account of the relation between the Kantian faculties, what Coleridge means by method is clear: an ordering of particulars such that a universal is expressed in each of them as the principle of their arrangement.[22]

Like Marsh, who hoped to get out of the Unitarian schism through Coleridgean evangelizing, Ralph Waldo Emerson was also excited by what he found in the *Aids to Reflection* and Hedge's review, which he referred to in a letter to his brother Edward as "a leaping living Logos."[23] It was not a dogmatic adoption of the Reason-Understanding distinction that Emerson took from the *Aids*, despite Marsh's efforts to guide the reader in his long introduction. Still searching for what he called, in a journal entry made just before entering Divinity School in 1824, the "strains of ecstasy & eloquence," Emerson saw in Coleridge's idea of method an ordering principle for his own emerging method of composition; one that particularly suited his needs in a moment of vocational doubt. If it is method that both Hedge and Coleridge make explicit in relation to Kant's effort to deduce the conditions of possibility for experience, Emerson will make the link between method and experience a matter of moving from pulpit eloquence to essayistic experiment.[24]

THE USES OF NATURAL HISTORY

Emerson's interest in the way method informs both literary composition ("progressive arrangement" as the "best words in the best order") and the principles underlying the science of classification (rather than the mere "aggregate") came together during a trip to Europe made just after he resigned his pulpit in the Second Unitarian church in 1832. On this visit he met Coleridge, whose insular monologues on the folly of Unitarianism did not prevent Emerson from assuring him that "many Unitarians read [his] books with pleasure & profit," asking him if he "had had any correspondence with [James] Marsh."[25] Not yet making regular appearances on the lyceum circuit, Emerson turned to his journals to test out new directions in his thought, transforming the problem of experience animating the Unitarian schism into his own concern with arriving at a compositional method suitable to his desire for "ecstasy & eloquence."

While he did not like Paris (a "loud modern New York of a place" he called it), Emerson underwent something of a conversion experience there, upon seeing Georges Cuvier's exhibit of comparative anatomy. His journal entry of July 13, 1833, reads:

I carried my ticket from Mr. Warden to the Cabinet of Natural History in the Garden of Plants. How much finer things are in composition than alone. 'Tis wise in man to make cabinets.... I saw amber containing perfect mosquitoes, grand blocks of quartz, native gold in all its forms of crystallization,—threads, plates, crystals, dust; and silver, black as from fire.... The universe is a more amazing puzzle than ever, as you glance along this bewildering series of animated forms,—the hazy butterflies, the carved shells, the birds, beasts, fishes, insects, snakes, and the upheaving principle of life everywhere incipient, in the very rock aping organized forms. Not a form so grotesque, so savage, nor so beautiful but is an expression of some property inherent in man the observer,—an occult relation between the very scorpions and man. I feel the centipede in me,—cayman, carp, eagle, and fox. I am moved by strange sympathies I say continually "I will be a naturalist."

The prose here combines the ecstatic rhetoric of Coleridge's descriptions of the ascension from matter to mind ("upheaving principle") with genuine curiosity about the science of classification. When Emerson writes "how much finer things are in composition than alone," he sounds as struck by the image of the cabinet as an arranging principle as by the objects it contains.[26] The tone of amazement in the entry is then not only in response to the wild diversity of nature but of seeing an organizing principle in an object as available to perception as the specimens displayed within it. To be "moved by strange sympathies" is to have an encounter with an object that stands for a principle previously thought of as furnished by the mind alone. In this way "composition" will be coupled for Emerson with an attempt to navigate between two clashing ideas of experience: the sensualist Lockeanism that would deal only with empirical particulars and a transcendental idealism in which the organizing categories of the mind are required for the apprehension of any object at all.

Just four months after seeing the cabinets in Paris, Emerson gave his first lyceum lecture before the Natural History Society in Boston.[27] A piece of the July 13 entry has been spliced into the lecture:

> I am impressed with a singular conviction that not a form so grotesque, so savage, or so beautiful, but is an expression of something in man the observer. We feel that there is an occult relation between the very worm, the crawling scorpions, and man. I am moved by strange sympathies. I say I will listen to this invitation. I will be a naturalist.[28]

If method for Emerson means realizing a "progressive transition from one step in the course to another," then here progressive transition occurs as the cutting of material from the journal directly into the lecture.[29] And it leads to telling modifications. The first added line imagines a relation between being "impressed" and the formation of a "conviction." If in the earlier entry, to be "moved by strange sympathies" was to have a perceptual encounter with an organizing principle (the cabinets) of the sort Coleridge stressed could only be provided by the mind, then here Emerson fuses an empirical impression with an inner principle—a conviction. The strangeness of feeling an impression crystalize into a principle is acknowledged in Emerson's changing the journal's "properties inherent in man" to the lecture's "something in man." To move from "properties" to "something" is to turn properties into processes, as if what had been taken to be inherent has turned out to be mutable and in the making. Changes like these show Emerson moving from a conception of experience as the mind's bringing order to aggregates of particulars to the "strange sympathies" of composition. Even as he reflects on the limits of Coleridgean method, Emerson experiments with the way a journal entry becomes a building block for a lecture.

Describing Emerson's revelation in the *Jardin* as decisive for his beginning to treat journal entries as starting points for lectures and addresses, Lee Rust Brown notes that with the July 13 entry we get a glimpse of Emerson's "critical abilities of discernment and composition,"[30] leading to "the kind of writing to which [Emerson] had long aspired."[31] This was nothing less than a "new model of...experience" as well as a "method of collection, preservation and composition," that led to Emerson's "mature vocation as journalizer, lecturer, essayist and poet."[32] I agree with this, but want to say something more about what Brown calls Emerson's "new model of experience." If Emerson's crisis of vocation was in part a matter of working through the tension between Unitarian empiricism and an emergent transcendentalism (different ways of thinking about experience), then a provisional solution to that crisis occurs as the *alignment* of a "new model of experience" with the "establish[ment] of the framework of possibility in which the...practice of writing 'up' from journals and notebooks could take place."[33] Rather than as a form of representation—of squaring inner with outer matters— Emerson now imagines experience as a way of *doing* something. And if, according to Brown, Emerson "treats the facts of his own writing as natural objects," thus opening up a "new world of...compositional practice,"[34] then in this first public lecture Emerson abandons both empiricism and transcendental idealism in favor of experience understood as the way the cabinets' embodiment of a general principle leads him to treat his journal as a collection of specimens to be arranged into new compositions. The impression in the *Jardin* becomes the condition of possibility for the move from journal to lecture.

Shortly after cutting the July 13 journal entry into the first lyceum lecture, Emerson began working on his first book, *Nature*, published anonymously in 1836. In the book's fourth chapter, devoted to 'Language,' Emerson imagines a bond between 'moral and intellectual facts' and natural phenomena:

> Every word which is used to express a moral or intellectual fact, if traced to its root, is found to be borrowed from some material appearance. *Right* originally means *straight*; *wrong* means *twisted*. *Spirit* primarily means *wind*; *transgression*, the crossing of a *line*; *supercilious* the *raising of the eye-brow*.[35]

If, as Brown put it, the cabinets' "meeting his eye" led Emerson to "treat the facts of his own writing as natural objects," then here he finds a progressive arrangement, not only from journal entry to lecture (and now to book), but from the "material appearances" of nature to the meanings of words. Indeed, the lines from *Nature* outlining his philosophy of language are themselves transposed phrases, borrowed from journal entries and lectures from late 1833. In a November 2, 1833, journal entry Emerson describes nature as a "great book" to be "put together" in language; a process he called, in another entry made during the composition of *Nature*, "the passage from the language of nature to the language of convention."[36] The trying out of phrases and sentences, subject to ongoing transposition and recombination, recast for different occasions and venues, is Emerson's way of enacting the idea that our meanings are "borrowed from some material appearance". Earlier in the book, in the chapter on "Commodity," he described this as the way "Nature, in its ministry to man, is not *only* the material but is also the process and the result...the useful arts are...new combinations by the wit of man, of the same natural benefactors."[37]

The concern with composition as an organizing frame within which material appearances are converted into the "new natural objects" of writing is, at a later point in *Nature*, brought explicitly back to the July 13 entry, where Emerson says he wants,

> to show the relation of the forms of flowers, shells, animals, architecture to the mind and build science upon ideas. In a cabinet of natural history, we become sensible of a certain occult recognition and sympathy in regard to the most bizarre forms of beast, fish and insect...[a] writer will feel that the ends of study and composition are best answered by announcing undiscovered regions of thought.[38]

Here Emerson appends to the list of the original journal entry the word "architecture," as if a formal principle followed from the series of flowers, shells, and animals. Internally marking the progressive arrangement from nature to the "writer," Emerson alludes to the cabinets, linking them again to "composition." And there is now the announcement that the writer seeks "undiscovered regions of thought," as if to specify that composition is not so much a matter of arriving at a fixed or final order but of carrying out an open-ended search.

Even if Emerson will shortly replace the metaphysical treatise with his preferred medium of the essay, the series running from the epiphany in the *Jardin* to the new declaration of vocation ("I will be a naturalist"), to the cutting of that material into the text of his first public lecture, to the philosophy of language and the new role imagined for composition that goes with it, leads to an idea of experience not reducible to a problem of representation. Rather than think of experience as a matter of securing a correspondence between inner and outer matters, experience is one with the doing of composition.

THE MIRACLES CONTROVERSY

Nature was not well received within the Unitarian establishment. One of the harsher notices appeared in an 1837 issue of *The Christian Examiner*, the same venue in which Emerson found Hedge's introduction to transcendental idealism. Francis Bowen said of the book that it contained "defects [in] points of taste in composition"; that its language suffered from "spice[s] of affectation"; and that the "novelty" of the "manner of treatment"—what Bowen called its "peculiar diction" and "cloud-capped" prose—was distracting.[39] Neatly registering the factions comprising the Unitarian schism, Bowen criticized what he took to be the book's stylistic infelicities through an appeal to John Locke. Quoting from the *Essay concerning Human Understanding* in which Locke compares "legions of obscure and undefined words" to "the learned gibberish [which] prevailed mightily in these last ages,"[40] Bowen used Unitarianism's preferred intellectual authority to attack what he took to be the dogmatic obscurantism of *Nature*, knowing that an enthusiasm for speculative metaphysics could be traced back to Hedge's widely read essay on Coleridge.[41] Characterizing Coleridge's mind as "medieval," Bowen wrote that "the bitterness and scorn, with which Coleridge...has replied to modest doubts and fair arguments, no parallel can be found, save in the scholastic controversies of the Middle Ages."[42]

In wanting both to identify *Nature* as an emblem of the "New School" in Unitarian intellectual life, and publically to denounce the movement, Bowen's reaction makes vivid the wider consequences of Emerson's search for a method of composition.[43] That *Nature* could provoke this sort of reaction is evidence that he was becoming a threateningly experimental thinker and writer whose works did not fit the grid of what Marsh had called Unitarian "orthodoxy." For Bowen in particular, it was Emerson's *way* of writing he found troubling; a style of expression inseparable from the method he had been developing in his journals, lyceum lectures, and in *Nature*.

Emerson's 1837 address on the "American Scholar," and especially his 1838 Divinity School address, take all of this a step further.[44] Just as he turned to his journals as a starting point for the lectures that led him away from the pulpit and onto the lyceum circuit, so with the Divinity School invitation Emerson turned again to his journals in search of a starting point for the address. He began with an entry made after attending Unitarian service, in which he laments the preaching style he hears coming from the pulpit:

> At Church all day but almost tempted to say I would go no more.... The snowstorm [outside] was real the preacher merely spectral. Vast contrast to look at him & then out of the window...evidently he thought himself a faithful searching preacher [but] he had lived in vain. He had no one word intimating that ever he had laughed or wept, was married or enamored, had been cheated or voted for or chagrined...it seemed strange that [anyone] should come to [this] Church.[45]

If by the end of June the journal "tended to be neglected, and the frequency and length of the entries dropped off as he applied himself to the task" of composing the address, by July 8, one week before the address, Emerson acknowledges the transition, referring to "the discourse now growing under my eye to the Divinity School."[46] The March 18 entry made it, again slightly altered, into the text of the Address, with Emerson using the figure of the "snowstorm" as a way of making explicit the difference between a formalist preaching style and the method he has been honing since his break with the ministry:

> Whenever the pulpit is usurped by a formalist, then is the worshipper defrauded and disconsolate....I once heard a preacher who sorely tempted me to say, I would go to

.....A snow storm was falling around us. The snow storm was real; the
spectral; and the eye felt the sad contrast in looking at him, and then
ow behind him, into the beautiful meteor of the snow. He had lived in
l secret of his profession, namely, to convert life into truth, he had not
fact in all his experience, had he yet imported into his doctrine.[47]

If "formalism" here captures the relation of preaching style to experience, then
an antidote to formalism occurs in the way Emerson cuts the March 18 journal
entry into the Address and then makes to it a revision: the journal entry's "snow
storm...falling" becomes "the beautiful meteor of the snow." Again, the method
works through transposition, as the reuse of journal entries (the declaration of
vocation in the *Jardin*), lyceum lectures (the reset passages in "The Uses of Natural
History"), books (*Nature*'s philosophy of language), and even the reworking of
a review of *Nature* (Bowen's emphasis on "manner") advances another step as a
snow storm becomes a meteor.[48] While perhaps a catachresis, or even an instance
of early *symbolisme* (the image would not be out of place in Arthur Rimbaud's
Illuminations), the phrase is most importantly a product of recombination, in
which a fresh image is discovered in the process of composition.[49] For Emerson the
experimental writer, experience is no longer the eye-witness report or the bringing
of empirical particulars under general categories, but something done and undergone: from seeing a cabinet or hearing a sermon, to recording one's impressions
in a journal, returning to those sentences or passages as themselves new objects to
be encountered, then putting *those* into new arrangements in lectures, addresses,
and books. Experience is not the front end of this process; it is the process in its
entirety.

After the critique of Unitarian preaching style, Emerson turned to a discussion
of the meaning of the word "miracle." Again he drew on his journals for language
in which to cast the discussion, and again he turned to an entry made after hearing
what he took to be a dull sermon. On June 20 Emerson wrote in his journal that "the
faith should blend with the light of rising & of setting suns, with the flying cloud,
the blooming clover & the breath of flowers."[50] Three weeks later in Divinity chapel,
he takes up the sensitive subject of miracles:

> The idioms of [Christ's] language, and the figures of his rhetoric, have usurped the place
> of his truth; and churches are not built on his principles, but on his tropes. Christianity
> became a Mythus, as the poetic teaching of Greece and of Egypt, before. He spoke of
> miracles; for he felt that man's life was a miracle...and he knew that this daily mira-
> cle shines, as the character ascends. But the word Miracle, as pronounced by Christian
> churches, gives a false impression; it is Monster. It is not one with the blowing clover
> and the falling rain.[51]

What made this passage the most incendiary moment of the Divinity School
address was the way it linked Unitarianism's understanding of the role of miracles

for establishing the truth of Christianity to the issue of preaching style. To think of miracles as being "one with the blowing clover and the falling rain," is to think of them as one with nature. In turning the June 24 journal entry's "blooming clover" into "blowing clover," and converting the earlier entry's "snow storm...falling" to "falling rain," Emerson aligns his argument about miracles with the unfolding of his own compositional practice. Rather than a spectral formalism, the diction and design of Emerson's address arises from processes he takes to be a continuation of falling snow, blowing clover, and falling rain. To be a naturalist—to resign a pulpit that has been "usurped by formalists"—is to continue the course of nature in a method of composition. This is why Emerson couples the question of preaching style with his alternate understanding of what a miracle is.

In rejecting the idea that a miracle is a monstrous aberration of nature, something cordoned off and separate from the "daily," Emerson attacked the core beliefs of the Unitarian community he was addressing. To doubt that a miracle was a suspension of the laws of nature, was in effect to doubt the veracity of the reports of the Gospels, which tell of Christ's controlling the weather, turning water into wine, giving sight to the blind, and being resurrected from the dead. Emerson's claim here is not only that a focus on the historical person of Jesus leads to the petrifying of his teachings into dead formalisms but that it is misguided to try to find evidence for miracles—understood as the suspension of the course of nature—in the form of eye-witness verification. Since Locke's sensationalism led Unitarians to "place a heavy emphasis on sense experience as the source of religious ideas," they "defended miracles and other supernatural evidences by arguing that God had no mode of conveying specific religious truths to the human mind except by manifestations which men could see or hear."[52] As Barbara Packer notes, the established church "clung to shreds of historical evidence, writing laborious volumes seeking to demonstrate that the Godhead had once dwelled on earth, while for Emerson all around them its epiphanies were perpetual."[53] If Unitarianism's understanding of the problem of reason and revelation hinged on an appeal to Lockean empiricism, which Marsh, Hedge, and later (and in a different way) Emerson found unsatisfactory, then in the Divinity School address Emerson continues to pursue the task of finding an alternate account of experience; one inseparable from what he called "being a naturalist." In replacing formalism with naturalism, he imagines an expression that would be "one with the blowing clover and the falling rain." If formalism was preaching insufficiently suffused with experience, then his own idea of experience treats it as continued, and realized, in composition.

Emerson's disregard for the empirical importance of miracles led Unitarian minister Andrews Norton to attack the Divinity School address in print. Norton stands as a kind of synecdoche for Unitarian doctrine in Cambridge circa 1838 (it would have been directly against his views that Marsh's "Preliminary Essay" was intended).[54] As with Bowen's review of *Nature*, Norton's first instinct was to attack the *manner* of expression issuing from what he called the "New School in

Literature and Religion." In his August 1838 review of the Address in *The Boston Daily Advertiser*, Norton wrote of Emerson's "crabbed and disgusting obscurity [picked up from] the worst of German speculatists," from that "hasher up of German metaphysics Cousin, and the hyper-Germanized Englishman Carlyle," and "the veiled image of the German pantheist Schleiermacher."[55] Norton goes on to call Emerson's address a "disavowal of learning or reasoning as sources of higher knowledge," and as provoking "disgust," "strong approbation," and amounting to "personal insult."[56] But Norton was most fearful of the effects such speech could have on the young, who might mistake Emerson's "incoherent rhapsody as a specimen of fine writing," having specifically in mind Emerson's calling religious sentiment "myrrh and storax and chlorine and rosemary."[57] Invoking the entire history of modernity as a series of challenges to ecclesiastical authority, and cementing the reception of Emerson's address as a heresy within the Unitarian community, Norton finally warned: "We well know how shamefully [the words of Christianity] have been abused in modern times by infidels and pantheists...whose philosophy is bound to break out in obscure intimations, ambiguous words, and false and mischievous speculations....Should such preachers abound, and grow confident in their folly, we can hardly overestimate the disastrous effect upon the religion and moral state of the community."[58]

While self-identifying transcendentalists like Orestes Brownson and George Ripley came to Emerson's defense in the *Boston Quarterly Review* and in privately printed pamphlets, this did not convince, or quell the ire, of Andrews Norton. As a man whose life's work was the multivolume *The Evidences of the Genuineness of the Gospels*, he tried again to bring down the "new school in literature and religion," this time in the genre that had set the debate going, a Divinity School address. Norton deepened and elaborated his condemnation of Transcendentalism in a talk called "The Latest Form of Infidelity," given to alumni of Harvard Divinity School on July 19, 1839. In this address, Norton compares Emerson to the "celebrated atheist" Baruch Spinoza, calling Spinoza "the first writer, as far as I know, who maintained the impossibility of a miracle."[59] Norton's comparison of Emerson to Spinoza is not a farfetched one. If "the Unitarian God stood above and beyond the natural order," and was not to be "confused with nature itself [and so] to apply his name to either the universe itself or to inanimate abstractions was a pitiful disguise for atheism,"[60] then in the Divinity School address Emerson offended Unitarian doctrine precisely in the way he imagines God as immanent in, or identical with, nature.[61] Spinoza's aim in the *Tractatus Theologico-Politicus* (1675) was also one of "detaching Christ from the churches," and was as such an "attack on ecclesiastical authority and priestcraft."[62] And it too linked an aversion to petrifying ritual with a critique of miracles understood as divine suspensions of the natural order. In the sixth chapter of the *Treatise*, "On Miracles," Spinoza states that "no event can occur to contravene nature, which preserves an eternal, fixed and immutable order."[63] Denying that "there ever have been, or ever could be, miracles," Spinoza asserts that "something that goes outside the bounds of the normal laws of nature affords no knowledge of

God [a concept] far better comprehended from the unchanging order of Nature."[64] He goes on:

> The people imagine that the power and providence of God are most clearly evident when they see something happen contrary to the usual course of things and their habitual views about nature, especially should it turn out to their benefit or advantage [but] since nothing is necessarily true except by divine decree alone, it most clearly follows that the universal laws of nature are simply God's decrees and follow from the necessity and perfection of the divine nature. If anything therefore were to happen in nature that contradicted its universal laws, it would also necessarily contradict the decree and understanding and nature of god.[65]

Spinoza's argument is a simple one: if God and the order of nature are identical it is absurd to think of God as suspending that order. If natural series follow from the necessity and perfection of God's decrees, then the idea of a miracle, as either an anomalous rupture in the causal order or as the basis for divine revelation, is an absurdity. Spinoza's argument is close to Emerson's, and Norton was right to hear Spinozist strains in the Divinity School address, particularly on the issue of miracles.[66]

Consider, then, the double assault of the Divinity School Address: On the one hand, it is jeremiad against a passionless and pedantic Unitarian preaching style, demanding that pulpit eloquence be charged with "experience." On the other, it is a replacement of the idea of miracles as monstrous suspensions of the natural order with an understanding of them as "one with the blowing clover and the falling rain"; that is, one perpetual miracle (God *or* nature). Considered together, the linked critiques are a function of Emerson's growing conviction that experience is to be thought of as the continuation of the course of nature in a method of composition. Rather than an empiricism that would search out the historical evidence for miracles (scholarly proofs built upon the eye-witness accounts of the past), or one that would make experience a matter of what is already given in the structure of the mind (Kant's "conditions of possibility"; Coleridge's "principles"), Emerson's naturalism is consonant with his quest for "ecstasy & eloquence."[67] Thus when Emerson complains about the thinness of lived experience in the formalist sermon, he complains of an expression that is not itself the effect of the "daily miracles" of nature; a preaching not arising from processes of transposition and recombination of the sort he has been experimenting with since the epiphany in Cuvier's *Jardin*. In this way he has turned the problem of miracles from a theological into a literary one. Building up and deriving new uses for terms he has been collecting from Hedge, Marsh, Coleridge, and the declaration of vocation triggered by his seeing first hand the Parisian cabinets, Emerson transfers the meaning of a miracle, understood as an aberrant suspension of the laws of nature, into oratorical provocation. It is no accident that an address that begins by celebrating the "fruitful soil, navigable seas; mountains of metal and stone... forests of all woods, in its animals, in its chemical ingredients; in the powerful path of light [and] heat attraction of life" leads to one of Emerson's most striking aphorisms: "Truly speaking it is not instruction but provocation that I can receive from another soul."[68] It is as if the capacity to be provoked—and to provoke oneself—arose from the "powerful paths" of nature; the "outrunning laws" at work in processes like falling snow, blowing clover, and falling rain.[69] Being a naturalist is here the way the search for an alternate preaching style occurs in parallel with the argument that divinity is immanent in nature.

Not long after the Divinity School Address, Emerson read his lecture "The Method of Nature," at Waterville (now Colby) College in Maine. Absorbing more fully the language of the reviews, and their specific pitting of sound argumentation against the "moonshine" and "disgusting obscurity" of the "new school in literature and religion," Emerson returns to the idea that nothing is fixed; that everything is always changing:

> When we are dizzied with the arithmetic of the savant toiling to compute the length of her line, the return of her curve, we are steadied by the perception that a great deal is doing; that all seems just begun; remote aims are in active accomplishment. We can point nowhere to anything final; but tendency appears on all hands; planet, system, constellation, total nature is growing like a field of maize in July; is becoming some[thing] else; is in rapid metamorphosis. The embryo does not more strive to be a man, than yonder burr of light we call a nebula tends to be a ring, a comet, a globe and parent of new stars.[70]

Everything Emerson says about nature here can be said about his own prose; it too has been in "metamorphosis" from earlier journal entries, through lectures and addresses, and on to the protean, musical sentences of the *Essays*. One of the essays of the first series, "Self-Reliance," contains an image metamorphosed from the Divinity School Address. "Man," he writes in the later essay, "is ashamed before the blade of grass or the blowing rose [and] cannot be happy and strong until he too lives with nature in the present."[71] In another lecture from the period, "The Poet," Emerson says that "poetry finds its origin in the need of expression which is a primary impulse of nature. In nature there is no rest. All things are in perpetual procession, flow and change…to be unfolded, explained, expressed"; and that "all the facts of the animal and organic economy…are emphatic symbols of this eternal fact of the passage of the world into the soul of man to suffer there a change."[72] When the lecture was recast for the essay "The Poet," these lines themselves underwent mutation: "What we call nature is a certain self-regulated motion of change," and then "it is not meters but a meter-making argument that makes a poem—a thought so passionate and alive that like the spirit of a plant or an animal it has a new architecture of its own and adorns nature with a new thing."[73] Here the move from lecture to essay partakes of the same metamorphosis Emerson celebrates in nature. Always lighting out for the new combination, experimenting in words with "motions of change," finding the directions of his own writing merging in a fluid procession,

Emerson's sentences become nature's own adornments.[74] When, in the last line of "Self-Reliance," he says "nothing can bring you peace but yourself...nothing can bring you peace but the triumph of principles," one sees that while the need to find a style has all along been a matter of "principle," principle itself has been in metamorphosis: from the early journal entries striving for "ecstasy & eloquence," to Coleridge's progressive arrangements, to Cuvier's classifications, to the new idea of experience that arises from the vocational announcement "I will be a naturalist."[75] If that idea of experience finds its realization in processes of composition, then Emerson now names this, at another point in "The Method of Nature," a "work of ecstasy"; an ecstatic merger of natural with literary processes he will later describe, in the essay "Love," as a scene in which "the stars [are] letters, the flowers ciphers and the air...coined in song."[76] With the Divinity School Address, and lectures and essays like "The American Scholar," "The Method of Nature," "Self-Reliance," "Love," and "The Poet" experience has become for Emerson something other than empirical acquaintance or transcendental deduction: it has become synonymous with the making of a prose attuned to the "one fact the world hates, that the soul becomes."[77]

JOYOUS SCIENCE

Emerson acknowledged the controversy surrounding the Divinity School address in an October 1838 letter to Thomas Carlyle, referring to the "outcry...against [my] infidelity, pantheism, & atheism," labeling the whole thing the "storm in our washbowl."[78] Later he made an angrier, more personal allusion to it in his journal:

Ah, ye old ghosts! Ye builders of dungeons in the air! Why do I ever allow you to encroach on me a moment; a moment, to win me to your hapless company? In every week there is some hour when I read my commission in every cipher of Nature, and know that I was made for another office, a professor of the Joyous Science, a detector and delineator of occult harmonies and unpublished beauties, a herald of civility, nobility, learning, and wisdom; an affirmer of the One Law, yet as one who should affirm it in music or dancing.[79]

Emerson reused the entry six months later for his 1842 lecture "Prospects," given at the Masonic Temple in Boston:

I hate the builders of dungeons in the air....Ascending souls congratulate each other on the admirable harmonies of the world. We read another commission in the cipher of nature: we were made for another office, professors of the Joyous Science, detectors and delineators of occult symmetries and unpublished beauties, heralds of civility, nobility, learning and wisdom, affirmers of the One Law. Cannot the great laws of the Universe be celebrated without sighing and groans, by the beauty of health, by musical harmonies.[80]

Lines like, "I read my commission in every cipher of Nature," condense and rearrange previously used phrases, images, and ideas, through the process Emerson calls "becoming a naturalist"; elaborated in the philosophy of language outlined in *Nature*, and later called the "method of nature." But the problem of vocation is given its most willful recasting here, in the announcement: "I am a professor of the Joyous science." Emerson's declaration reads as a rebuke to those "builders of dungeons in the air" who complained of *Nature*'s affected diction and of the "crabbed obscurity" of the Divinity School address (as much as detecting in these works the influence of pantheists like Spinoza). In shifting, in what remains of this chapter, from the New England reception of *Nature* and the Divinity School address to a very different context of reception for his writing, I want to elaborate some of the consequences of Emerson's naturalism, and the new understanding of experience that goes with it. Taking the declaration "I am a professor of the Joyous science" as a cue for turning to the question of Emerson's decisive role in the development of Friedrich Nietzsche's thought and writing, I consider Emerson's importance to a writer who called one of his most stylistically daring and personal books *Die fröhliche Wissenschaft* (1882/1886) [*The Gay Science*]. If Nietzsche's own thinking became more and more indissociable from the demands of arriving at a prose style suited to what he called "becoming what one is," Emerson's role in this transformation was not so much a matter of influence as it was what Cavell calls Nietzsche's "transfiguring" the pitch of Emerson's prose directly into his own.[81]

While revising in early 1881 material from his commonplace notebooks that would eventually become *Die fröhliche Wissenschaft*, Nietzsche returned in earnest to a full rereading of Emerson's essays, freshly annotating all of them. As Ralph Bauer notes, Nietzsche began at this time "an intensive study of [the *Essays*], entering...the most significant phase of his apprenticeship to [Emerson]," pointing out that Nietzsche collected quotations from the German translation of the *Essays*.[82] Bauer is building upon Eduard Baumgarten's work in the Nietzsche archive in Weimar, which revealed how the marginal notes in the German editions of Emerson's essays "proceed without any interruption from Emerson's text into Nietzsche's own meditations"[83]; evidence that Nietzsche's approach to composition "develop[ed] naturally from [a] method of collecting literary material."[84] More recently, Benedetta Zavatta has claimed that "rather than constituting merely an occasional stylistic influence, Emerson's philosophy informed the development of the very grounds of Nietzsche's own philosophy"[85]; an intimate relation Jennifer Ratner-Rosenhagen calls Nietzsche's way of "using Emerson to get closer to himself."[86]

As a clue to what it would mean to treat Nietzsche's scrupulous reading of Emerson as an effort to "get closer to himself," or as constituting, not simply an influence, but the very grounds of his philosophy, we might look at three explicit moments where Emerson is mentioned in Nietzsche's writing in late 1881 and early 1882. In a commonplace book dated "Herbst 1881" Nietzsche has written, at the top of the page, "Emerson-Exemplar."[87] The announcement in the autumn of 1881, as he is beginning to work on *The Gay Science*, that Emerson is to serve as a model to be imitated seems to confirm that late 1881 was for Nietzsche a time of re-immersion in the *Essays*. The second mention of Emerson, also from late 1881, is in the first edition of *The Gay Science*, which takes as its epigraph a quote from the essay "History": "To the poet, the philosopher, all things are friendly and sacred, all events profitable, all days holy, all men divine."[88] The line echoes the complaint from the Divinity School address that a formalist pulpit is a lifeless one; and that rather than settle for the divine at second hand, we ourselves are "newborn bards of the holy ghost."[89] To say that all events are miraculous and so profitable [*Erlebnisses nutzlich*] also suggests putting literary "Exemplars" to new use. The third explicit mention of Emerson from around this time is also from *The Gay Science*, where Nietzsche names him as one of those in the nineteenth century who had attained "mastery in prose" [*Meisterschaft der Prosa*], making explicit his admiration for Emerson as a stylist.[90]

While *gaya scienza* refers traditionally to style manuals compiling rules of versification, rhyme, and stanza structure in medieval love poetry, Emerson seems to be using the phrase to name the making of a prose that would have in it the qualities of song and rhythm; a thinking and writing along the lines of what Nietzsche elsewhere calls a "Socrates who makes music."[91] In his 1854 lecture on "English Poetry," Emerson calls this process, simply, "poetry," saying that "Poetry is the *gai science* [and] the trait and test of the poet is that he builds, adds, and affirms."[92] In his own reappraisal of *The Gay Science* in the idiosyncratic autobiography *Ecce Homo*, Nietzsche described the ecstatic month of January during which he wrote much of its last section, referring to the "Provençal concept of *gaya scienza*—that unity of singer, knight and free spirit."[93] For both Emerson and Nietzsche, then, to practice *gaya scienza* is to become attuned to the rhythms of poetry (in the broad sense Emerson uses the word, which would include prose) as it is being set down sentence by sentence. This is, I think, what Poirier is getting at when he says that it is not so much a matter of whether Nietzsche in fact read the "Prospects" lecture in which Emerson announces his vocation as the "professor of the Joyous science" (let alone the highly unlikely case that he somehow came across the 1841 journal entry), but rather that there can be heard in both "a particular tone of voice... a particular sound."[94]

If Emerson's method emerges from his sense that composition involves adding to and affirming the course of nature, read through Nietzsche's absorption of his ideas it ends up looking like a specific kind of compatibilism. If what got Emerson on the path of his method was Marsh's caution about blurring the boundary between experience understood as a passive receptivity (a capacity we share with "brutes") and the kind of spontaneous rationality that would allow one to be *free* from the causal determinations of nature, then for Marsh, the turn to Kantian idealism was a matter of securing a place for human freedom within nature. But in Emerson's naturalism, determinism and freedom are not mutually exclusive.[95] In what remains of this chapter I want to look closely at Emerson's particular brand of compatibilism, specifically in relation to the way the "Joyous science" of composition finds its condition in what Emerson calls a "deeper cause," and what Nietzsche will later call *amor fati*.

Nietzsche takes up the question of freedom and determinism, and the relation of these words to "experience," in two key passages from *The Gay Science*. At section 319 he writes:

> *As interpreters of our experiences*: One sort of honesty has been alien to all founders of religions and their kind: They have never made their experiences a matter of conscience for their knowledge. But we others...are determined to scrutinize our experiences as severely as a scientific experiment.[96]

The passage is echoed in a later section of the *Gay Science* where he complains: "How many people know how to *observe* something?":

> Your judgment "this is right" has a pre-history in your instincts, likes, dislikes, experiences [so] let us stop brooding about the "moral value of our actions"...let us leave such chatter and such bad taste to those who have nothing else to do but drag the past a few steps further through time and who never live in the present.... We, however, *want to become those we are*—human beings who are new, unique, incomparable, who give themselves laws, who create themselves. To that end we must become the best learners and discoverers of everything that is lawful and necessary in the world.[97]

If Emerson's joyous science imagines expression as being "one with the blowing clover and the falling rain"—we, like nature, are in a state of continual becoming—then Nietzsche's lines turn Emerson's naturalism into the injunction to "become those who we are." Amplifying Emerson's concern with the question of vocation, Nietzsche calls for a project of self-discovery; a kind of experiment in creating oneself, of shaping becoming into a style. Instead of submitting experience to the tribunal of judgments (making it synonymous with knowledge; with the phrase "this is right") experience for Nietzsche is a matter of "creation." And creation for Nietzsche is inseparable from "conscience," with conscience understood as our obligation to look—with the severity of a "scientific experiment"—into the way our judgments have a "pre-history in [our] instincts," and so are bound up with "everything that is necessary and lawful in the world." But here Nietzsche's understanding of experience arrives at what looks like a paradox. What does it mean to say that becoming those who we are—those who give themselves laws and who create themselves—at the same time involves succumbing to everything that is necessary and lawful in the world? How is it that becoming what one is involves both free creation and acknowledging that one is conditioned by necessary laws?

The beginnings of an answer can be found in Nietzsche's admiring description of what he calls Emerson's "cheerfulness." In contrast with the "noisy"

Thomas Carlyle, who practices an "ardent dishonesty towards himself," Emerson is, as Nietzsche puts it in *Twilight of the Idols*, "much more enlightened, eclectic, refined, much more given to wandering . . . above all happier . . . the sort of person who instinctively lives only on ambrosia and leaves behind anything indigestible. Compared to Carlyle a man of taste . . . [Emerson] has that sort of kind and witty cheerfulness [*Heiterkiet*] that discourages any seriousness."[98] In the word "cheerful" is a connection to "*froliche*," to gaiety and joyousness; to "lighthearted defiance of convention,"[99] and what Nietzsche later described as the "highest degree of the *gaya scienza* [in which] profundity and exuberance go hand in hand."[100] If joyous science is the search for a method of freely affirming our place in the series of nature—what George Kateb calls "affirming all sides of an unstoppable struggle" by "giving it good words"—then Nietzsche imagines the compatibility of freedom and necessity as a coupling of profundity (the depths of nature) and exuberance (a cheerful art of affirmation).[101]

In section 109 of *The Gay Science*, Nietzsche offers an explicitly naturalist provocation: "When may we begin to *naturalize* humanity with a pure, newly discovered, newly redeemed nature?"[102] This peculiarly "redemptive" naturalism is made more explicit in two quotes from *Beyond Good and Evil*, which continue the discussion of freedom and necessity from section 319 of *The Gay Science*. Here it is geared more specifically to the matter of composition:

> the genuinely philosophical compatibility between a bold and lively spirituality that runs along *a presto*, and a dialectical rigor and necessity that does not take a single false step—this is an experience most thinkers and scholars would find unfamiliar and, if someone were to mention it, unbelievable. . . . Artists might have a better sense of smell even in this matter: they are the ones who know only too well that their feeling of freedom, finesse and authority, of creation, formation, and control only reaches its apex when they have stopped doing anything "voluntarily" and instead do everything necessarily—in short, they know that inside themselves necessity and "Freedom of the will" have become one.

A few pages later Nietzsche puts this coupling of freedom and necessity directly in relation to literary art:

> Just remember the compulsion under which every language so far has developed strength and freedom: the compulsion of meter, the tyranny of rhyme and rhythm. Look at how much trouble the poets and orators of every country have to go through! . . . the strange fact is that everything there is, or was, of freedom, subtlety, boldness, dance, or masterly assurance on earth, whether in thinking itself, or in ruling, or in speaking and persuading, in artistic just as in ethical practices, has only developed by virtue of the "tyranny of arbitrary laws" . . . there is no small probability that precisely this is "nature" and "natural."[103]

Freedom, finesse, rhythm, rhyme—all arise from the arbitrary laws Nietzsche equates with "nature." That the artist has a "better sense of smell" in the matter of the inseparability of free creation and necessity is for Nietzsche the way "formation and control only reaches its apex when [one has] stopped doing anything 'voluntarily' and instead does everything necessarily."[104] Composition is here imagined as a form of freedom that is at bottom a compulsion. Nietzsche thus inherits and transforms the way his "exemplar" wondered, in the lecture in which he announced his vocation as a practitioner of the "Joyous science," why "the great Laws of the universe [must] be celebrated with sighing and groans?," offering his own remedy as that of "affirming the One Law in singing and dancing."[105]

These lines of Emerson's—and their transfiguration in Nietzsche—show him still working through the core problem of the Unitarian schism. Marsh worried that human freedom as self-determination, when blurred with the natural order of mere causal occurrences, would fatally compromise a moral human existence. Emerson, beholden neither to the Lockean premises Marsh attacked nor to the Kantianism he invoked to take their place, practices a gay science of composition in which freedom and necessity—caprice and gravitas—are one. Put differently, if gay science is, for both Emerson and Nietzsche, an art of affirming necessity, then it is also a naturalism arising from the compatibility, in composition, of freely creating and doing everything by "compulsion." While this begins in Emerson as a rejection of the sort of freedom that would by definition remain above or outside nature, it becomes vivid in the full-blown compatibilism he shares with Nietzsche.[106]

AMOR FATI (BEAUTIFUL LIMITS)

Assembled again from journal entries and passages transposed from lectures, Emerson's great essay "Experience" continues to imagine the move from experience understood as either eye-witness testimony or justified knowledge to one of affirming the laws of nature in joyous science. Just as the Divinity School address made method "one with the blowing clover and the falling rain," so the naturalist idea that freedom is compatible with necessity informs the essay's opening lines:

> Where do we find ourselves? In a series, of which we do not know the extremes, and believe that it has none. We wake and find ourselves on a stair; there are stairs below us, which we seem to have ascended; there are stairs above us, many a one, which go upward and out of sight.... Sleep lingers all our lifetime about our eyes, and night hovers all day in the boughs of the fir tree. All things swim and glitter.... Ghostlike we glide through nature.... Did our birth fall in some fit of indigence and frugality in nature, that she was so sparing of her fire and so liberal of her earth, that it appears that we lack the affirmative principle, and though we have health and reason, yet we have no superfluity of spirit for new creation?[107]

The dazed voice here worries that the series in which we find ourselves—the natural course of things—will overtake us, perhaps already has overtaken us, leaving us listless and stupefied. The fear that implication in the series is so deep that we "lack the affirmative principle" to meet or match it is a fear that we will not have the resources to meet the series with a "new creation." Attuned to the presence in the word experience of "peril," Emerson registers here the danger that the series may leave us overwhelmed; a danger he describes elsewhere in the essay as an "onward trick of nature...too strong for us." Lost amid the succession of events, zombified, depleted, powerless to counterbalance the onrush, the opening paragraph of "Experience" imagines a failure to respond to nature with "superfluity of spirit." Experience here is not our looking on at the passing show; nor a worry over whether the flux of phenomena is real or a dream; nor even the trauma of the loss of a child.[108] Experience is what we undergo in attempting to affirm the series in which we necessarily find ourselves. This is why, as George Kateb puts it, "to have experiences in the world is [for Emerson] inordinately difficult."[109] Such difficulty is inseparable from the way finding ourselves on stairs, which seem stretched over a void, requires of us a reciprocal affirmation. The worry is that one will not be sufficiently superfluous to meet the demand; that if the new creation doesn't occur, then neither will experience.[110]

Emerson calls our bond with necessity "temperament." Reimagining the stairs of the series in which we find ourselves as "a train of moods like a string of beads," which, as we pass through them, "prove to be many-coloured lenses which paint the world their own hue," temperament names the "iron wire on which [the beads] are strung."[111] Temperament reveals itself in the way what seems impulse in the moment "turns out to be a certain uniform tune which the revolving barrel of the music box must play....I thus express the law as it is read from the platform of ordinary life."[112] Finding at the bottom of impulse a necessity (a "must") Emerson says that in "view of nature, temperament is final."[113] Closely connected to temperament, but not identical with it, is what Emerson calls "character." In the essay of that title, Emerson tells us that when character is at work, we are no longer "pendants to events, only half attached to the world [but] share in the life of things [as] an expression of the same laws which control the tides and the sun, numbers and quantities...[character is] nature in its highest form."[114] An aspect of Emerson's naturalism is then the way temperament gets expressed in manifestations of character; a dynamic Emerson also calls self-reliance (and the negation of which he names "conformism").[115] The relation of temperament to character is also an expression of his compatibilism: we are not free either to have or not have a temperament, but we *are* free to affirm our temperament in manifestations of character, or "nature in its highest form." And it is just this affirmation of the compatibility of freedom with necessity that Emerson is afraid will not occur, when he speaks of nature requiring of us a "new creation."

Indeed, near the midpoint of "Experience" Emerson shifts his focus from the "iron wire" of temperament to the need for a new creation. Returning to the idea of method as a way or road, Emerson now says "everything good is on the high-way," extending this to a more expansive "equator of life" as a figure for "thought, spirit, poetry."[116] If this equatorial highway is poetry (in the broad sense), then the purpose of poetry is to trace the "beautiful limits" of our place in the series: "How easily, if fate would suffer it, we might keep forever these beautiful limits, and adjust ourselves, once for all, to the perfect calculation of the kingdom of known cause and effect."[117] For Emerson, to keep our beautiful limits, to adjust our place in the kingdom of cause and effect, is to "give good words" (Kateb) to our necessary implication in the series of nature.

Later, Emerson offers a more detailed account of what he means by "keeping our beautiful limits":

> That which proceeds in succession might be remembered, but that which is coexistent, or ejaculated from a deeper cause, as yet far from being conscious, knows not its own tendency. So is it with us, now skeptical, or without unity, because immersed in forms and effects all seeming to be of equal yet hostile value, and now religious, whilst in the reception of spiritual law, [but] underneath the inharmonious and trivial particulars, is a musical perfection, the Ideal journeying always with us.[118]

The "deeper cause" journeying always with us seems a version of the wire of temperament, along which slide our variable moods. Being a naturalist, arriving at a method of nature, achieving *Meistershaft der prosa*, practicing "Joyous science": all are ways of getting into a resonant relation with the "musical perfection" of the Ideal. And all are an antidote to the desire for anchorage agitating the skeptic and the passive reception of the religionist. These latter attitudes remain dazed by suc-cession; or worry, not only about helpless implication in the series, but about the impossibility of knowing its ultimate origin or endpoint. But the deeper cause from which temperament springs, as Emerson reminds us, "does not know its own tendency"; indeed, it does not "know" anything at all—it shapes, arranges, transposes, combines. No longer confined to a more or less accurate report on "inharmonious and trivial particulars," experience for Emerson names the search in composition for a harmony between the swim and glitter of succession and the iron wire of temperament.[119] Like the soul's becoming, the wording of that work keeps changing: being a naturalist, the method of nature, joyous science, ecstasy, poetry, power.

When Emerson says, in the closing paragraph of "Experience": "But far be it from me the despair which prejudges the law by a paltry empiricism" he comes full circle in naming the problem that got his method underway. That the problem of empiricism comes back to him here, and that Marsh's incompatibilism—his caution about mixing a receptivity to affects with the rationality constitutive of human freedom and autonomy—is answered in "Experience" with a naturalism that does not see a choice between freedom and necessity. Bound up with this response to Marsh is a replacement of the notion of experience as knowledge or correspondence— linked, not only to Kant's idea of *Erfahrung* as our capacity for judging, but to the form of verification Norton brought to his understanding of miracles—with the realization that while we are implicated necessarily in nature we are at the same time free to affirm that implication in a method of composition. If empiricism is for Emerson paltry, it is not, as Cavell reminds us, because of "its reliance on experience, but rather because of its paltry idea of experience."[120] It is "paltry" because it treats experience as either spectatorial detachment before a series of outer successions, or (when empirical realism is coupled with transcendental idealism) the deduction of the categories which constitute the objects of possible experience. What Emerson is after in his method is a remedy for the helplessness of the position he identifies, first as "empiricism," and then as "skepticism." Skepticism, as Emerson uses the word here, names the falling out of attunement with the coupling of freedom and necessity gay science seeks to affirm. Hence the essay's last line, that the "world exists to realize . . . the transformation of genius into practical power."[121] If "practical power" names a certain fit between temperament and character, "genius" suggests an ecstatic communion with a deeper cause.

This compatibilist response to the Unitarian schism—neither empiricism nor transcendental idealism but a joyous science of freely affirming the series in which we find ourselves—is made more explicit in Emerson's later essay "Fate," from *The Conduct of Life*. Taking up again the imagery of stairs or steps as serial increments, Emerson writes that in "our first steps to gain our wishes, we come upon immovable limitations . . . that is to say, there is Fate, or laws of the world."[122] While we are free to take steps (they arise from "our wishes") we must nevertheless come up against necessary laws. Emerson calls these laws an "irresistible dictation": "But if there be irresistible dictation, this dictation understands itself. If we must accept Fate, we are not less compelled to affirm liberty, the significance of the individual, the grandeur of duty, the power of character."[123] We cannot resist the dictation because it issues from the bond between our temperament and a "deeper cause." But we are free to affirm that bond in manifestations of character; in becoming what we are. Thus when Emerson says in "Fate" that "we are sure . . . though we know not how, necessity does comport with liberty," it is both the clearest statement of his compatibilism and another step toward a new understanding of experience. Not reducible to affective impressions, nor to rationally justified knowledge, experience for Emerson is the achievement of a certain "comportment" between our implication in nature and an experiment in creating ourselves; what he describes in "Spiritual Laws" as the way a "man is a method, a progressive arrangement, a selecting principle."[124]

If the naturalist account of experience leads for Emerson to joyous science—to building up, adding to, affirming the series in which we find ourselves as journal entry becomes lecture and lecture becomes essay through selection, transposition, and recombination—then that becomes philosophically intelligible as the making synonymous of freedom and necessity. Returning to the beautiful limits he sought in the essay "Experience," Emerson now offers the following injunction:

> Let us build altars to the Beautiful Necessity. If we thought men were free in the sense, that, in a single exception one fantastical will could prevail over the law of things, it were all one as if a child's hand could pull down the sun. If, in the least particular, one could derange the order of nature,—who would accept the gift of life? Let us build altars to the Beautiful Necessity....Why should we be afraid of Nature...why should we fear to be crushed by savage elements, we who are made up of the same elements? Let us build to the Beautiful Necessity...to the Necessity which rudely and softly educates him to the perception that there are no contingencies; that Law rules throughout existence.[125]

Like the beautiful limits poetry establishes, showing us ways of arriving at a meas-ure of our implication in nature, "Building altars to Beautiful Necessity" allows, as Steven Meyer puts it, for "all the difference between a deadening determinism and a determined freedom."[126] Of these two options I think Emerson offers in "Fate" a determined freedom. One way to build altars to our necessary implication in the series of nature is to build essays like "Experience" and "Fate" up from jour-nal entries, lectures, addresses, and other, previous, essays, such that composition itself is the form freedom takes (for Emerson) when one embraces the injunction to become what one is. The apprehension, in "Experience," that the series in which we find ourselves might leave us sleepwalking spectators left to puzzle out a life reduced to a "bubble and a skepticism" becomes, in "Fate," the irresistible hearing and affirmation of a "dictation"; the beautiful necessity to which our temperament is attached and to which we say yes. This is the pitch of thought Nietzsche takes directly from Emerson when he writes, at the opening of the St. Januarius section of *The Gay Science:* "I want to learn more and more how to see what is *necessary* in things as what is beautiful in them....*Amor fati*: let that be my love from now on!...I do not want to accuse; I do not even want to accuse the accusers. Let *looking away* be my only negation! And, all in all and on the whole some day I want only to be a Yes-sayer [*Ja-sagen*]."[127] There is serene logic in Nietzsche's New Year affirma-tion: if you announce yourself to be a lover of fate you can *only* say "yes" to your implication in the series of nature, since your freedom takes the form of an affirma-tion. What Emerson called "building altars to necessity" Nietzsche transmutes into an ecstatic affirmation: *Amor fati!*

The well-known line from "The Poet"—"art is the way from the creator to his work"—is a good description of how Emerson arrived at the distinctive sound of the *Essays.* That "way," or method, I have claimed, involves a shift in the meaning of experience. If the Unitarian schism arose from an appeal to transcendental idealism as an alternative to an empiricism thought to blur the line between rational freedom and mere receptivity to sensory affects, Emerson got out of that schism by locat-ing the conditions for experience in a method of writing up from journal entries; a shift from representation to making, captured in "out-running" words like "experience," "experiment," "expression," and "ecstasy." If Emerson is in the end some kind of transcendentalist, it is in the way he hangs onto the idea that experience is had on condition. But rather than find those conditions as already given in the mind, he searched them out in the wording of the world. This was nothing less than the invention of a style.

CHAPTER 2

Nonreasoning Creatures

Those problems that at first blush appear utterly insoluble receive, in that very circumstance—as Edgar Poe remarked in his "Murders in the Rue Morgue"—their smoothly fitting keys.

Charles Peirce

ANTEBELLUM AI

"Perhaps no exhibition of the kind has ever elicited so general attention as the Chess-Player of Maelzel. Wherever seen it has been an object of intense curiosity to all persons who think."[1] So begins an unsigned editorial Edgar Allan Poe contributed in 1836 to a new Virginia magazine called *The Southern Literary Messenger*. In it Poe attempts to infer correctly the workings of Bavarian inventor Johann Maelzel's chess-playing automaton, a traveling exhibition he saw on a number of occasions during one of its tours of the United States.[2] Observing the way the automaton won chess games against volunteers picked from the audience, Poe was fascinated by the effect the performance had on a paying spectator and was convinced the machine was a fake.

As many scholars have pointed out, the attempt to debunk Maelzel's machine was a first step toward Poe's invention of the analytic detective story.[3] "The Murders in the Rue Morgue," which appeared in *Graham's Magazine* in the spring of 1841, carries over many of the concerns of the earlier essay, and already contains a remarkable number of the devices that characterize the genre to this day: the ratiocinative mind at the center of a criminal enigma in which police toil in search of solution available only by a creative leap of inference; a dutiful and observant friend, often the narrator, who reports on the detective's feats of analysis; and the locked room mystery, in which the plot hinges on a perpetrator's egress and ingress to and from what seems to be a hermetically secure room.[4]

But what is never commented on in the scholarship pointing out the importance of "Maelzel's Chess-Player" for the composition of "The Murders in the Rue Morgue" is the *way* the tale turns the essay on the chess player into the logic of a new genre. If Poe's editorial is a matter of making inductive inferences about whether a piece of physical mechanism could be said to be doing something like "thinking," then the first modern detective, C. Auguste Dupin, makes inferential leaps from particular perceptions to correct explanations: first inferring the contents of another's thoughts, then making sense of a double murder in a Paris apartment. In imagining the relation of perception to inference like this, Poe anticipates at the level of literary form the category Charles Peirce believed to be the logical basis of pragmatism. Adding a third type of inference to deduction and induction, Peirce termed "abduction" the way "inference shades into perceptual judgment," such that when "we find some very curious circumstance, which would be explained by the supposition that it was a case of a certain general rule [we] adopt that supposition."[5]

Like Poe's derivation of the detective story from an editorial about whether or not a machine could play good chess, Peirce's idea of abductive inference developed from his curiosity about whether or not a machine could think. Indeed, Poe and Peirce, in their different ways, were beginning to ask the questions that continue to animate the field of artificial intelligence a century and a half later. If the artificial intelligence (AI) research program stems from two basic questions: What is compatible with physical mechanism? and What is required for meaningfulness?, Peirce thought that if you looked at what human beings do when they reason, you would see the *limits* of how far mechanism can explain meaning.[6] In his essay on the chess player, in which, as Shawn Rosenheim puts it, he was "striving after a notion of artificial intelligence,"[7] Poe takes up these same questions. By the time he writes "The Murders in the Rue Morgue" he starts to imagine the underlying principle of pragmatism: that reasoning is itself an experimental process shading into perception. That Poe was concerned with just these matters—a curiosity that led him to invent a genre built around flashes of hypothesis—is made explicit in Peirce's mentioning him in the course of a discussion of the relation of perception to inference, writing that the "problems that at first blush appear utterly insoluble receive, as Edgar Poe remarked in his 'Murders in the Rue Morgue,' their smoothly fitting keys."[8] If Peirce treated the question of what we do when we reason as a jumping off point for inventing a new type of inference, Poe used it as a catalyst for inventing a literary genre.

Poe begins his essay on the chess machine by stressing the difference between mere mechanism and human agency: "Everywhere men of mechanical genius, of great general acuteness, and discriminative understanding," he writes, "make no scruple in pronouncing the Automaton a pure machine, unconnected with human agency in its movements."[9] He then compares the chess-playing automaton to Charles Babbage's difference engine, saying that a machine able to win at chess is something very different from a machine that churns out sums:

> It will perhaps be said in reply that a machine such as [Babbage's calculating machine] is altogether above comparison with the Chess-Player of Maelzel. By no means—it

is altogether beneath it [since] arithmetical or algebraical calculations are, from their very nature, fixed and determinate. Certain data being given, certain results necessarily and inevitably follow. These results have dependence upon nothing, and are influenced by nothing but the data originally given. And the question to be solved proceeds, or should proceed, to its final determination, by a succession of unerring steps liable to no change, and subject to no modification. This being the case we can without difficulty conceive the possibility of so arranging a piece of mechanism, that upon starting it in accordance with the data of the question to be solved, it should continue its movements regularly, progressively and undeviatingly towards the required solution, since these movements, however complex, are never imagined to be otherwise than finite and determinate.[10]

Poe's concern here with the distinction between Babbage's machine and Maelzel's chess player is about the difference between determined calculations and inferences about data that cannot be known in advance. A machine like Babbage's calculator "proceeds...to its final determination, by a succession of unerring steps liable to no change, and subject to no modification," since it treats the data fed into it in a fixed manner, with the conclusion implicit in the premises from the beginning; just as a deductive inference moves by necessity from a major premise, to a particular case, to a conclusion. Maelzel's chess player, on the other hand, would have to respond in real time to an opponent's chess moves and convert those data into meaningful moves of its own. Thus with the chess player,

> there is no determinate progression. No one move in chess necessarily follows upon any one other. From no particular disposition of the men at one period of a game can we predicate their disposition at a different period. Let us place the first move in a game of chess in juxtaposition with the data of an algebraical question, and their great difference will be immediately perceived. From the latter...the second step of the question, dependent thereupon, inevitably follows. It is modeled by the data. It must be thus and not otherwise. But from the first move in a game of chess no especial second move flows of necessity.[11]

If algebraic data, according to Poe, advance inexorably from premise to conclusion, moves made by the mechanical chess player would have to occur without such predeterminations. Poe's contrasting Babbage's difference engine with Maelzel's chess-playing machine is thus a matter of spelling out the difference between a priori deductions and a posteriori inductions, a distinction that will serve as the basis for his argument attempting to show up the machine as a fake.

For Poe's readership, the most captivating question concerned whether or not somebody is concealed within the machine; a question that amounts, for the antebellum audience, to "Could a mechanical contraption actually play good chess?" or, to update the wording, "Is there such a thing as artificial intelligence?" Poe takes up this question in a discussion of inductive reasoning:

> Some *person* is concealed in the box during the whole time of exhibiting the interior. We object, however, to the whole verbose description of the manner in which the partitions are shifted, to accommodate the movement of the person concealed. We object to it as a mere theory assumed in the first place, and to which circumstances are afterwards made to adapt themselves. It was not and could not have been arrived at by any inductive reasoning. In whatever way the shifting is managed, it is of course concealed at every step from observation.[12]

As with the distinction between the determinate calculations of Babbage's engine and the more improvisatory making of chess moves, Poe avoids the inference based on a "mere theory assumed in the first place." One should not speculate about hidden partitions because one should not assume what cannot be observed. In fact Poe was only partly correct in his assessment of the chess player's mechanism: there *was* somebody concealed within the cabinet guiding the movements of its mechanical arm, and his remaining concealed during Maelzel's exposition of the cabinet's interior *did* depend on movable partitions. But what concerns us here is less the final accuracy of Poe's inferences than the way the observed effects of Maelzel's performance led him to write a certain kind of magazine editorial. In making explicit the link between the mechanical chess player's enchanting spectators with the effect of artificial intelligence and a kind of magazine writing that would entice potential readers of the *Southern Literary Messenger,* Poe translated the illusion of the exhibition into his own essay of inductive performance. And if it is observation rather than a theory assumed in the first place that makes all the difference in the possibility of there being a chess-playing machine, then it is precisely Poe's insistence on induction that leads him to the kinds of inferences that show the machine to be a mere substitution of surface effects for actual machine intelligence.[13] What a machine must be able to do in order to play chess is the very thing Poe is doing in making inferences based on observation alone. This conversion of the exhibition's effects into a certain kind of writing is a crucial step on the way to Poe's invention of the analytic detective story; a tale that in turn anticipates Peirce's idea of the abductive inference.[14]

PEIRCE MACHINES

Before turning to look in detail at how the essay on Maelzel's chess player gets formally elaborated in "The Murders in the Rue Morgue," I want first to consider how Peirce's own writing on reasoning machines echoes Poe's ideas about the relation of mechanism to inference. In his 1887 paper "Logical Machines," Peirce wonders whether a piece of mechanism might be designed that could carry out deductive inferences, and if so whether such machines might be steps toward other machines that would be capable, not only of reasoning, but of choice, hypothesis, creativity, and learning. Echoing Poe's assessment of the difference between Babbage's calculating engine, and the chess-playing machine, Peirce writes:

> A [reasoning machine] is destitute of all originality...it cannot find its own problems, it cannot feed itself...the machine is utterly devoid of original initiative and would only do the special kinds of things it had been calculated to do. This...is no defect in a deterministic machine [since a] deterministic machine has been contrived to do a certain thing, and it can do nothing else.[15]

Peirce then considers the relation of deterministic machines to certain kinds of inferences, describing a piece of mechanism that "embodies" relations of necessity in syllogisms. Again sounding close to Poe's contrasting Babbage's calculating engine with the chess-playing automaton, Peirce says of the syllogism that it "can be embodied in a machine where pushing the lever A activates the piston B, which in turn rotates the wheel C, so that pushing A in effect activates C. Machines then, are capable of reasoning, in the sense of drawing inferences."[16] Peirce goes on:

> The secret of all reasoning machines is after all very simple. It is that whatever relation among the objects reasoned about is destined to be the hinge of a ratiocination, that same general relation must be capable of being introduced between certain parts of the machine. For example, if we want to make a machine which shall be capable of reasoning in the syllogism If A then B, If B then C, Therefore, if A then C we have only to have a connection which can be introduced at will, such that when one event A occurs in the machine, another event B must also occur. This connection being introduced between A and B, and also between B and C, it is necessarily...introduced between A and C.[17]

If in a deductive syllogism there is a relation of necessity between premise, case, and conclusion, then in principle a piece of mechanism could carry out an analogue of that relation.[18] Peirce was here building upon the work of Allan Marquand, a student in his logic course at Johns Hopkins University in 1881–82;[19] and Marquand had himself become interested in, and sought to make improvements upon, a logical machine designed by Stanley Jevons.[20] Aside from serving as an interesting (and largely neglected) chapter in the prehistory of the computer, Peirce's paper on logical machines, with its Poe-like attention to the difference between inference as formal validity and inference as inseparable from observation, begins to lay the groundwork for imagining the process by which initial, tentative hypotheses turn into general explanations; of how reasoning arises from the way "perception shades into inference."

In a definition he contributed to the *Century Dictionary* Peirce wrote that a logical machine was one which "being fed with premises produces the necessary conclusions from them [but] the value of logical machines seems to lie in their showing how far reasoning is a mechanical process, and how far it calls for acts of observation."[21] In this typically idiosyncratic definition, Peirce claims that while such machines physically embody a logic of formal necessity, what they really show is the way reasoning is ultimately more a matter of observation and experiment than determinate calculation.[22] This claim involved for Peirce making the move from formal logic to what he began to call "expanded logic," or the "logic of relations." For Peirce, a logic of relations was one that would treat reasoning as a "living, non-mechanical process."[23] As the basis for pragmatism—what Peirce, wanting to distinguish his method from his friend William James's popular elaboration of pragmatism, will later call "pragmaticism"—such logic stressed the role of experiment in reasoning itself. Peirce spelled out what he meant by this distinction in an 1887 letter to J. M. Hantz: "For my part, I hold that reasoning is the observation of relations...it is a living process [and] a kind of experimentation."[24] The letter to Hantz marks an initial turn for Peirce away from the essay "Logical Machines"—where he follows Poe in thinking that a reasoning machine could only perform determinate calculations—to a new emphasis on a logic of relations in which reasoning is thought of as living process. Kenneth Ketner sums up what's at stake in Peirce's conception of expanded logic with the question: "To what extent is the method [of reasoning] mechanical, deterministic, and unbending in nature; and to what extent do [such methods] include factors like observation, experiment, induction, creativity, serendipity, free choice, judgment, discernment and originality?"[25] Ketner's distinction ought to remind us, not only of the difference Peirce describes in his letter to Hantz between reasoning as mechanical and deterministic and reasoning as a living process, but of Poe's doubt that a pure machine could play good chess.

Peirce's "living process" is not incompatible with a notion of method, as he makes clear in an unpublished piece, "Our Senses are Reasoning Machines." There method is linked to learning as an experimental openness to making revisions on the fly: "In genuine reasoning, we are not wedded to our method. We deliberately approve it, but we stand ever ready and disposed to reexamine it and improve upon it."[26] Peirce here notes the difference between "arbitrary methods (which would bear close resemblance to mechanical, deterministic algorithms)...and scientific methods which admit of a reality and a creative, experimenting, observing critical inquirer whose beliefs are adjusted to that reality in unpredictable ways."[27] In this second type of reasoning, there is always, as Ketner puts it, a "non-deterministic step, which often involves creativity, discernment...even serendipity"; what he calls the "experimental design phase" of inquiry.[28] Peirce, then, is wondering if there could be a machine that would be capable of implementing method understood on this latter account; that is, a machine that could learn.[29] Ketner calls such learning machines "Peirce machines." Again, the contrast between a deterministic and nondeterministic reasoning machine was exactly the angle of Poe's essay "Maelzel's Chess-Player," and the basis for Poe's skepticism about whether a pure machine could win chess games against spectators randomly picked from the audience.[30]

Insofar as a Peirce machine (to stick with Ketner's term) would treat thinking as the trying out of hypotheses—as testing, experimentation or guessing—it also becomes clear how it serves for Peirce as a jumping off point for what he called "abductive" inferences; a term he so much as equated with the meaning of pragmatism. An abductive inference, according to Peirce, is one that shades into perceptual judgment, with the implication that perceptual judgments themselves contain general elements.[31] Peirce says abductive inferences "come to us like a flash" and arise from a choice or preference for one hypothesis over another. Abduction is the postulating of a hypothetical rule that will explain some perceived particular; an attempt at coming up with the general category under which some particular may be made intelligible.[32] Abduction, then, could be described as a conjecture at a general category that may or may not account for some perceived particular through an intuitive guess at hypotheses.[33]

JUMPING TO CONCLUSIONS

The parallels sketched here between Poe and Peirce directly inform the treatise-like opening paragraphs of "The Murders in the Rue Morgue." Again taking up the tone of the explanatory editorial, Poe begins the tale with the claim that "the mental features discoursed of as the analytical are, in themselves, but little susceptible of analysis. We appreciate them only in their effects."[34] Here reasoning power ("analysis") is thought of as split between mental features and observable effects. In the introductory paragraph that appeared in the original April 1841 *Graham's Magazine* version (which Poe omitted from later reprintings), the narrator refutes the "vulgar dictum...that the calculating and discriminating powers (causality and comparison) are at variance with the imaginative...but although thus opposed to received opinion the idea will not appear ill-founded when we observe that the processes of invention or creation are strictly akin with the processes of resolution."[35] In these lines from the original opening paragraph, Poe is already moving beyond the dyad of deduction ("calculating power") and induction ("discriminating" observation), claiming it vulgar to presume that invention and resolution (with this last term understood as analytical disentangling) are mutually exclusive. Though the idea will return when Poe describes his detective Dupin as a "Bi-part soul: the creative and the resolvent,"[36] what one notices about the language of this trial run for Poe's first tale of detection is the way he has revised the question of determinism that served as the criterion for the analysis of the chess machine, to one of showing how invention and reasoning shade into one another. The remainder of the revised paragraph elaborates upon this idea, with Poe saying that the man who delights in disentangling "enigmas, conundrums, and hieroglyphics" achieves "results, brought about by the very soul and essence of method [but] have in truth, the whole air of intuition."[37] Knowingly mixing the language of experimental guessing (intuition) with calculation (method, results), Poe, in these opening lines of the first detective story, both builds upon and undoes the division underpinning the earlier editorial on the chess machine.

The second paragraph of "The Murders in the Rue Morgue" then explicitly revisits the example of chess, and again flips the values of the analogy. Specifically, playing chess now serves, not as a criterion for thinking, but as a certain kind of observation—what Poe simply calls "attention"—to be contrasted with something he calls "acumen" and "analysis." If the idea of machine intelligence with which Poe grappled in "Maelzel's Chess-Player" (and which Peirce is concerned with in his paper on Marquand's machine) was a matter of imagining kinds of nondeterministic inference, then in "The Murders in the Rue Morgue" the issue is no longer that of contrasting deductive calculation with inductive experiment. With chess now used as a counterexample, Poe moves beyond induction toward something like guessing:

> To calculate is not in itself to analyze...In [the game of chess], where the pieces have different and bizarre motions, with various and variable values, what is only complex is mistaken (not an unusual error) for what is profound....In draughts [checkers], on the contrary, where the moves are *unique* and have but little variation, the probabilities of inadvertence are diminished, and the mere attention being left comparatively unemployed, what advantages are obtained by either party are obtained through superior *acumen*.[38]

In an inversion of the argument found in "Maelzel's Chess-Player," chess is here the ruse under which an "elaborately frivolous" effect of thinking appears, which Poe now aligns with mere calculation.[39] Conversely, "acumen" now names an attention to that which exceeds the formalities of the game as closed and rule-bound; a free, associative attention, open to improvisation and experiment. From this freely surveying attention Poe shifts to a comparison of chess to the card game whist:

> When I say proficiency [in whist] I mean that perfection in the game which includes a comprehension of *all* the sources whence legitimate advantage may be derived. These are not only manifold but multiform, and lie frequently among the recesses of thought altogether inaccessible to the ordinary understanding.[40]

In summarizing the opening minitreatise on the difference between calculation (chess) and analysis (draughts and whist) by saying that "it is in matters beyond the limits of mere rule that the skill of the analyst is evinced [and he] makes, in silence, a host of observations and inferences," Poe's narrator begins to imagine what Peirce called "abduction."[41] Later in the tale, Dupin will comment on his own skill as an analyst, saying that it is "by deviations from the plane of the ordinary that reason feels its way, if at all, in its search for the true."[42] This going "beyond the limits of mere rule," and "deviation from the plane of the ordinary," these conjectural leaps beyond the canons of deduction and induction, leaps which may account for some confounding particular, is just what gives Dupin his skill as an analyst.

After remaking chess into an example of calculation, and with analysis now standing for a kind of inference that would include "deviations from the plane of the ordinary," Dupin's first ratiocinative performance tests out the opening paragraph's move beyond deduction and induction. In a famous episode, Dupin uncannily completes the narrator's thoughts after a long silence during an evening stroll on a Paris boulevard, saying to him: "He is a very little fellow, that's true, and would do better for the *Théâtre des Variétés*."[43] Intuiting that the narrator thinks the actor Chantilly's "diminutive figure unfitted him for tragedy,"[44] Dupin reveals the steps that got him from discrete observations to the narrator's associative chain of reflection, claiming to elucidate the "illimitable distance and incoherence between the starting point and the goal."[45] After explaining how he had noticed that the narrator collided with a fruiterer in the street, Dupin shows how he arrived at the inference that he (the narrator) had been thinking of the actor Chantilly:

> You kept your eyes upon the ground—glancing, with a petulant expression, at the holes and ruts in the pavement (so that I saw you were thinking of stones) until we reached a little alley called Lamartine which had been pavement . . . with overlapping and riveted blocks. Here your countenance brightened up, and, perceiving your lips move, I could not doubt that you murmured the word "stereotomy," a term very affectedly applied to this species of pavement. I knew that you could not say to yourself "stereotomy" without being brought to think of atomies and thus of the theories of Epicurus; and since, when we discussed this subject not very long ago, I mentioned to you how singularly, yet with how little notice, the vague guesses of that nobel Greek had met with confirmation in the late nebular cosmogony, I felt that you could not avoid casting your eyes upward to the great *nebula* in Orion. . . . You did look up; and I was now assured that I had correctly followed your steps. But in that bitter *tirade* upon Chantilly, which appeared in yesterday's "*Musée*" the satirist, making some disgraceful allusions to the cobbler's change of name upon assuming the buskin, quoted a Latin line about which we have often conversed. I mean the line *perdidit antiquum litera prima sonum*. I had told you that this was in reference to Orion, formerly written Urion; and from certain pungencies connected with this explanation, I was aware that you could not have forgotten it. It was clear therefore, that you would not fail to combine the two ideas of Orion and Chantilly. That you did combine them I saw by the character of the smile that passed over your lips. . . . So far, you had been stooping in your gait, but now I saw you draw yourself up to your full height. I was then sure that you reflected upon the diminutive figure of Chantilly. At this point I interrupted your meditations to remark that as, in fact, he *was* a very little fellow . . . he would do better at the *Théâtre des Variétés*.[46]

Dupin's explanation can be broken down into a series of abducted hypotheses that all turn out, for the first fictional detective, to be correct.[47] Abductions like the one that sets off the series rely on provisional rules such as: "If you're looking at something, you're thinking about it"; and "If your lips are moving then you're saying something to yourself."[48] By far the most precarious leap in the series, and one that depends on the validity of abductions like the two just mentioned, occurs when Dupin says: "I knew that you could not say to yourself 'stereotomy' without being brought to think of atomies and thus of the theories of Epicurus." As Nancy Harrowitz points out, this hypothesized rule would have to be something like: "if you think of 'stereotomy' you must think of 'atomy,' and then you must be thinking of Epicurus' theories."[49] In accord with the narrator's description of Dupin as a "Bi-part soul: the creative and the resolvent," there is a double aspect to inferences like these: Dupin is able both to "resolve" his perceptions into discrete components (to break down his surroundings into particulars), and then recombine the selected particulars in a single conjectural jump.[50] Here it is not just observed patterns that enable Dupin to guess correctly the narrator's thoughts, but inductions from a "discussion not very long ago" about "the noble guesses" of the atomist Epicurus. The steps from paving stones, to stereotomy, to "atomies," to Epicurus, and on to the discussion of Chantilly's being suitable for the *Theatre des Variétés*, are thus in part the result of a recollected conversation (and one which, appropriately, happens to be about "guessing"). As conjecture at a new explanatory category, abduction is also an art of resolution and synthesis; a selecting of elements from perception and memory, and their recombination in hypothetical leaps that, if valid, render patterns of apparently disconnected particulars intelligible. If "stereotomy" is the accident that sets off the chain of inference (the contact between the narrator's foot and a piece of pavement), it is also its status as an "affected" word that enables it to serve as the starting point from which different elements—recollected prior conversations; facial expressions and posture, phonetic resemblances—turn into the inferences that allow Dupin to read the narrator's thoughts.

But there is, in this scene, a more formally reflexive way Poe stages the abductive jump from perceived particular to explanatory category. Insofar as this is a first glimpse of Dupin in the act of making inferences, with the amazed narrator looking on and reporting on those inferences, the episode marks a turn into the modern, analytic detective story. And insofar as the scene of mind reading carries forward the effect Maelzel's performance had on spectators (and the way it led Poe to compose a certain kind of essay), so this first appearance of Dupin's uncanny skill as an analyst completes the move from perceived particular ("Maelzel's Chess-Player") to the unveiling of a new genre ("The Murders in the Rue Morgue"). And if a defining attribute of this genre is the presence of a character with a certain kind of ability—the amateur detective preternaturally skilled in making correct inferences—then the genre's identity as a genre depends on its depiction of the abduction of hypotheses. Poe's experimental writing between 1836 and 1841 can thus be understood as his turning the perceptual encounter with the chess machine into the general category of the detective story, such that the relation of "Maelzel's Chess-Player" to "The Murders in the Rue Morgue" looks like a single, unbroken abduction.

Not long after the performance of what seems to be mind reading (but is in fact just a series of valid inferences), Dupin and the narrator find themselves "looking over the evening edition of the 'Gazette des Tribunaux.'" There they read of how the "inhabitants of the Quartier St. Roch were aroused from sleep by a succession of terrific shrieks," and of the double murder of a Madame L'Espanaye and her daughter Mademoiselle Camille L'Espanaye.[51] The mother, having been thrown out a window, is found in the courtyard with her head nearly severed; the daughter is discovered wedged feet first up into the chimney.[52] The apartment is in total disarray. On a chair is a "razor besmeared with blood," and scattered over the floor are found "four Napoleons, an ear-ring of topaz, three large silver spoons, three smaller *métal d'Alger*, and two bags, containing nearly four thousand francs in gold."[53] As with the scene of mind reading, the solution to the crime will depend on Dupin's ability to conjecture from perceptual patterns—here the aftermath of a double murder—to correct inference.

Following the detailing of the crime scene in a second newspaper report, Dupin and the narrator read the testimony of a series of deposed witnesses about what they have heard coming from within the apartment. Each of them describes having heard a gruff voice which each believes to be in a different language. None can decide if the shrieks, and the few intelligible words, have been uttered by a man or a woman. But they all agree that it was a "very strange voice," the voice of a "foreigner," a "shrill voice" in which one "could not distinguish the words," and that could not be differentiated from "scraping and scuffling."[54] The lack of agreement about the gender and nationality of the voice or voices heard, and their "gruff" and "shrill" character, along with the odd fact of the valuables left behind on the apartment floor (the murders do not appear to be the result of an attempted robbery), seems to create a problem of motive. But at a later point in the tale Dupin will mock the Parisian police for precisely this assumption; what he calls their "blundering idea of motive," as if motive were the wrong general category through which to assess observed particulars in the apartment.[55] Harrowitz describes this as the way the police do not go "beyond the assumption that the murder was a human being [and so the police are] unable to understand ... the clues, or even to realize what the clues were."[56] The procedural appeal to the wrong general category for inferring the meaning of the crime scene prevents the police from knowing, not just what has occurred, but what is to count as a clue at all.

Refusing the predetermined general category of motive, Dupin takes an approach more suited to what he calls the "excessively *outré*" aspects of the crime.[57] In a piece of inferential theatrics worthy of "Maelzel's Chess-Player," Dupin again brings to a set of observed facts improvised hypotheses making possible valid inference. Considering at once the extreme strength required to perform the acts of violence, the problem of getting in and out of a high locked room (and locked windows), the fact that money and jewels are left upon the floor, and the inability of the twelve deposed witnesses to agree on either the nationality or the gender of the voices coming from within the apartment, Dupin unfolds the steps of his analysis:

> If now…you have properly reflected upon the odd disorder of the chamber, we have gone so far as to combine the ideas of an agility astounding, a strength superhuman, a ferocity brutal, a butchery without motive, a *grotesquerie* in horror absolutely alien from humanity, and a voice foreign in tone to the ears of many nations, and devoid of all distinct or intelligible syllabification. What result, then, has ensued? What impression have I made upon your fancy?[58]

Like the scene of mind reading, in which Dupin exhibits the steps from paving stones to the narrator's thoughts, it is again a matter of moving from perceived particulars to general explanation, as we approach the tale's dénouement. But here Poe imagines the move from particular to general as a move from a shriek "foreign in tone to the ears of many nations" to what he calls "intelligible syllabification"; from unpartitioned sounds to articulate speech. With this distinction in mind Dupin points out the width of the finger marks on Madame L'Espanaye's neck by mapping them onto a piece of paper laid flat on a table top. In what he describes as an "experiment," Dupin again exhibits the steps of his reasoning. The narrator reports:

> "You will perceive," continued my friend, spreading out the paper upon the table before us, "that this drawing gives the idea of a firm and fixed hold. There is no *slipping* apparent. Each finger has retained—possibly until the death of the victim—the fearful grasp by which it originally embedded itself. Attempt, now, to place all your fingers, at the same time, in the respective impressions as you see them."
>
> I made the attempt in vain.
>
> "We are possibly not giving this matter a fair trial," [Dupin] said. "The paper is spread out upon a plane surface; but the human throat is cylindrical. Here is a billet of wood, the circumference of which is about that of the throat. Wrap the drawing around it, and try the experiment again."
>
> I did so; but the difficulty [of getting my hands around it] was even more obvious than before. "This," I said, "is the mark of no human hand."
>
> "Read now,' replied Dupin," this passage from Cuvier."
>
> It was a minute anatomical and generally descriptive account of the large fulvous Ourang-Outang of the East Indian Islands. The gigantic stature, the prodigious strength and activity, the wild ferocity, and the imitative propensities of these mammalia are sufficiently well known to all. I understood the full horrors of the murder at once.[59]

Combining the problem of an absence of motive with an absence of "intelligible syllabification," Dupin dramatizes the way inductive testing bears out the validity of an abducted hypothesis: that an Ourang-Outang has committed the double murder in the Rue Morgue. Moving from bruises on Madame L'Espanaye's neck, to a two-dimensional pattern drawn on paper, to a three-dimensional model of those markings, and then, in a last decisive step, to the classificatory logic that arranges living beings according to species, Dupin's experiment shows how a guess at a rule can turn out to right. And if, as Shawn Rosenhiem points out, acoustical perception in the tale "runs on a continuum from the orangutan's grunts to Dupin's 'rich tenor' with its 'deliberateness and entire distinctness' of enunciation,"[60] then here *sound* tracks the abducted premise guiding Dupin's inferences, differentiating him from a too procedural police ("motive" as a category outside of which certain percepts do not register). We could say, then, that the scene marks out parallel paths along a perceptual continuum: the first, based on sound, moves from unpartitioned shrieks to "intelligible syllabification" (this latter phrase itself an extravagant performance of the thing it names, packing eleven syllables into two words)[61]; the second, based on sight, moves from bruises on a murder victim's neck, to finger widths traced, first on paper, then cylindrically. Taken together, the two series form an experiment designed to test the correctness of the abduction that the murder has been committed, not by a deliberative human being, but, as the volume of Cuvier confirms for Dupin, by a motiveless "Ourang-Outang of the East Indian Islands." If Dupin's first inferential performance was a matter of getting from patterns in paving stones to another person's thoughts, then here that same logic works in the way sound runs along a graduated scale from "shrieks" to articulate ("syllabic") utterance; and in the way marks on a victim's body move to a graphic representation (first in two, then in three dimensions), to the taxonomic grid through which disordered particulars are brought under general categories and so made intelligible.

Dupin's ability to come up with a rule for rendering observed particulars intelligible—for figuring out what such sounds and markings *mean*—is again formally enacted in the way Poe invents a new kind of literature. If we agree with those who treat the essay on the chess player as a rehearsal for the first analytic detective story, then we should treat the move from the one to the other as a move from a striking perception provoking attempts at inference to a tale that brings into focus a new generic category. The passage from the handprint to the page of Cuvier, by which Dupin makes the jump from one species to another, enacts the very formal features—*outré* crime; inferential drama; dénouement—of a new genre as it is becoming recognizable *as* a genre. If, as Rosenhiem puts it, Cuvier "provide[s] a methodological justification for Poe's cryptographic reading of the world," then that "justification" occurs in the way the shape of an abductive inference is formally embodied in the experiment of inventing a genre.[62] The moment of dénouement—motiveless animal rather than rational agent—is then also a throwing into relief the difference that makes a difference for determining what is to count as a detective story. What Poe called, in an 1846 letter, "something in a new key," is also a distinct "species" of literature.[63] In this way, inferential steps from paving stones to another's thoughts, from shrieks to "intelligible syllabification," from handprints on the neck of a corpse to a volume of Cuvier, are analogous to the move from the essay on the chess machine to the invention of the detective story. "The Murders in the Rue Morgue" is that peculiar literary experiment which, while being an individual example, at the same time creates the general category of which it is an instance.[64]

THE PHILOSOPHY OF COMPOSITION

If in "The Murders in the Rue Morgue" the criterion for distinguishing between one kind of creature and another is a capacity for "intelligible syllabification" (a distinction made vivid in the tale's dénouement), Poe continues to exploit this distinction in his poem "The Raven" (1845). In the essay he wrote explaining how he composed the poem, Poe claimed that he had arrived at a point that required a "non-reasoning creature capable of speech" to utter the poem's single word refrain, "nevermore."[65] The move from the first detective story's criterion of "intelligible syllabification" to the alliterative density and jagged rhythms of the poem's trochaic octameter persists as the difference between a nonreasoning creature's repeated word and a compulsively syllabic narrator. Indeed "The Raven" is a poem that flaunts and indulges in gratuitous "syllabification"; a poem about the difference between a creature that blindly repeats a meaningless sound, and a narrator who, in trying to figure out what the sound means, surrounds it with an excess of syllables. In "The Raven" the tension between "non-reasoning" utterances and "intelligible syllabification" occurs in the way the narrator invests what he hears with meanings inconsistent with the sound the bird makes. The drama of the poem thus hinges on the way meaning is projected onto meaningless sounds. Since we presume the raven to be squawking the word by rote, the meaning of "nevermore"—of being gone forever—is something *added* to the sound. Extending the problem Poe has been honing from the essay on the chess player and the first detective story—how, in Peirce's words, "perception shades into inference"—"The Raven" recasts it as an assignation of significance to the rote reiteration of something that sounds like, but doesn't mean, "nevermore."[66]

Mourning the death of "the rare and radiant maiden whom the angels name Lenore," Poe's grief-stricken, melancholic narrator sits in his study, "pondering...over many a quaint and curious volume of forgotten lore." Like many of Poe's nervous narrators, he is hypersensitive to sound, and is soon disrupted by a "tapping" and a "rapping."[67] In the immediately following stanza he says he feels "thrilled" by the "silken sad uncertain rustling" of the curtains in his room, taking this excessively sibilant rustling to be "some visitor entreating entrance at [his] chamber door."[68] Already in these opening stanzas can be found the organizing tension that will run throughout the poem, from the narrator's state of grieving remembrance (perhaps exacerbated by whatever is in those "volumes of forgotten lore") to sound patterns that seem, but are not in themselves, meaningful.

Soon there arrives at the narrator's door a "stately raven," and we get the first instance of the poem's single-word refrain:

> Then this ebony bird beguiling my sad fancy into smiling,
> By the grave and stern decorum of the countenance it wore
> "Though thy crest be shorn and shaven, thou," I said "art sure no craven,
> Ghastly grim and ancient Raven wandering from the Nightly shore—
> Tell me what thy lordly name is on the Night's Plutonian shore!"
> Quoth the Raven "Nevermore."[69]

The beat of the trochaic lines—which move from octameter acatalectic in the first, to heptameter catalectic in the second, back to octameter in the third, again to octameter acatalectic in the fourth and fifth, and finally to tetrameter catalectic in the sixth—seem designed to dramatize the impact of the last word of the last line, "Nevermore."[70] In this stanza, each of the catalytic lines end on the phoneme "or," and so rhyme and meter combine to capture the incantatory effect of the raven's refrain. "The Raven"'s trochaic lilt is always reminding us that a nonreasoning creature could learn to utter sounds that seem like intelligible syllables but are in fact just phonetic patterns learned by rote. But the syllabic here takes on a peculiar logic, bound up with the poem's central predicament: what does it mean to find sounds uttered by an animal saturated with the deepest human longing and remorse? In marking this move initially as the regular beat from stress to unstress, and the way the variable meter of the lines set up each stanza's one-word refrain, sound in "The Raven" is continuously on the verge of usurping sense. To render two consecutive feet as "*bird* be | *guil*ing," for example, is to show meter halving a word so that it leans on a prior alliteration ("bird be"), while at the same time splicing together deceptive charm ("beguile") with cunning ("guile"). What is here "be*guil*ing" to the narrator is the way a creature presumed to be incapable of rational discourse is asked what its name is and replies "Nevermore." The same tension between meter and sense is then amplified in the stanza, where the enjambment from the third to the fourth line splits the bird's list of attributes at precisely the point where an internal rhyme ("craven"; "raven") jumps to alliterative adjectives ("ghastly"; "grim"), causing meter to grate against sense. Given the way the poem's extravagant diction and metronomic trochees are always threatening to dissolve into brute sound effects, it is fitting that what "beguiles" the narrator is the way the bird's response seems poised between a meaningless phonetic pattern and intelligible speech.[71]

The next stanza further develops the relation of sound to sense, as the narrator reflects upon what he has heard and tries to infer the bird's meaning:

> Much I marveled this ungainly fowl to hear discourse so plainly,
> Though its answer little meaning—little relevancy bore;
> For we cannot help agreeing that no living human being
> Ever yet was blessed with seeing bird above his chamber door—

Bird or beast up on the sculptured bust above his chamber door
With such name as "Nevermore."[72]

The narrator justly "marvels" at the fact that the bird responds to his question with an intelligible word (its "discourse"), but at this stage refuses to grant the sound "meaning" or "relevancy." Rather, he simply wonders what to make of the actions of an animal presumed to be incapable of rational discourse, such that "no living human being ever yet was blessed with seeing bird" respond when asked its name. But the distinction between a discoursing human being and a creature presumed to be without that ability (even if still capable of making sounds that resemble speech) is just what the stanza starts to blur. The "marveling" at the bird's capacity to respond with a sound that seems full of meaning is heightened in the way the partitions of the trochees bring out the "b" sound at the expense of the word divisions. "Bore" "bird," "beast," "being," "blessed," and "bust" are, in the midst of a discussion about what kinds of species make intelligible sounds (human "beings" versus "beasts"), twice rhythmically cut into "a | bove"; a splitting of a word that casts back over the stanza to words like "being" and "beast" (and "blessed, "bore," and "bust") in a way that privileges sonic resemblance over semantic distinctness. Interior echoing of this kind also informs the way the opening stanzas of the poem anticipate the meaning of the word "nevermore." In six out of the seven opening stanzas the narrator rationalizes the rustling he hears outside his door as being, alternately, "some visitor," "darkness," an "echo," "the wind," and *nothing more*.[73] When we get to the eighth stanza—involving the narrator's beguilement at the bird's discourse, and its first utterance of "Nevermore"—we find his earlier words of explanation, "nothing more," blending with the sound the raven makes (and that the narrator will soon repeat) in each of the poem's remaining stanzas. "Nothing more" both sounds like and means something close to "nevermore," but its significance is completely different from (even as it anticipates) the bird's refrain. If the move from "nothing more" to "nevermore" amounts to the difference between a trifle ("nothing more" than an echo, the wind, etc.) and what Poe called "mournful and never-ending remembrance," such glitches in the relation of sound to sense are just what the narrator finds beguiling.[74]

In the next stanza, the narrator changes his views about the bird's stubborn monotone:

But the Raven still beguiling my sad fancy into smiling
Straight I wheeled a cushioned seat in front of bird, and bust and door
Then, upon the velvet sinking, I betook my self to linking
Fancy onto fancy, thinking what this ominous bird of yore—
What this grim, ungainly, ghastly gaunt and ominous bird of yore
Meant in croaking "Nevermore."[75]

If in the former stanza the narrator shrugged off the possibility that the bird's word had any sense, now he begins to wonder aloud about what the bird "*meant* in croaking

Nevermore." This hedging about the possibility that the bird "meant" something in making the sound plays out in two ways in the stanza. First, the narrator's description of the raven spills over the edges of the trochaic divisions in excessive alliterative runs like "grim ungainly ghastly gaunt," as if to flaunt the way meaning fluctuates in sonic differences, and how such effects alter meaning at the level of individual words, parts of words, and even individual letters. Second, the poem's involuted syntax seems here to lift up into the semantic, such that "Nevermore" now *means* grief, loss, the permanence of death; and such that the narrator is led to make a series of inferences based on how the same sound can mean different things depending on his own (progressively despairing) inner states. Again, like the first detective story (which Rosenheim says places "grunts" and "discourse" on a continuum), Poe puts the narrator's concern with meaning on a continuum with "croaking," such that the poem is about a compulsion to furnish a nonsemantic croak with the mournful ring of "Nevermore": a sound the bird makes, but not a word that it says.

Falling more and more into a state of spellbound entrancement before the bird's single-word refrain, the narrator struggles to hang onto his sense of what "Nevermore" means:

> Thus I sat engaged in guessing, but no syllable expressing
> To the fowl whose fiery eyes now burned into my bosom's core
> This and more I say divining, with my head at ease reclining
> On the cushion's velvet lining that the lamp-light gloated o'er,
> But whose velvet-violet lining with the lamp-light gloating o'er,
> *She* shall press, ah, nevermore![76]

If "syllables" are now explicitly placed in juxtaposition with "guessing," it is because the narrator feels provoked to make inferences about sounds that seem to flicker in and out of significance. The poet will go through a good many more of these changes in attitude toward the bird, based on his shifting attributions of sense to its single-word refrain, in an attempt to hypothesize ("guess") what the bird might mean. Here, though, there is a last effort at fixing the meaning of the word, in his reminder to himself that it is "*she*," his lost Lenore, that will "Nevermore" press her head upon the pillow, nor see the glow of the lamps. In a move of desperate logic the narrator buttresses his guesses with new manipulations of sound. The two lines leading up to the mournful reclaiming of the meaning of "nevermore" from the oblivion of mindless repetition, are formed from a retaliating repetition of his own: "On the cushion's velvet lining that the lamp-light gloated o'er / But whose velvet-violet lining with the lamp-light gloating o'er." Attempting here to marshal resources of sound comparable to the bird's—the mechanically doubled full line with its proliferating "l" echoes (velvet-lining-lamp-light-gloated), and with the second line's "violet" heightening further the effect—the narrator has been lured away from sense into brute acoustics. When we finally reach the refrain line, with Poe's italicized "*she*" (the narrator straining for still further effects), the "ah" in "*She* shall press, ah, nevermore," seems a sound emptied of sense; a stray phoneme lodged in the line's struggle to reclaim the meaning of "nevermore."

By the final stanza's realization that the raven, "still is sitting, *still* is sitting upon the pallid bust of Pallas just above my chamber door," the twining of sound and sense takes the narrator to a point from which he does not return. As with the penultimate stanza, Poe again adds to the trochaic pulse both the repetition of a single phrase—"still is sitting"—and heightened emphasis in italicizing the second occurrence of the first word of the phrase. That doubly emphasized word—*still*—layers a second rhythm over the troches, creating a kind of phase shift in the poem. Since the word means simultaneously stasis and duration its single syllable both freezes and preserves the flow of time. That the narrator repeats the word, and then adds to it further italic emphasis ("*still* is sitting" suggests the bird is sitting there still, even now; as if eternally stilled), suggests that for him space and time have been squeezed into a single syllable. In this final stanza of the poem, it appears the bird has succeeded in driving the narrator mad, and that from his state of entranced hallucination he shall "nevermore" return.

If the relation of "The Raven"'s narrator to a "non-reasoning creature" is an inversion of Dupin's to the ape—in the latter the inference bootstraps from "shrieking," to a solution to the murders; in the former, the sound, while "syllabific," is furnished with meanings that cannot be what the bird means—then these are two sides of Poe's way of thinking through the problem of how "perception shades into inference." In "The Raven" Poe continues to explore the abductive jump from perception (sound) to the general categories under which perceptions become meaningful ("intelligible syllabification"). And he has clearly had the earlier tale of detection in mind in "The Raven," not only in his remaking the problem of species understood as the difference between sounds that mean something and sounds that are just sounds (shrieks, grunts, croaks), but in the bird's backstory. When we turn to the essay in which Poe alleged to explain the steps by which he composed the poem, we find out that in planning it he found he needed a creature that "having learned by rote the single word 'nevermore,' and having escaped from the custody of its owner, is driven, at midnight, through the violence of a storm to seek admission at a window from which a light still gleams."[77] Poe's tendency to recycle and transpose his own ideas from previous pieces becomes clear when we recall that the Ourang-Outang, captured in Borneo by a French sailor and brought back to Paris, startled by the return of its owner from an evening debauch, springs into the street with a shaving razor in its hand, where an illuminated window leads it to commit the double murder in the Rue Morgue.[78]

Just prior to the publication of "The Raven," Poe wrote a short article in which he proposed an idea for a magazine essay:

> An excellent Magazine paper might be written upon the subject of the progressive steps by which any great work of art—especially literary art—attained completion. How vast

a dissimilarity always exists between the germ and the fruit—between the work and its original conception! Sometimes the original conception is abandoned, or left out of sight altogether [but] pen should never touch paper, until at least a well-digested general purpose be established. In fiction, the dénouement—in all other composition the intended effect should be definitely considered and arranged, before writing the first word: and no word should be then written which does not tend, or form a part of a sentence which tends, to the development of...the strengthening of the effect.[79]

Much of his essay, "A Chapter of Suggestions," which appeared in *The Opal* magazine in 1845, was reworked for the larger audience Poe had gained with the intervening appearance of "The Raven" in the *Evening Mirror*, a poem that brought him wide fame. Levine writes that "The Raven" was a "crowd-pleaser [and its] fame [was] probably critical [to Poe's] decision to write an essay on how a poem is made."[80] Poe's sense of an expanded audience for the just previously published idea about an essay that would explain the compositional process led to the more knowing performance of "The Philosophy of Composition."

Modifying slightly the language of "A Chapter of Suggestions," Poe turns his emphasis on a "strengthening of effect" into an axiomatic starting point. Claiming now that in all of his writing he has "prefer[red] to commence with the consideration of an *effect*,"[81] Poe, in the "The Philosophy of Composition," says that he has

often thought how interesting a magazine paper might be written by any author who would...detail step by step, the processes by which any one of his compositions attained its ultimate point of completion....Most writers—poets in especial—prefer having it understood that they compose in a fine frenzy—an ecstatic intuition—and would positively shudder at letting the public take a peep behind the scenes, at the elaborate and vacillating crudities of thought...in a word, at the wheels and pinions—the tackle for scene shifting—the step ladders and demon-traps—the cock's feathers, the red paint and the black patches, which, in ninety nine cases out of the hundred, constitute the properties of the literary *histrio*.[82]

In offering to reveal to his audience how the "The Raven" had been composed—his claim that he is going to expose the "wheels and pinions" and the "tackle for scene shifting" behind the process of composition—Poe perversely exacerbates the logic of abduction. If, in "The Murders in the Rue Morgue," abduction occurs in the way Dupin is able to come up with hypotheses by which perceived patterns become valid inferences, and in "The Raven" the way the narrator, in an inversion of that process, invests the sounds made by a nonreasoning creature (the rote squawk "Nevermore") with meaning, then in the move from "The Raven" to "The Philosophy of Composition," the poem is submitted to an explanation of the process by which it was composed. Poe's decision to unveil the compositional steps of the poem—which he says unfolded with the "rigid consequence of a mathematical problem"—is thus his providing the explanatory categories for making sense of its effects. Indeed, when he claims to have started from the axiom "I prefer commencing with the consideration of an effect," he offers a general explanatory category under which the poem's particular sounds become intelligible. Here, then, "The Raven" begins to mean something very different from saying it means (for example) that a bereaved narrator, in a state of near hallucination, assigns significance to a word a bird utters by rote, because he begins to confound the sound the bird makes ("Nevermore") with a "mournful and never-ending remembrance" of his lost love Lenore. With the appearance of "The Philosophy of Composition," "The Raven" begins to *mean* what Poe offers as an account of how he *made* it.

Poe is fastidious in his description of how he arrived at the sound of the poem, specifically the selection of the phoneme "or" for the refrain:

> I next bethought me of the nature of my refrain. Since its application was to be repeatedly varied, it was clear that the refrain itself must be brief, for there would have been an insurmountable difficulty in frequent variations of application in any sentence of length [such a refrain had] to have force, must be sonorous and susceptible of protracted emphasis, admitted no doubt: and these considerations inevitably led me to the long *o* as the most sonorous vowel, in connection with *r* as the most producible consonant.[83]

While this sound—*or*—captivates the narrator and leads him to project a series of personal meanings onto a meaningless croak, Poe tells us that *or* has been selected in accordance with the principle that a refrain should be "sonorous and susceptible of protracted emphasis." This decision, according to Poe, has been deduced from certainties that "admit of no doubt" and are arrived at "inevitably"; necessary calculations following from the axiom of "commencing with a consideration of an effect." It is as if the beguiling variability of sound and sense in the poem—the way its lines lock into assonant, alliterative, and rhythmic patterns that cut across the meanings of individual phrases and words—were now made to mean in accordance with Poe's explanation of why he made the compositional decisions he did.

This might seem an odd sort of abductive inference, since it implies that Poe is making a conjecture at how he composed his own poem. But that is exactly what he claims to be doing in "The Philosophy of Composition." In telling us that "no point in the composition [of "The Raven"] is referable either to accident or intuition," and that "the work proceeded step by step, to its completion with the precision and rigid consequence of a mathematical problem," Poe is claiming to offer the explanatory categories under which the particular effects of the poem become intelligible. More specifically, in claiming to have composed "The Raven" according to predetermined axiomatic rules, Poe puts to new use his own earlier essay on the chess machine, such that the effect Poe is after in "The Philosophy of Composition" is to convince his readers that he is himself a poetry-making machine.[84] Realizing he had gained a large audience with "The Raven," Poe casts about over his own previous work in search of striking material to recycle; a regular practice, as we've seen with the escaped Ourang-Outang that, like the talking bird, seeks refuge at a glowing window (indeed, the poem's lost mistress is recycled from a just previously published poem, "Lenore"[85]), and the remaking of the paragraph from "A Chapter of Suggestions" into the premise of "The Philosophy of Composition." With the introduction of the language of mechanism, concealment, unveiling, and theatrics, we find Poe in the act of conjuring the earlier editorial's concern with mechanical reasoning for use in an essay purporting to expose the wheels and pinions of composition. But rather than an effort at inductively inferring the truth about the difference between a pure machine and human agency, it is now a matter of deliberately confounding that distinction so as to create the effect that Poe has composed "The Raven" by following a set of predetermined steps. To put it the other way around: if the illusionism of Maelzel's exhibition is reimagined in Poe's essay as the claim that "The Raven" has been composed with the "rigid precision of a mathematical problem," then what is here being *concealed* are the ideas, devices, tricks, and imagery Poe has been testing out, in a number of different forms (editorial, tale, poem, critical review) in the columns of magazines since his editorship at the *Southern Literary Messenger*. The claim that "The Raven" had been composed in accordance with a set of "universal" rules (putting to new use language Poe had previously used to deride calculation in the essay debunking the chess player), here we find those falsely theoretic starting points resurrected as props for the "literary histrio" of "The Philosophy of Composition." Again, this is just the effect Poe hoped to create in the essay—that "The Raven" *had* been so composed.

In the dénouement of "The Murders in the Rue Morgue" Dupin exhibited the steps of reasoning, from material markings, to a drawing, to a cylindrical model of the drawing, to a textbook of comparative anatomy enabling a completion of the inference that the murderer was not a human being with a motive, but a frenzied Ourang-Outang. But in "The Philosophy of Composition," Poe makes himself into a different kind of reasoner. Like Dupin, he makes explicit the discrete steps of an inferential series. But unlike Dupin, the poetry-making automaton moves through steps that are alleged to have been predetermined beforehand, following by necessity from the axiom of the "consideration of an effect" (contrast this with Dupin's conjectural jumps from perceptual particulars to general explanations). In keeping with Poe's appeal to the illusion of artificial intelligence as a way of creating the effect of a poetry-making machine, "The Philosophy of Composition" imagines composition as the following out of an algorithm. If an algorithm is "an infallible, step-by-step recipe for obtaining a pre-specified result,"[87] then Poe echoes this definition, not only in his description in the essay on Maelzel's chess player that a pure machine would have to move through its calculations in a "succession of unerring steps,"[88] but in the way he describes how he wrote his poem step by step.[89] Sticking close to Poe's account in "The Philosophy of Composition," an algorithm for composing "The Raven" might look something like this:

1. Intend to compose a poem that should suit at once the critical and popular taste.
2. Conceive the proper length of the intended poem.
3. Select the length of about 100 lines.
4. Design the poem in accordance with the universally appreciable maxim that Beauty is the sole legitimate province of the poem.
5. Select the tone of the poem in accordance with the maxim that melancholy is the most legitimate of poetic tones.
6. Employ the device of the refrain in the poem.
7. Variably apply the refrain throughout the poem.
8. Find a sound for the refrain.
9. Select the phoneme "or."
10. Find a word embodying this sound.
11. Select "Nevermore."
12. Find a nonreasoning creature capable of speech to utter the refrain.
13. Select a raven.
14. Find the most melancholy topic according to the universal understanding of mankind.
15. Select the death of a beautiful woman.
16. Combine the idea of a lover lamenting his deceased mistress and a raven continuously repeating the word "Nevermore."
17. Begin to compose "The Raven."[90]

In an illusionism worthy of Maelzel, a series of predetermined steps—deduced from axioms like "melancholy is the most legitimate of poetic tones," and "the death of a beautiful woman" as the most melancholic topic—are offered to explain the making of a poem that has in fact been built up from a number of previous literary experiments. From the essay on the chess player, to the abductive theatrics of "The Murders in the Rue Morgue," to the way the tale's problem of intelligible syllabification is remade in "The Raven" into the problem of the repetition of a single-word refrain: all these steps are, in "The Philosophy of Composition," looped back through the surface effects of the chess-playing machine. We are told we are reading an essay about the composition of "The Raven," but in fact we are—if we pay close enough attention to Poe's literary illusionism—witnessing the increments by which the analytical essay of literary theory arises from the earlier "steps" of "Maelzel's Chess-Player," "The Murders in the Rue Morgue," and, of course, "The Raven." If the witnessing of Maelzel's machine led, on the one hand, to the invention of a genre marked in its defining scenes by a certain kind of inference (first mind reading, then the solving of a murder), here Maelzel's machine is reimagined in an essay that adopts as its formal premise the surface effect of an algorithm, designed to conceal the ongoing toil of a work-a-day magazinist.

If, as I suggested above, the move from "Maelzel's Chess-Player," to "The Murders in the Rue Morgue," to "The Raven" has been one long abduction, then that pattern culminates in the way "The Philosophy of Composition" fully conceptualizes the compositional logic of those earlier instances. In offering as a guiding axiom his "preferring to commence with the consideration of an effect," Poe both accurately describes the origin of certain of his literary experiments (the witnessing, and writing about, the chess-playing automaton), and tells us what he is really up to in "The Philosophy of Composition": creating the effect of having composed "The Raven" as if he were following out an algorithm. And since in returning to the spectacle of the chess machine Poe also implicitly returns to his own critique of calculation as a "succession of unerring steps," the effect of the essay is that of making *himself* into a "non-reasoning creature." If the human agency required for reasoning was, in "Maelzel's Chess-Player," based on the idea that one cannot play a game like chess (well) from a theoretical staring point assumed in the first place, but must rather rely on observations of an opponent's moves; and if reasoning in "The Murders in the Rue Morgue" was imagined as Dupin's ability to arrive at correct inference through guesses at explanatory categories; and reasoning in "The Raven" was a matter of the narrator's guessing at the meaning of the rote repetition of single sound, and its confounding and hallucinatory phonetic resemblance to the name of his lost mistress; then in "The Philosophy of Composition" there isn't any reasoning at all. There is only a poetry-making machine moving through a series of predetermined steps; only the following out of an algorithm, which proceeds with "the determination and rigid precision of a mathematical problem"—the very determinism Poe and Peirce each reject as a model for what it means to reason.[91]

If the aim here has been to show how Poe's seeing Maelzel's chess player, in Richmond in 1836, set off a series of writing experiments leading to things like the essay of inductive performance, the detective story, and the essay of literary theory, then I have tried to make explicit how experience itself has shifted from eye-witness observation to a search for a kind of writing that, while being an particular example, at the same time invents the general category of which it is an instance. In this sense we could say that for Poe the experimental magazinist experience is analogous to the invention of a genre. Poe offers various enactments of this logic: his conversion of the spectacle of the chess machine, first into an essay of inductive debunking, then into a new genre, and finally into an essay purporting to explain the process of composition (but which in fact sets out to create the effect of poetry-making automaton). The "non-reasoning creatures" that populate these pieces—the blindly calculating automaton, the motiveless ape, the bird that speaks by rote, and finally Poe himself in the role of a lyric algorithm—each play their part in what we might think of as one long abductive inference, as those problems that at first appear insoluble receive their smoothly fitting keys.

CHAPTER 3
Unearthing *Pierre*

He would climb Parnassus with a pile of folios on his back.
Herman Melville, *Pierre*

MOBY-DICK REVIEWED

In his series of sketches on the "Literati of New York City," Poe described Wiley & Putnam editor Evert Duyckinck as "one of the most influential of the New York *littérateurs*, distinguished...especially for an almost Quixotic fidelity to his friends."[1] Duyckinck, who in 1846 assembled and brought out an edition of Poe's *Tales* in his short-lived Library of American Books series, was nevertheless later repaid with Poe's assertion that this selection was made "by a gentleman whose taste does not coincide with my own."[2] Poe's often prickly column itself amounted to a series of tactical (and sometimes tactless) moves in a complex politics of literary allegiance, in part centered on Duyckinck's magazine *The Literary World* and the Young America movement he helped to found.[3]

It was also in 1846 that Duyckinck published a first novel by an unknown writer named Herman Melville, also included in the Wiley & Putnam Library of American Books series. While Duyckinck thought Melville's *Typee, A Peep at Polynesian Life* unrefined and "not overphilosophical,"[4] he nevertheless considered it a good example of descriptive verisimilitude, and thought the author an expert in all things nautical.[5] While he was later able to reconcile the more metaphysical passages of *Mardi* (1849) and *Moby-Dick* (1851) with the recognizable outlines of the sea adventure, the ostentatiously melodramatic prose of *Pierre; or, the Ambiguities* (1852) horrified him.[6]

While the first draft of *Pierre* was a focused attempt at imitating the formal devices of the gothic romance (a strategy Melville believed would win him a popular audience and make him money), the final design of the novel was the result of an impulsive experiment. In early 1852, Melville spliced over 160 pages of new material into the center of a nearly finished manuscript. Though it has not once been mentioned or alluded to anywhere in the first sixteen chapters of *Pierre*, the added pages reveal that the eponymous protagonist has all along been a renowned author:

> In an earlier chapter of this volume, it has somewhere been passingly intimated, that Pierre was not only a reader of the poets and other fine writers, but likewise—and what is a very different thing from the other—a thorough allegorical understander of them, a profound emotional sympathizer with them; in other words, Pierre himself possessed a poetic nature; in himself absolutely, though but latently and floatingly, possessed every whit of the imaginative wealth which he so admired.... But it still remains to be said that Pierre himself had written many a fugitive thing, which had brought him, not only vast credit and compliments from his more immediate acquaintances, but the less partial applauses of the always intelligent, and extremely discriminating public [and] the high and mighty Campbell clan of editors of all sorts had bestowed upon him those generous commendations, which, with one instantaneous glance, they had immediately perceived was his due.[7]

While reviewers were exasperated by what they took to be *Pierre's* clotted, unwieldy prose and potboiler plot, they found the sudden revelation of Pierre's authorship simply baffling.[8] Alongside Melville's "egregiously belated announcement that young Pierre was already an author,"[9] we have Melville's facetious allusion to the "always intelligent and extremely discerning public," and the "mighty Campbell clan of editors," suggesting that the decision to add the material on Pierre-as-author began as a reaction to what he took to be the indifferent, if not outright hostile, reception of *Moby-Dick*.

Particularly stinging for Melville was a review by his friend and patron Duyckinck, in two consecutive issues of the *Literary World* in November of 1851. In what Hershel Parker calls the novel's "single most influential American review,"[10] Duyckinck listed off a few of what he called Melville's "infelicities," complaining of his tendency to muddy his prose with "opaque allegorical veils":

> [Mr. Melville's books have] a double character. In one light they are romantic fictions, in another statements of absolute facts. When to this is added that the romance is made a vehicle of opinion and satire through a more or less opaque allegorical veil, as particularly in the latter half of *Mardi*, and to some extent in [*Moby-Dick*], the critical difficulty is considerably thickened. It becomes quite impossible to submit such books to a distinct classification.[11]

While Duyckinck was genuinely troubled by the problem of classifying works like *Mardi* and *Moby-Dick*, he nevertheless took some time to single out what in *Moby-Dick* he still found worthy of praise—Melville's mastery of verisimilitude:

> With this we make an end of what we have been reluctantly compelled to object to this volume. With far greater pleasure, we acknowledge the acuteness of observation, the

freshness of perception [and] the salient imagination which connects...the world of books and the life of experience.[12]

In rewarding the author of *Moby-Dick* for his "acuteness of observation" and "freshness of perception," Duyckinck makes clear the way accurate depiction is appealed to as a corrective to "opaque allegorical veils."[13] And in explicitly offering a categorical distinction between "the world of books" and "the life of experience"— and the proper way to connect these separate orders—he extends that evaluative distinction to the way travel literature as veridical reportage must be cleanly differentiated from, even as it faithfully mirrors, experience understood as concretely lived events. Any blurring of these orders would risk obstructing a report on life, making "allegory" an obstacle to perception itself. For Duyckinck, a failure to respect this distinction amounted to bad taste bordering on the immoral.

In a January 1852 letter to Sophia Hawthorne, sent two months after he'd seen Duyckinck's review and just weeks before had added the new material to *Pierre*, Melville thanked her for a letter she sent him telling him how much she admired *Moby-Dick*. If "allegory" had been used as a word of reproach in the review, Melville has transformed it into something else in the letter to Sophia:

> I had some vague idea while writing [*Moby-Dick*] that the whole book was susceptible of an allegoric construction...but the specialty of many of the particular subordinate allegories, were first revealed to me after reading [Nathaniel] Hawthorne's letter, which, without citing any particular examples, yet intimated the part-&-parcel allegoricalness of the whole.[14]

The concern here to analyze the role of allegory in his own earlier novel will be amplified in the pages Melville adds to *Pierre*, some of the first of which are careful to point out that Pierre was "not only a reader of the poets and other fine writers, but likewise—and what is a very different thing from the other—a thorough allegorical understander of them." Given that the new material unexpectedly reveals Pierre to be a revered novelist and man of letters, allegory is keyed more explicitly to the vicissitudes of Melville's career, and at just the moment he is grappling with the tension between established criteria of literary evaluation and his own formal and stylistic ambition.[15]

Here then is what literary experiment amounts to for Melville in early 1852. *Pierre*'s dense, allusive prose, along with the cutting of pages directly into the middle of the finished manuscript—with little effort at hiding the seams of the cut—are part of refusal of the criteria of unity and verisimilitude. In adding pages aimed explicitly at the literary-critical dogmas of the *Literary World* Melville rejects its terms of aesthetic validation by insisting on "opaque allegorical veils."[16] And in converting particular lived events from late 1851 and early 1852 into what Richard Poirier has called an "allegory of his thwarted career as a novelist," Melville does something very different from what he did with the raw material of his time at sea in the earlier novels

Duyckinck preferred (with the exception, of course, of *Mardi* and *Moby-Dick*); that is, report them with a mixture of alluring romance and perceptual acuteness. The refusal of the *Literary World*'s criteria involves a shift from acuteness of observation to the veiling effects of allegory.

What I am describing as Melville's replacement of verisimilitude with allegory is in part an extension of Poirier's linking an "allegory [of the] activity of the writer" to a "foregrounding of literary technique"; a foregrounding that, in the case of *Pierre*, results in a prose of "formidable density."[17] In his introduction to the recent *Pléiade* edition of Melville's work, Phillipe Jaworski echoes Poirier's description, saying that in both *Moby-Dick* and *Pierre* the novels' "narrative apparatus [*dispositive*]" is "part of its vision, and factors directly in [its] ordering of meaning."[18] Given the way Melville added the pages on Pierre as an author as "an interpolation into the narrative [which] seems to have begun with a delayed and petulant reaction against parts of his friend... Duyckinck's review of *Moby-Dick*," we should see Melville as setting out to create an unmanageably dense—even "opaque"—novel about the making of a novel, and one that would irreverently reject the idea that the relation of lived experience to literary form were a matter of documentary accuracy.[19]

What exactly does it mean to say that allegory obstructs verisimilitude? Angus Fletcher notes that allegory "destroys the normal expectation we have about language [so that] when we predicate quality x of person Y, Y really is what our predication says he is [whereas] allegory turns Y in to something other (*allos*) than what the open and direct statement tells the reader."[20] Fletcher links allegory's conversion of the direct statement into "something other" to Johan Huizinga's claim that if symbolism "expresses a mysterious connection between two ideas," allegory "gives visible form to the conception of such a connection."[21] To say that allegory gives visible form to the connection between two ideas is to identify the *way* it converts the direct statement into something other as its rendering sensuous—its causing to appear—the connection between the ideas. Fletcher alludes to Eric Auerbach's discussion of "*figura*" in relation allegory's making sensuous the connection between ideas, such that *figura* names a bringing forth into appearance, whether as a plastic form or a figure of speech.[22] Each of these claims are, in their different ways, close to Jaworski's telling us that in *Moby-Dick* and *Pierre* the narrative "apparatus" is part of what the novels show us; what Poirier means by Melville's "foregrounding" of literary technique; and what Duyckinck may have meant in diagnosing Melville's tendency toward "opaque allegorical veils." If allegory is imagined to impose some recalcitrant literary matter in the way of the accurate depiction—obstructing *vraisemblance* in making sensuous the process by which one thing is made to stand for another—then we are invited to treat the separate accounts in Jaworski, Poirier, and (in a very different context) Duyckinck as finding in Melville's prose circa 1851–52 a use of allegory designed to undo the aesthetic criteria he found himself rebelling against.

Consider all of this in relation to some claims Sacvan Berkovich makes in a seminal essay on *Pierre*: First, that the novel treats of such "elaborately artful forms they might be taught as allegory"; that allegory in *Pierre* stems from its being a novel made up of "words about words" and "surfaces stratified upon surfaces of literary reference...layered in a broad archaeological sequence"; that this archaeological layering is given expression in the novel's "persistent reference to mountains, hills, rocks and stones"; and that the stacking up of registers is what led to the "outrage of the 1852 reviews [of *Pierre*]."[23] While Berkovich's description of *Pierre*'s stratified layers is close to Jaworski and Poirier's description of the novel's style, he adds to their accounts the idea that the pile up of inherited forms is expressed in the novel's recurring references to rocks, stones, and mountains.[24] But what none of them make explicit is the *way* the novel's amassed rock and stone figures are keyed to Melville's use of allegory. If what Poirier calls the effort, in *Pierre*, to "cope with the cultural accumulations that over the centuries have been building up within literary practice...the accumulated weight of inherited forms and models,"[25] occurs in the novel as the piling up of different styles—Elizabethan mannerism, the metaphysical prose of Sir Thomas Browne and Thomas De Quincey, the devices of gothic romance, the teachings of the Gospels, the dream visions of Bunyan and Dante, Greek myth, and up to and including the correspondence with editors, publishers, and the magazine reviews Melville happened upon in the weeks just prior to the addition of the new material on Pierre as an author—then this is just what Duyckinck was complaining about: the casting of a "veil" (of style, of literary manner) before the faithful portraiture of novels like *Typee* and *Omoo*. But in *Pierre* such vieling is more willful and deliberate. Keyed to the effects of allegory, the novel gives form to the styles and devices that over the centuries have accumulated in literary practice by replacing oceanic verisimilitude with an obsession with the terrestrial: from its dedication to Mt. Greylock, to the many vivid descriptions of rock formations and mountain ranges, to the Memnon stone's strange hieroglyphic, and finally in Pierre's climactic dream vision of rock faces coming to life.

If Melville's irreverence in *Pierre* involves pitting the whole of pitting the whole of Western literary history against what he took to be the parochial aesthetic criteria by which *Moby-Dick* had been judged, then he does this by making a term of reproach—allegory—into the guiding formal principle for a novel about the making of a novel. And since the events that most impressed him in late 1851—just the moment when he was, as Walker Percy puts it, "breaking through into the freedom of his art"[26]—were the uncomprehending reviews of what he took to be the most ambitious writing of his life, his refusal of those criteria ends up as an allegory of his thwarted career.

TALKING PICTURES (GOTHIC METAPHYSICS)

Before looking in detail at the pages Melville spliced into the middle of *Pierre* after seeing the reviews of *Moby-Dick*, I want to consider some general features of the prose of the novel's opening chapters. During the initial planning stages of *Pierre*

Melville set out to imitate the conventions of gothic and sentimental romance, with the intention of making a book "calculated for popularity... being a regular romance, with a mysterious plot to it, and stirring passions."[27] But that plan seems to have given way at some point to the experiment of merging the tone and devices of the sentimental romance with the ornate metaphysical rhetoric carried over from the composition of *Moby-Dick*.[28] An immensely impressionable reader, Melville was, while at work on *Pierre*, still pouring over his large-print edition of Shakespeare,[29] Thomas De Quincey's *Confessions of an English Opium Eater* (1821),[30] and especially Sir Thomas Browne's *Religio Medici, Urn Burial*, and *Garden of Cyrus* (1642). Brian Foley says it was none other than Duyckinck who encouraged Melville to read Browne, and that a three-volume edition of his works were "among [Melville's] earliest selections" from Duyckinck's private library of twenty thousand volumes.[31] The discovery of Browne came at "a crucial juncture in Melville's career," leading to the experiment of *Mardi*, a novel Foley says began as a 'realistic' travel narrative in the manner of *Typee* [but was] expanded into an allegorical satire interspersed with philosophical speculations and teeming with obscure allusions."[32] The description spells out precisely the terms of approbation and critique of Melville's antebellum milieu, as "realistic" travel narrative becomes "obscure" and "speculative" allegorical satire. An ability immediately to convert his reading into new directions in composition, combined with his growing dissatisfaction with the formulaic strictures of writing sea adventures of the sort that made him a popular author in the late 1840s, resulted in the formal and stylistic ambition of *Moby-Dick* and *Pierre*.[33]

In the opening chapters of *Pierre* Melville abandons any pretense of verisimilitude, telling us, in a voice arising from a fusion of sentimental mannerism and involuted Brownean rhetoric, of Pierre Glendinning's landed estate at Saddle Meadows.[34] During a treacly chronicle of the protagonist's aristocratic lineage, the narrator informs us that

> the metaphysical writers confess, that the most impressive, sudden and overwhelming event, as well as the minutest, is but the product of an infinite series infinitely involved and untraceable foregoing occurrences. Just so with every motion of the heart. Why this cheek kindles with a noble enthusiasm; why that lip curls in scorn; these are things not wholly imputable to the immediate apparent cause, which is only one link in the chain; but to a long line of dependencies whose further part is lost in the mid-regions of the impalpable air.[35]

In layering an allusion to "metaphysical writers" with vexed meditation upon the vicissitudes of the "heart," Melville casts elements of the genre he was claiming to parody in an overtly "metaphysical" prose.[36] Direct echoes of Brownean syntax—looping patterns like "an infinite series infinitely involved"—are superimposed onto generic mannerism, fusing cloying whimsy with dense speculation. If the particular kind of speculation offered in the passage concerns the way the whims of the "heart" cannot be explained merely through an appeal to what can be observed on the surface ("this cheek kindles"; "that lip curls"), then that claim is given form in a writing that replaces a report on surfaces with a prose so opaquely "involved" it bars access the heart's hidden whims. What Bercovich described as *Pierre*'s "surface stratified upon surface of literary reference," and Poirier the "cultural accumulations that over the centuries have been building up with literary practice," is here made sensuous as the superimposition of two distinct, overtly literary, layers.

Melville goes on to concretize the layering of the metaphysical and the gothic in a specific image:

> There has long stood a shrine in the fresh-foliaged heart of Pierre, up to which he ascended by many tabled steps of remembrance; and around which annually he had hung fresh wreaths of a sweet and holy affection. Made one green bower of at last, by such successive votive offerings of his being; this shrine seemed, and was indeed, a place for the celebration of a chastened joy, rather than for any melancholy rites. But though thus mantled, and tangled with garlands, this shrine was of marble—a niched pillar, deemed solid and eternal, and from whose top radiated all those innumerable sculptured scrolls and branches, which supported the entire one-pillared temple of his moral life; as in some beautiful gothic oratories, one central pillar, trunk-like, holds up the roof. In this shrine, in the niche of this pillar, stood the perfect marble form of his departed father; without blemish, unclouded, snow-white, and serene; Pierre's fond personification of perfect human goodness and virtue.[37]

While the superimposition of literary layers again "veils" verisimilitude, here it does so in a decisive shift toward allegory, as the handling of a particular idea—the vicissitudes of the heart—condenses into a series of emblems: marble shrines, gothic oratories, pillared temples, sculptured scrolls. What is shown in the passage is the *likening* of Pierre's heart to marble, pillars, temples, and scrolls, such that the layering of metaphysical intricacy with the clichés of gothic romance both creates an extravagant obstacle to the faithful report and turns allegory itself into a source of experience. This effect, by which allegory gives sensuous form to the process by which one thing is made to stand for another, insists on precisely the kind of "opacity" Duyckinck complained of in his review of *Moby-Dick*.[38]

The description of the heart as a whorled, stratified stone is followed by a description of a portrait of Pierre's remembered father:

> there hung, by long cords from the cornice, a small portrait in oil, before which Pierre had many a time trancedly stood. Had this painting hung in any annual public exhibition, and in its turn been described in print by the casual glancing critics, they would probably have described it thus, and truthfully: "An impromptu portrait of a fine-looking, gay-hearted, youthful gentleman. He is lightly, and, as it were, airily and but grazingly seated in, or rather fittingly tenanting an old-fashioned chair of Malacca. One arm confining his hat and cane is loungingly thrown over the back of the chair, while the fingers of the other hand play with his gold watch-seal and key. The free-templed head is sideways turned, with a peculiarly bright, and care-free, morning expression. He seems as if just dropped

in for a visit upon some familiar acquaintance. Altogether, the painting is exceedingly clever and cheerful; with a fine, off-handed expression about it. Undoubtedly a portrait, and no fancy-piece; and, to hazard a vague conjecture, by an amateur."[39]

Here Melville adds to Brownean rhetorical extravagance and sentimental gothic parody an imagined art review; and one that would purport to "describe truthfully" the portrait of Pierre's father. Continuing to literalize his agon with the dogma of *vraisemblance*, Melville now overtly casts metaphysical and gothic modes in a language of pictorial copying. At just the moment the narrator takes up the issue of the truthful rendering of Pierre's father, the prose swerves into the added register of imagined ekphrasis.[40] This obstruction of the portrait's power to depict works in the way the fictional review exploits one of the novel's recurring tics of diction— adverbial neologisms like "trancedly," "grazingly," "loungingly," "peculiarly"—as if the disruption of verisimilitude by allegory were registered in a wild accretion of suffixes. Rather than a "faithful" relation between portrait and subject, we get, to use Bercovich's phrase, "words talking to words."

But we soon find out that there is *another* portrait of Pierre's father, and one his mother prefers because it is a "far more truthful and life-like presentation."[41] Pierre stands "trancedly" before this second portrait, trying to figure out what it is about the alternate rendering that leads his mother to think of it as the more accurate one. Considering again the merits of the first portrait, Pierre now hears his father speaking directly to him from the painting, in what he takes to be a "conceit." The voice offers advocacy in favor of the first portrait as being the more accurate, despite his mother's preference for the second.

> And yet, ever new conceits come vaporing up in [Pierre], as [he looks] on the strange chair-portrait: which, though so very much more unfamiliar to me, than it can possibly be to my mother, still sometimes seems to say...Look again. I am thy real father, so much more truly, as thou thinkest thou recognizest me not, Pierre. To their young children, fathers are not wont to unfold themselves entirely, Pierre. Here are a thousand and one odd little youthful peccadilloes, that we think we may as well not divulge to them, Pierre. Consider this strange and ambiguous smile, Pierre....Consider, for a smile is the chosen vehicle for all ambiguities, Pierre. When we would deceive, we smile, when we are hatching any nice little artifice, Pierre....There was a certain, oh, but too lovely young Frenchwoman, Pierre. Youth is hot, and temptation strong, Pierre; and Time sweeps on, and the thing is not always carried down by its stream and may be left stranded on the bank....Once upon a time, there was a lovely young Frenchwoman, Pierre.[42]

After re-establishing the criterion of verisimilitude—the first portrait now argued to be "more truly...thy real father"—Melville again methodically undercuts it in mannered accumulations. Here, the obsessive, punctuating repetition of the words "smile" and "Pierre," in conjunction with the affectedness of "thy" and "-est," are compounded for the ushering in of another gothic device: Pierre's father's illicit dalliance with a "Frenchwoman," the consequence of which is his illegitimate half-sister, Isabel. What the passage calls a "nice little artifice," then, is the way a second, more "ambiguous" portrait is thought to be the more faithful one, but only insofar as it reveals a narrative hidden in the picture. That the accurate rendering of the father paradoxically appears in the transition from pictographic truth to "gothic" (and parodic) truth is disclosed through what the portrait names as a "conceit"; one which pits its revelation against an allegedly "faithful" representation.[43] In introducing the gothic formula of the illegitimate half-sister through a painting that announces secret patrimony in the form of a conceit, Melville again turns a layering of literary devices into a "veil" of the sort about which Duyckinck complained. That Pierre should imagine a painting speaking to him, and that its speech should be a countersource for the truth about his father, amounts finally to an allegory in which Melville takes the measure of, and irreverently refuses, the evaluative criteria by which *Moby-Dick* had failed.

Reeling from the portrait's revelation of a half-sister, Isabel, we find Pierre in a "haze of ambiguities":

> the strangeness of the portrait only served to invest his idea with a fine legendary romance [but now] Pierre saw all preceding ambiguities, all mysteries ripped open as if with a keen sword, and forth trooped thickening phantoms of an infinite gloom. Now his remotest infantile reminiscences—the wandering mind of his father...the mystical midnight suggestions of the portrait itself...all overwhelmed him with reciprocal testimonies. And now, by irresistible intuitions, all that had been inexplicably mysterious to him in the portrait, and all that had been inexplicably familiar in the face, most magically these now coincided, the merriness of the one not inharmonious with the mournfulness of the other, and, as it were, melted into each other, and thus interpenetratingly uniting, presented lineament of an added supernaturalness.[44]

Extending what Poirier called "the accumulated weight of inherited forms and models" to "romance," Melville continues to unleash on his confused protagonist layer upon layer of literary artifice. As the revelation of his half-sister comes "trooping forth" from behind the smile of the portrait, in a procession of "phantoms of an infinite gloom," the portrait's power to give a faithful account is now a matter of the way it stands for Pierre's "infantile reminiscences"; dimly remembered episodes now equated with a "legendary romance." In a perverse flourish, Melville finally tells us that these different scales or units of measure of the accurate, the faithful, the truthful, "coincided [and] melted into each other, and thus interpenetratingly uniting, presented lineament of an added supernaturalness." That the stock generic truth of Pierre's father having sired his half-sister with a mysterious Frenchwoman is finally "united" in an "added supernaturalness," is Melville's way of replacing unity as a formal principle enforced by antebellum reviewers by "interpenetratingly uniting" sentimental romance, Brownean rhetorical extravagance, the critical journalism of the art review, and now throwing in for good measure "legendary romance."

Such style-clusters again leave their mark in the way an abuse of the substantive ("mournfulness"; "supernaturalness") is wed to further adverbial inventions ("inexplicably"; "interpenetratingly"), as if the words were displaying on their surface an accretion of lexical matter.[45]

After brooding in front of the two portraits Pierre visits a rock formation remembered from his youth roaming the forests of Saddle Meadows. Arriving at a barn-sized stone that "was something like a lengthened egg, but flattened more; and, at the ends, pointed more; and yet not pointed, but irregularly wedge-shaped," he makes a strange discovery:

> Pierre happened to brush aside several successive layers of old, gray-haired, close cropped, nappy moss, and beneath, to his no small amazement, he saw rudely hammered in the rock some half-obliterated initials—"S. yᵉ W." Then he knew, that ignorant of the stone, as all the simple country round might immemorially have been, yet was not himself the only human being who had discovered that marvelous impending spectacle: but long and long ago, in quite another age, the stone had been beheld, and its wonderfulness fully appreciated—as the painstaking initials seemed to testify—by some departed man, who, were he now alive, might possibly wag a beard old as the most venerable oak of centuries growth. But who,—who in Methuselah's name,—who might have been this "S. yᵉ W.?" Pierre pondered long, but could not possibly imagine; for the initials, in their antiqueness, seemed to point to some period before the era of Columbus' discovery of the hemisphere.[46]

Still in a haze of speculation about which of the two portraits of his father is the more accurate one, Pierre feels compelled to interpret the marking on the stone. What Melville calls the stone's "ponderous inscrutibleness" encodes impacted layers of pastiche and allusion that obstruct simple access to the meaning of the inscription. With the portrait's ambiguity now collapsed into a neologism of the sort that upset reviewers—"inscrutibleness"—*Pierre*'s replacement of pictographic exactitude with allegorical abstraction is literalized in a hieroglyph with no referent. It is not the point to try to figure out what "S. yᵉ W." means. Rather, Pierre puzzles over an inscription which, while inscrutable, nevertheless stands for the possibility of meaning as such. This is just what Bercovich, Poirier, Jaworski, and Duyckinck (in his disapproving way), have been telling us: that the obstruction of documentary accuracy through a deliberate imposition of artifice is what *Pierre* is, in some fundamental way, about. The novel's affected devices, piling up like so many rock formations, crystallize in the way a marking cut in stone gives form to the process by which one thing is made to stand for another. All of this is made more explicit in Pierre's act of naming the stone "Memnon":

> When in his imaginative ruminating moods of early youth, Pierre had christened the wonderful stone by the old responding name of Memnon, he had done so merely from certain associative remembrances of the Egyptian marvel, of which all Eastern travelers

speak.... But in after times, when placed in far different circumstances from those surrounding him at the Meadows, Pierre pondered on the stone, and his young thoughts concerning it... then an immense significance came to him, and the long-passed unconscious movements of his then youthful heart, seemed now prophetic to him, and allegorically verified by the subsequent events.[47]

The attraction to and fascination with the stone is for Pierre the way its "immense significance" casts back to Columbus and to the "Egyptian marvels" in writing and architecture. But his effort to decipher the hieroglyph also amounts for him to a "verification" of the events of own life. Now coupling allegory with the true or accurate depiction ("verification"/verisimilitude), Pierre imagines the ambiguities in which he is enveloped—the difference between the chair portrait and the drawing room portrait, the revelation of an illegitimate sister, the hieroglyph upon the Memnon stone, and now his own memories of his "youthful heart" christening the stone "Memnon"—as united in an inscrutible emblem. If allegorical artifice is in *Pierre* a way of giving form to the process by which one thing can be made to stand for another, then here Pierre takes a mysterious marking in stone to be an "allegorical verification" of his own lived experience.[48]

CHRONOMETRICALS AND HOROLOGICALS

Just prior to the events narrated in the pages Melville added to the novel in January 1852, we find Pierre abruptly leaving Saddle Meadows for the city. Equipped with the new knowledge of his half-sister, he has broken off an arranged marriage with blonde, innocent, Lucy, and taken up with his dark, mysterious sibling Isabel. Again manipulating the clichés of the sentimental gothic (light/dark imagery, incest intrigue, country/city, proliferating personification), Melville adds another item to the pile up of registers: a pamphlet that suddenly appears in Pierre's hand, in a coach bound for New York.

Entering the coach in a state of "horrid anarchy and infidelity," Melville likens Pierre's mood to a story he remembers having heard from a "reverend man of God."[49] The story concerns a priest who was "in the act of publicly administering the bread at the Holy Sacrament of the Supper when the Evil One suddenly propounded to him the possibility of the mere moonshine of the Christian Religion," but during which the priest nevertheless "holds to his firm Faith's rock."[50] Melville then tells us how Pierre happens by chance upon a strange pamphlet, written by one Plotinus Plinlimmon, enigmatically titled "*EI*" and subtitled "Chronometricals and Horologicals."[51] The contents of the pamphlet are not unrelated to Pierre's remembered story about the priest's resisting doubt and remaining true to his "faith's rock." Plinlimmon offers a series of arguments designed to show that "human life on this earth is but a state of probation; which among other things implies, that here below, we mortals have only to do with things provisional" and so accordingly "all our so-called wisdom is likewise but provisional."[52] Plinlimmon develops this argument through a discussion of heavenly or "Christian" time versus and earthly or "expedient" time;[53] a central claim rendered in elaborate conceits and a welter of allusions to Plutarch, Saint Paul, Plato, Bacon, Pascal, Jeremy Taylor, Shaftsbury, and Mandeville.[54] Just as the combining of gothic plot devices and metaphysical prose formed an allegory of style that rendered Pierre's sentimentalized heart a marble shrine; and just as the Memnon stone signified upon its surface a hieroglyph without any referent other than its own engraved "inscrutibleness," so this moment in the novel breaks off entirely from narrative reportage, swerving into the knotty arguments of Plinlimmon's treatise. The effect of the shift in register marks an abrupt change in the narrative, as the opening chapters detailing Pierre's idyllic existence at Saddle Meadows jump to a cab headed for the city.

"It seems to me, in my visions," writes Plinlimmon,

> that there is a certain most rare order of human souls, which if carefully carried in the body will almost always and everywhere give Heaven's own Truth, with some small grains of variance. For peculiarly coming from God, the sole source of that Heavenly truth, and the great Greenwich hill and tower from which the universal meridians are far out into infinity reckoned; such souls seem as London sea-chronometers...which as the London ship floats past Greenwich down the Thames, are accurately adjusted by Greenwich time.[55]

Here the idea of "Heavenly truth" is rendered as an elaborate comparison, in which different local times, labeled "Greenwich" and "Chinese," are placed under the name "Bacon," while a more universal time, immune to relative location, is placed under the name "Christ." Plinlimmon then compares the provisional variability of Baconian knowledge with the eternal Truth of the Kingdom of Heaven: "Bacon's brains were watch-maker's brains; but Christ was a chronometer; and the most exquisitely adjusted and exact one, and the least affected by all terrestrial jarrings, and any that have ever come to us."[56] If the exquisitely exact measure of Christian "chronometrics" marks an absolute time immune to the relative perspective of "terrestrial jarrings," then Plinlimmon goes on to criticize any view that holds such chronometrics—the teachings of Christ—to be anything more than provisional guidelines for "virtuous expediency" on earth.[57] Pierre's remembered story is thus in the pamphlet turned into an allegory of the difference between the timeless and the variable, both in the likening of types of temporality to the names Bacon and Christ and in earthly figures: from eternal truths (rock of faith) to the contingencies of a finite and perishable existence (terrestrial jarring).

Like Pierre's finding his life allegorically "verified" in the Memnon's stone's hieroglyphic, Melville here turns the events of his own life—not adventures on the south seas but the ups and downs of his career as a novelist—into fresh material to be added to his manuscript. Keeping in mind Poirier's claim that *Pierre*'s style arose from its being an "allegory of Melville's thwarted career," we should remember that part of the criticism Duyckinck brought against *Moby-Dick* in the second installment of his November 1851 review was the way it "mingled quaint conceit and extravagant daring speculation" with a "piratical running down of creeds."[58] Duyckinck's phrase is in fact an apt characterization of the arguments in Plinlimmon's pamphlet. If, as Parker tells us, Melville had to "stifle his anger at [reviews like Duyckinck's] if he were to preserve his aesthetic control" over *Pierre*, and so struggled "to concentrate on his manuscript after late November, by which time he had written much of or perhaps all of the rural opening section of the novel," then we can infer that the pages on Plinlimmon's pamphlet were composed shortly after the appearance of Duyckinck's review of *Moby-Dick*.[59] We ought then to treat Pierre's happening upon the pamphlet as a transposition of Melville's happening upon the reviews in the *Literary World* in late November 1851. Given Duyckinck's preferred categories of critical approbation, the pamphlet's pitting the absolute time of an "exquisitely adjusted" Christian chronometrics (Pierre's remembered "rock of Faith") against Baconian "virtuous expediency" ("terrestrial jarring") is Melville's way of dramatizing a "piratical running down of creeds" in pages added to *Pierre* in the aftermath of being accused of such irreverence in his own previous novel. It may seem as though Melville is mocking the sort of certainty that would "deride the preachers of a low, expedient, comfortable morality of compromise and adjustment."[60] But, as Parker notes, "Melville might often if not always agree with the ideas attributed to Plinlimmon while altogether dissociating himself from the blandly rational and self-satisfied tone in which Plinlimmon is reported to express them."[61] Given that all of this is part of Melville's building the vicissitudes of his own career into a novel in progress, it may just as easily be literary-critical "creeds"—Duyckinck's fusion of upstanding Christian decorum with the principles of unity and verisimilitude—that are "piratically run down" in Plinlimmon's argument about virtuous expediency.

Between smug expediency and the laws of the *Literary World*, the Rock of Faith and terrestrial jarring, allegory functions as a form of experience different from the perceptual acuteness for which Melville's earlier writing had been praised. Pierre's impulsive decision to leave Saddle Meadows, and the chance discovery of the pamphlet, is the grotesque double of Melville's surprise upon discovering Duyckinck's condescending reviews. Allegory here is not about aligning the referential coordinates of two levels of meaning, but of giving sensuous form to the technique by which one idea is made to stand for another. In this case, that alignment occurs in the way Pierre looking down to find "some paper protruding from his clutched hand" such that "he knew not how it got there, or whence it had come"[62] is the transposition of Melville's alarm at finding his patron and friend Duyckinck accusing him in print of irreligion. In his own "haze of ambiguities" upon discovering that disapproval, Melville impulsively transferred the points raised in the review to the contents of the fictional pamphlet.

While Melville converts the accusation that *Moby-Dick* indulges in a 'piratical running down of creeds' into a scene in which Pierre finds a pamphlet that might be similarly described, Plinlimmon offers his own summary of what the treatise means:

> This Chronometrical and Horological conceit, in sum, seems to teach this—That in things terrestrial (horological) a man must not be governed by ideas celestial (chronometrical)...but if any man say that such a doctrine as this I lay down is false [or] impious I would charitably refer that man to the history of Christendom for the last 1800 years; and ask him, whether in spite of all the maxims of Christ, that history is not just as full of blood, violence wrong, and iniquity of every kind, as any previous portion of the world's story? Therefore, it follows, that so far as practical results are concerned—regarded in a purely earthly light—the only great original moral (chronometrical) doctrine of Christianity...has been found (horologically) a false one.[63]

Again, Plinlimmon's point is that the teachings of the Sermon on the Mount are not timeless immutable laws, in serene isolation above the tumult of terrestrial jarring, but "conceits" to be put to use for expediency in one's earthly doings. In arguing for the merely allegorical nature of Christ's teachings, Plinlimmon both brings down to earth an absolute chronometrics and extends Melville's effort in *Pierre* to absorb the whole of Western literary history into an allegory of his own career, now reaching back to the Gospels and the whole "history of Christendom." Terrestrial jarring both names our earthly finitude—in a moral philosophy preached upon a "Mount"—and the literary experiment Bercovitch describes as "lead[ing] from Christian faith to...a world of fictive surfaces...interpretations whose levels of meaning seem to multiply in direct proportion to their absence of substance."[64] Melville's conversion of the accusations of "impiety," directed at what he took to be his masterpiece, to Pierre's discovery in a coach of an enigmatic pamphlet taking up similar issues, thus occurs as the displacement of a prose geared to fidelity to the deliberate construction of "opaque allegorical veils" (here woolly speculations about "Horologicals and Chronometricals"). That change in the relation of composition to experience—from faithful portrait to opaque veil—is heightened when Melville cuts 160 pages of new material into the finished manuscript of *Pierre*; a decision keyed even more explicitly to his relationship with Duyckinck.

THE REFUSED DAGUERREOTYPE

If the argument in the pamphlet transposes the criteria Melville found himself rebelling against—Pierre's entering the cab in a state of "horrid anarchy," only to find Plinlimmon's own "running down of creeds"—then when we get to the pages Melville rushed into his novel in the last weeks of January 1852, we find him cutting directly into his manuscript the language of the reviews and his own correspondence with Duyckinck. This is the experiment Parker and Howard take to be the disastrous last-minute decision that wrecked what would otherwise have been a "unified" and "hyper-controlled" parody of the gothic romance novel, amounting for them to the "greatest single tragedy in American literary history."[65]

As with Melville's keying compositional decisions in *Pierre* to the appearance of Duyckink's review of *Moby-Dick* in late November, so the much more substantial addition of pages on Pierre as an author were added after a visit to Duyckink's home at 20 Clinton Place. Parker tells us that Melville was to "walk directly from Cliff Street," the location of Harpers where Melville was in final negotiations for the royalties on *Pierre*, then to the "Clinton place [home of the] friend who had acted as his literary advisor since [the publication of *Typee* in the] spring of 1846."[66] Parker and Higgins conjecture that Duyckinck obliged Melville "by reading the manuscript of *Pierre* within a day or two and then told him honestly how much he disapproved of it," since Duyckink was still the "earnest Christian who a few weeks earlier in the *Literary World* had condemned the irreligion of *Moby-Dick*."[67] Parker surmises that only a "dramatic confrontation just at this time" could account for Melville's decision to rush 160 pages of new material into a novel that was far enough along toward completion to bring him to New York for contractual negotiations with the Harpers in the first weeks of January 1852.[68] If *Pierre's* mood of anarchy upon entering the coach transposes into allegory Melville's reading with angry alarm Duyckink's review of *Moby-Dick*, then the hastily added pages on Pierre-as-author does something comparable with the final break with his friend and patron.

The first added chapter, "Young America In Literature"—a direct allusion to the nationalist clique in which Duyckinck was the central figure—explains how Pierre is already a well-established and respected author, in demand from all quarters of the antebellum literary marketplace, and uniformly praised by the "high and mighty Campbell clan of editors of all sorts had bestowed upon [Pierre] those generous commendations, which, with one instantaneous glance, they had immediately perceived was his due."[69] In describing Pierre's literary success, Melville borrows directly from the reviews of *Moby-Dick*, methodically inverting their diction to reflect praise for Pierre's (up to now unmentioned) literary fame. Indeed, each instance of fictional praise for Pierre's writing is a direct transposition from some actual review: the *Democractic Review* complained of *Moby-Dick's* "incoherent" and "involved syntax," while a reviewer for the London *Athenaeum* complained of the novel being "disfigured by mad...English"; Pierre is in turn praised for his "command of language," the "euphonious construction of sentences," and the "pervading symmetry of his...style."[70] The *New York Tribune* complained of Melville's "lawless flights, which puts all regular criticism at defiance"; Pierre is commended for his "never permit[ting] himself to astonish; is never betrayed into any thing coarse or new; as assured that whatever astonished is vulgar, and whatever is new must be crude."[71] Where Duyckinck in the *Literary World* called *Moby-Dick* "reckless at times of taste and propriety," Pierre is "characterized throughout by Perfect Taste." And where Melville had "just been denounced by clerical critics or pious lay reviewers for 'sneering at the truths of revealed religion,' and for 'sneers at revealed religion and the burlesquing of sacred passages of Holy Writ,'" Pierre's "predominant end and aim" is declared to be "evangelical piety."[72] In each case, critical judgments of the sort that scolded Melville for daring the kind of writing he aspired to—the kinds of appraisals that continually referred his experiments in form and style back to the master categories of "unity," "propriety," "symmetry," and "verisimilitude"—are transposed into praise for Pierre's stylistic grace and decorum. Just as Plinlimmon's irreverent claim that Christ's "chronometric" understanding of time was but a mere allegory designed to bring about expediency in one's local jarrings (a reimagining of Duyckinck's scolding Melville for a "piratical running down of creeds"), so in these added pages Melville turns the reviews of *Moby-Dick* into a fictional account of Pierre's literary success. In both cases it is a matter of converting the dominant literary critical "creeds" into raw material for a fresh burst of composition. And if the addition of the pages amounts to a sabotage of whatever unity had already been in place in the manuscript, then this is also a move from understanding the relation of literature to experience as one of documentary accuracy to one in which lived events are continued—altered, intensified—in the process of composition.

The deliberate undoing of unity in *Pierre* functions in a more direct way with Pierre's refusal to have his daguerreotype taken. Here, rather than transpose the language of newspaper and magazine reviews into the texture of his novel, Melville converts his own previous correspondence with Duyckinck into a decisive episode in Pierre's career. In a February 1851 letter Duyckinck had asked Melville to have his daguerreotype taken so that an engraved portrait could be made for *Holden's Dollar Magazine*, where he and his brother George were to become editors.[73] In a letter dealing specifically with the (still relatively new) technology of the daguerreotype, Melville wrote back to Duyckinck:

> How shall I go about refusing a man?—Best be round-about, or plumb on the mark? ... as for the Daguerreotype (I spell the word right from your sheet) that's what I can not send you, because I have none. And if I had, I would not send it for such a purpose, even to you.—Pshaw! you cry—& so cry I.—"This is intensified vanity, not true modesty or anything of that sort!" ... The fact is, almost everybody is having his "mug" engraved nowadays; so that this test of distinction is getting to be reversed; and therefore, to see one's "mug" in a magazine, is famous throughout the world—I respectfully decline being oblivionated by a Daguerretype (what a devel of an unspellable word!).[74]

Melville used the text of this letter for some of the first material he added to *Pierre*, and the changes he made lay bare the process by which lived events are generalized into allegories. Describing an encounter with a certain "chief mate," an editor of a magazine called "Captain Kidd Monthly," Melville has Pierre refusing to have *his* daguerreotype taken for the magazine:

> Upon one occasion, happening suddenly to encounter a literary acquaintance—a joint editor of the "Captain Kidd Monthly"—who suddenly popped upon him round a

corner, Pierre was startled by a rapid—"Good-morning, good-morning;—just the man I wanted:—come, step round now with me, and have your Daguerreotype taken;—get it engraved then in no time;—want it for the next issue." So saying, this chief mate of Captain Kidd seized Pierre's arm, and in the most vigorous manner was walking him off, like an officer a pickpocket, when Pierre civilly said—"Pray, sir, hold, if you please, I shall do no such thing."—"Pooh, pooh—must have it—public property—come along—only a door or two now."—"Public property!" rejoined Pierre, "that may do very well for the 'Captain Kidd Monthly';—it's very Captain Kiddish to say so. But I beg to repeat that I do not intend to accede."—"Don't? Really?" cried the other, amazedly staring Pierre straight in the countenance; —"why bless your soul, *my* portrait is published—long ago published!"—"Can't help that, sir"—said Pierre. "Oh! come along, come along," and the chief mate seized him again with the most uncompunctious familiarity by the arm. Though the sweetest-tempered youth in the world when but decently treated, Pierre had an ugly devil in him sometimes, very apt to be evoked by the personal profaneness of gentlemen of the Captain Kidd school of literature. "Look you, my good fellow," said he, submitting to his impartial inspection a determinately double fist,—"drop my arm now—or I'll drop you. To the devil with you and your Daguerreotype!"[75]

If we follow Parker's conjecture that the early January visit to Clinton Place led to Duyckinck's advising Melville not to publish *Pierre* in any version at all, and so to a "dramatic confrontation," then here we find Melville turning those events into Pierre's "sudden encounter" with an influential New York *littérateur*. Fusing correspondence from a year earlier with an event from a few weeks before, Melville recasts his walk from the Harpers' offices to Duyckinck's Clinton Place address as Pierre's running into the "joint editor of the Captain Kidd Monthly." In calling the paper the 'Captain Kidd Monthly' Melville again absorbs into the doing of composition Duyckinck's having chastised him for his "piratical running down of creeds" in his review of *Moby-Dick*.[76] But more importantly, Melville's decision to use the correspondence requesting and refusing the daguerreotype for the first of the added pages heightens *Pierre*'s preoccupation with the question of representation begun in the chapter on the portraits of his father. Remembering reviewers' praise of Melville's earlier novels for their "daguerreotype-like naturalness" and "fidelity" of description, the scene of the refused daguerreotype becomes a generalized allegory for a career that has moved from moderately successful, oceanic verisimilitude (*Typee, Omoo, White-Jacket, Redburn*) to a kind of writing that would mar documentary accuracy through ostentatious artifice.[77] But here Melville's adaptation of the language of the letter shows him straining to keep separate literal and allegorical levels. The staccato repetitions ("good morning, good morning"; "pooh, pooh"; "come along, come along"; "my portrait is published, long ago published"); and jumpy sentence fragments set off with clusters of dashes, colons, and semi-colons (";—just the man I wanted:—"; "—must have it—"; "—public property—"), make of the transposed correspondence a kind of collage, as if the technique by which one thing is made to stand for another were both breaking down and being put more and more on display. Even Melville's joke, from the earlier correspondence, about that "devel of an unspellable word!," while used as a vehicle to acknowledge the sting of accusations of irreligion ("to the devil with you and your daguerreotype"), seems to undercut the *vraisemblance* implicit in the daguerreotype in glitches of textual reproduction, and in a neologism—"oblivionated"—of just the sort that rankled antebellum reviewers. To refuse to have one's "mug engraved," then, is to refuse a logic of copying that is both a criterion of literary evaluation and an antebellum technology linked to career-building. In making the request for, and refusal of, the daguerreotype into new material to be added to *Pierre*, Melville turns experience understood as copying into the doing of composition. The episode thus enacts irreverence toward ideas of perceptual and promotional precision, as they were bound up with a politics of taste (call them "creeds") preached in magazines like *The Literary World* and *Holden's*. The extent to which the author's picture (as daguerreotype or engraving) could contribute to the building of a career—the fame Melville pined after, but at the same time distrusted—is finally ironically acknowledged in the way *Pierre's* massive literary fame is, in these added pages, so flimsily contrived.

If the daguerreotype perpetuates the novel's concern with accurate representation, Melville soon extends this into a justification of Pierre's refusal of the logic of copying:

> This incident, suggestive as it was at the time...had a surprising effect upon Pierre. For he considered with what infinite readiness now, the most faithful portrait of any one could be taken by the Daguerreotype, whereas in former times a faithful portrait was only within the power of the moneyed, or mental aristocrats of the earth. How natural then the inference, that instead of, as in old times, immortalizing a genius, a portrait now only *dayalized* a dunce...when every body has his portrait published, true distinction lies in not having yours published at all. For if you are published along with Tom, Dick, and Harry, and wear a coat of their cut, how then are you distinct from Tom, Dick, and Harry?[78]

The "surprising effect" of the encounter with the editor of the Captain Kidd Monthly is the way it provokes in Pierre a dramatic shift from "ugly devil" to "considered...infinite readiness"; an altered state of mind that leads him to meditate on the meaning of "distinction." If the dagguereotype turns every "mug" into a "dayalized dunce," then Melville (as Pierre) renders that leveling effect in generalized allegorical types—"Tom, Dick, and Harry." Unlike those singular "aristocrats of the earth," immune to the protocols and criteria of the *Literary World*, Pierre laments the reign of "engraved" dunces, as fads puffed in nationalist periodicals usurp "immortal genius." Again: in *Pierre* Melville pushes events away from faithful portraiture toward abstract, emblematic types (here "Tom, Dick, and Harry"; "immortal genius"). Hurt by the dismissal of a novel Melville took to be the masterwork of a "natural aristocrat," Melville turns the rejection of marketing strategies (and the technology that supports them) into a defense of art made for the ages.[79]

ENCELADUS AND ALLEGORY

The use of allegory in *Pierre* for creating both a generalizing typicality and a foregrounding of literary technique leads to a climax in the novel far more intense than the off-the-cuff pastiche of *Romeo and Juliet* with which the first version ends. Even Parker, who bitterly laments Melville's destroying the "hyper-controlled" first draft of *Pierre*, calls the concluding sections of Book XXV the "most remarkable prose" in the novel. Newton Arvin claims they contain "eloquence comparable to some of the great stretches of *Moby-Dick*"[80]; and Poirier says the description of Pierre's dream vision of the Titan Enceladus is "one of the most powerful passages Melville ever wrote."[81]

After the revelation of Pierre's authorship and literary fame and his run-in with the editor of the "Captain Kidd Monthly," we find him in a converted church in Lower Manhattan, full of "artists of various sorts, painters, or sculptors, or indigent students, or teachers of languages, or poets, or fugitive French politicians, or German philosophers."[82] In this intellectual bohemia (where he will meet, among others, Plotinus Plinlimmon) we learn, in the chapter "Pierre Immaturely Attempts a Mature Work," that he is "lodged in three lofty adjoining chambers of the Apostles"; a mise-en-scène, Parker reminds us, which is a thinly veiled version of Melville's own writing room at Pittsfield. It is in this room that Pierre "resolves to give the world a book, which the world should hail with surprise and delight"; one that will be the synthesis of "a varied scope of reading, little suspected by his friends, and randomly acquired by a random but lynx-eyed mind, in the course of multifarious, incidental, bibliographic encounterings."[83] This certainly seems a further nod to the Clinton Place basement where Duyckinck both leant Melville the books fueling the stylistic ambition of *Moby-Dick* and *Pierre*, and where there occurred the more recent falling out leading to the addition of 160 pages to the finished manuscript (a "multifarious" and "incidental...encounter" that Melville allegorized as his "sudden" run-in with the editor of the "Captain Kidd Monthly"). But here that run-in forms the basis of a minitreatise on the relationship of reading to composition: "All mere reading is apt to prove but an obstacle" to the budding novelist, and while Pierre thought of himself as having left behind the acquisition stage of a "varied scope of reading" passing into the "wonderful element of Beauty and Power," he "could not see...that already, in the incipiency of his work, the heavy unmalleable element of mere book knowledge would not congenially weld with the wide fluidness and ethereal airiness of spontaneous creative thought. He would climb Parnassus with a pile of folios on his back."[84] Climbing Parnassus with a pile of folios on his back is the generalized type for Melville's own compositional toil on *Moby-Dick* and *Pierre*, weighed down with the "heavy unmalleable elements" of Shakespeare, Browne, de Quincey, the Gospels, the sea adventure, the sentimental gothic, antebellum periodical culture, and up to recent reviews and correspondence. In imagining the novelist laboriously scaling the heights of "Parnassus"—a stock type of literary immortality from Athens to Montparnasse—Melville turns his own career into a vast, allegoric emblem.

The relation of allegory to mountains is soon wildly hyperbolized in an extended analogy between Pierre's inner life and "the Alps":

> the Alps do never in one wide and comprehensive sweep, instantaneously reveal their full awfulness of amplitude—their overawing extent of peak crowded on peak, and spur sloping on spur, and chain jammed behind chain, and all their wonderful battallionings of might; so hath heaven wisely ordained, that on first entering into the Switzerland of his soul, man shall not at once perceive its tremendous immensity; lest illy prepared for such an encounter, his spirit should sink and perish in the lowermost snows. Only by judicious degrees, appointed of God, does man come at last to gain his Mont Blanc and take an overtopping view of these Alps; and even then, the tithe is not shown....Appalling is the soul of man! Better might one be pushed off into the material spaces beyond the uttermost orbit of our sun, than once feel himself fairly afloat in himself![85]

In likening what Parker calls Pierre's "perilous inner terrain" to a vast mountain range, Melville continues his experiment in imagining the relation of literature to experience, not as faithful portraiture, but as a giving form to the process by which one thing is made to stand for another.[86] As with the allegoric conversion of Pierre's heart into a series of stone figures, the prose here is not so much a matter of likening Pierre's inner life to a vast mountain range as of making sensuous that likening itself. Mountains here give form to the *allos* by which the "inner" turns into "terrain"; a conversion again made manifest at the lexical level, in unwieldy neologisms ("battalionings"; "overtoppings"); more abuse of the substantive ("awfulness"); Browne-like doublings ("peak...peak"; "spur...spur"; "chain...chain"); and densely assonant composites ("lowermost snows").[87]

What Poirier called Melville's attempt to take on "the accumulated weight of inherited forms and models," what Bercovich called "words talking to words," and what Duyckinck complained of, in his review of *Moby-Dick*, as Melville's propensity for "opaque allegorical veils," is made still more explicit later in the chapter:

> Yet now, forsooth, because Pierre began to see through the first superficiality of the world, he fondly weens he has come to the underlayered substance. But, far as any geologist has yet gone down into the world, it is found to consist of nothing but surface stratified on surface. To its axis, the world being nothing but superinduced superficies.[88]

As with the transposition of the correspondence refusing the daguerreotype into Pierre's run-in with the editor of the "Captain Kidd Monthly," Melville's prose becomes more effortly artificial the more *Pierre* approaches direct reportage. But here the process by which lived events become general emblems is explicitly a concern with "geological" phenomena; of "superinducement" and "underlayering."[89] The alignment of style and geology is made sensuous in a Brownean doubling reaching giddy excess in phrases like "superinduced superficies." The thinking together of "geology," "inner landscapes," and literary allusion is given its most willfully allegoric cast when we learn of Pierre's vision of "The Delectable Mountain." Here Melville makes undeniably explicit the way *Pierre* is a book about books; a "superinducement" of literary layers to which the novel gives form in inscrutable stones and rock formations. Again coming close to the straight autobiographic report, Pierre, we learn, is suffering from overwork and eye strain from staring too long at the "progress of his book," and goes out for a walk to get some air. He is soon lost, staggering, and "before his eyes a million green meteors danced [and] when he came to himself he was lying crosswise in the gutter, dabbled with mud and slime."[90] The morning following this collapse, "during a state of semi-consciousness or rather trance a remarkable dream vision [comes] to him ... a baseless yet imposing spectacle of natural scenery."[91] But before the content of the dream vision is revealed there appears another of the narrator's disquisitions, this time on the relation of nature to meaning:

> Say what some poets will, Nature is not so much her own ever-sweet interpreter, as the mere supplier of that cunning alphabet, whereby selecting and combining as he pleases, each man reads his own peculiar lesson according to his own peculiar mind and mood. Thus a high-aspiring but most moody, disappointed bard, chancing once to visit the Meadows and beholding that fine eminence, christened it by the name it ever after bore; completely extinguishing its former title—The Delectable Mountain—one long ago bestowed by an old Baptist farmer, an hereditary admirer of Bunyan and his most marvelous book. From the spell of that name the mountain never afterward escaped; for now, gazing upon it by the light of those suggestive syllables, no poetical observer could resist the apparent felicity of the title. For as if indeed the immemorial mount would fain adapt itself to its so recent name, some people said that it had insensibly changed its pervading aspect within a score or two of winters. Nor was this strange conceit entirely without foundation, seeing that the annual displacements of huge rocks and gigantic trees were continually modifying its whole front and general contour.[92]

Beginning with the idea that Nature is the "supplier of that cunning alphabet" for each person to read their own "peculiar lesson," we learn that the Mount of the Titans has previously been known as the Delectable Mountain; a name given it by an "admirer of Bunyan."[93] This is of course to identify the mountain with one of the most overtly allegorical works in Western literary history, "that most remarkable book" *The Pilgrim's Progress*. As with the generalizing types "Tom, Dick, and Harry," "Nature, Meadows, and Delectable Mountain," are a series of substitutions of abstract emblems for specific individuals.[94] In making explicit reference to the Delectable Mountain, Melville, in his effort to persist at all costs in the deliberate abstraction of an allegoric mode—to ward off a too "faithful" mapping of Pierre's work on his novel with his own work on *Pierre*—points us to the moment in Bunyan's allegory at which Christian, in his journey on the road to the celestial city, meets the shepherds Knowledge, Experience, Watchful, and Sincere tending to their flocks on top of the Mountain.[95] That this is not an off-hand allusion, but rather placed at the center of Pierre's climactic dream vision, cements the novel's relentless obstruction of verisimilitude by allegory. Here that move occurs as the superimposition of three ways of foregrounding literary technique: making the materials of literature as immanent in a natural landscape ("Nature" as the "supplier of that cunning alphabet"); marking the equation of letters and Nature in a conspicuous allusion to Bunyan (an emblem of "allegory" itself); and leveling the relation of natural landscape to literary convention in a series of general types (Nature; Meadows; Delectable Mountain).

If Bunyan's allegory is claimed to be "delivered under the similitude of a dream," in which general meanings are revealed through particular experiences, then Pierre's dream vision unleashes its own version of the generalizing power of allegory:

> A terrific towering palisade of dark mossy massiveness confronted you; and trickling with unevaporable moisture, distilled upon you from its beetling brow slow thunder-showers of water drops, chill as the last dews of death...all round and round, the grim scarred rocks rallied and re-rallied themselves; shot up, protruded, stretched, swelled and eagerly reached forth, on every side bristlingly radiating with a hideous repellingness.[96]

As the stones become more imposing the prose contorts into more "hideously" artificial shapes. "Moss" and "mass" swallow each other in "mossy massiveness," giving way to odd inventions like "unevaporable." Accordingly, Melville pushes his sentences more and more toward brute sonority: "All round and round the grim scarred rocks rallied and re-rallied." As an alliterative pattern ("round and round") picks up momentum through an interior echo ("scarred rocks"), then further splits and replicates ("rallied and *re*-rallied"), it is as if the words were ricocheting off the rocks they describe. With the "re-rallying" rocks "bristlingly radiating" out into further inventions like "repellingness," the effect is of Bunyan's dream vision buckling under the density of an experimental prose. Such willful stylistic invention shows Melville straining to keep separate his allegorical tiers, as Pierre's literary labor threatens to mirror his own.

At the center of Pierre's vision appears what the narrator calls a "form of awfulness":

> Enceladus the Titan, the most potent of all the giants, writhing from out the imprisoning earth;—turbaned with upborne moss he writhed, still, though armless, resisting with his whole striving trunk, the Pelion and the Ossa hurled back at him;—turbaned with upborne moss he writhed, still turning his unconquerable front toward that majestic mount eternally in vain assailed by him, and which when it had stormed him off, had

heaved his undoffable incubus upon him, and deridingly left him there to bay out his ineffectual howl.[97]

Throwing "Titans" onto the pile of allusions, Pierre's climb up Parnassus now takes on the superinduced strata of the Gigantes, "writhing from out the imprisoning earth," heaving an "undoffable incubus." An invention like "undoffable incubus," while perhaps what antebellum reviewers were referring to when they complained of Pierre's "hideous" prose, is a vivid example of how a certain kind of verbal impactedness—seven syllables jammed into a two-word phrase—can itself take on the effects of allegory. This kind of compression is already going on in Moby-Dick. Describing the wild malice Ahab feels toward the whale Ishmael explains how Ahab had "pitted himself, all mutilated" against what the whale stood for: "all that most maddens and torments; all that stirs up the lees of things...all that cracks the sinews and cakes the brain; all the subtle demonisms of life and thought; all evil, to crazy Ahab, were visibly personified, and made practically assailable in Moby Dick."[98] While the whale is of course a real entity in the novel (it bashes apart boats, takes off limbs, and finally drags Ahab, caught in his own lines, out to sea) it is most concretely present in the novel as kind of allegoric potential. I say "potential" (as opposed to claiming that the whale is an allegory for, say, the inscrutable nature of existence, or raw anguished desire, or monomaniacal fury) because Ahab and Ishmael, for whom nothing in existence is unrelated to the whale, make of Moby Dick a general emblem for the possibility of one thing standing for another. When Duyckinck complained of Melville's propensity for "opaque allegorical veils," and when Melville mused in a letter to Sophia Hawthorne that Moby-Dick hung together by a diffuse "allegoricalness," both identify a volatile asymmetry between the faithful report and the abstract emblem. In Pierre that tension gets expressed in local prose effects: a phrase like "undoffable incubus," a representative instance of Pierre's mineralized style, is a compressed but no less abstractly totalizing emblem, here standing in for the vicissitudes of Melville's career: the pile of folios is undoffable—unremovable, stubbornly attached—because, like the appearance of Enceladus from out of the earth, the labor of composition is inseparable from the materials that form its substrate (the accumulation of styles building up since the Bible and the Greeks). And they are an "incubus" because, in giving form to the layers of allusion that led to novels like Moby-Dick and Pierre, such bookishness is just what dooms Melville's most ambitious literary experiments to fail before the evaluative criteria of the Literary World.[100]

Soon the narrator turns to consider Pierre's own impressions of Enceladus:

> [Pierre's] strange vision [now] displaced the four blank walls, the desk, the camp-bed, and domineered upon his trance. But no longer petrified in all their ignominious attitudes, the herded Titans now sprung to their feet; flung themselves up the slope, and anew battered at the precipice's unresounding wall. Foremost among them all, he saw a moss-turbaned, armless giant, who despairing of any other mode of wreaking his

immitigable hate, turned his vast trunk into a battering ram, and hurled his own arched out ribs again and yet again against the invulnerable steep. "Enceladus! it is Enceladus!— Pierre cried out in his sleep. That moment the phantom faced him, and Pierre saw Enceladus no more; but on the Titan's armless trunk, his own duplicate face and features magnifiedly gleamed upon him with prophetic discomfiture and woe.[101]

Pierre's heart becoming a marble shrine; the portrait's breaking through pictorial representation with a spoken conceit; the Memnon's stone's inscrutable hieroglyphic rendering a rock face meaningful (without signifying anything in particular); the discovery of a pamphlet arguing that Christ's teachings are, rather than the rock of faith, mere allegories of our terrestrial jarring; the mechanical precision of the daguerreotype remade into a hostile refusal to "have one's mug engraved"; the usurpation of Pierre's interiority by a vast expanse of rock—all of this culminates in Pierre's vision of his face in the trunk of Enceladus. Because the passage transposes into allegory the writing sessions during which Melville added the new material—first into a solitary atelier, then into a vision in which a writing room becomes a rock formation—the scene of composition has become a totally abstract tableau. And just as the psychodrama particular to the sentimental gothic (Pierre's "perilous inner terrain") turned into a meditation on mountain ranges, here an irreverent refusal of antebellum aesthetic criteria becomes Enceladus's "wreaking his immitigable hate" upon an "invulnerable steep," as an armless stone torso becomes the screen on which Pierre sees himself projected, "in duplicate face and features." The dogma of the faithful portrait—the "duplicate"—now terrorizes Pierre as a nightmare.

If, as Newton Arvin notes, "Melville's own life is [in *Pierre*] made into the stock types of fiction," then the novel exaggerates the making of such types in the stratifications of its style: from the language of reviews and correspondence, to the conventions of gothic and sentimental romance, to Browne's "metaphysical" prose, Shakespeare, Dante, *Pilgrim's Progress*, the Gospels, the Titans of Greek myth, and finally "Parnassus," the general type of literary glory.[102] That Pierre is himself finally imagined, not only as an emblem for the novelist's "thwarted career," but of literary ambition itself invites us to find in his name a different kind of hieroglyphic. Like the personifying projection of an inscription upon a rock (the "allegorical verification" of the Memnon stone), the more radically abstract dream vision has Pierre merging his own face with the face of a mountain (a hallucinatory hyperbole of "having one's mug engraved"). "Pierre"—stone—has been throughout the compact cipher for the obstruction of criteria that, if adhered to, would have made *Pierre* either an amusing pastiche of the sentimental romance or a faithful portrait of Melville's struggles as a writer. Instead, Melville wrote a novel of refusal and self-sabotage.[103]

Evert Duyckink's review of *Pierre* for the August 1852 issue of the *Literary World* was not an approving one. He described the novel as "a confused phantasmagoria of distorted fancies and conceits, ghostly abstractions and fitful shadows"; a novel that was but a "spectre of the substantial author of *Omoo* and *Typee*."[104] He is disturbed by how the "transformation" could have taken place, from the earlier writer of felicitously precise travel narratives to the "*diablerie*" of *Pierre*.[105] As he made explicit in his review of *Moby-Dick*, and as he must have implied in his face-to-face appraisal of the first version of *Pierre*, Duyckinck weds his literary criticism to classical ideals of "order, grace and proportion"; ideals that should never be confused with the grotesque distortions of allegory.[106] Grace and proportion meant above all, not just for Duyckinck but for most antebellum reviewers, the right ratio of romance to unity and *vraisemblance*.

In trying to arrive at the true structure of *Pierre*, Parker contends that the pages Melville added to the novel in late 1851 and early 1852 wrecked what would otherwise have been Melville's most "hyper-coherent" work, perhaps surpassing *Moby-Dick* in power and conception. In contrast to this view, I have tried to show how attention to the added pages is crucial to understanding Melville's most ambitious novel. Given the decisive events of late 1851 and early 1852 that led to their addition, and the explicitly allegorical way that material is put to use, we get a clue as to why Melville reacted as he did to Duyckinck's correctives in his review of *Moby-Dick*. If it was, as Parker puts it, "difficult if not impossible for Melville not to write about his own experience," then in *Moby-Dick* and *Pierre*, the relation of writing to experience shifts from faithful portraiture to the making sensuous of the way one thing can be made to stand for another.

CHAPTER 4

The Ambassador Effect

[T]here is only one primal stuff or material in the world, a stuff of which everything is composed...if we call that stuff "pure experience" then knowing can easily be explained as a particular sort of relation.

William James

[R]eally relations stop nowhere.

Henry James

THE GENTEEL TRADITION

In a 1911 address given before the Philosophical Union in Berkeley, California, George Santayana described what he took to be a telling fissure in the American intellectual temperament. It is one, he says, whose "wisdom [is] a little thin and verbal" but is at the same time "leaping down a sort of Niagara Rapids [of] invention and industry and social organization."[1] Santayana thought the latter the pragmatic spirit of innovative commercialism, the former a vestige of the Calvinist metaphysics from which American philosophy emerged, and which he called the "genteel tradition."[2] The lecture was Santayana's farewell to the United States, where he had always been "at once an outsider and an intimate of the rituals of Boston's elite society."[3] After receiving a small inheritance, he would seek relief from what he saw as the prim provincialism of Boston, resigning from Harvard's Philosophy Department to "assume the life of a perpetual stranger" in Europe.[4]

Santayana nevertheless identified his Harvard colleague William James as an American who had broken with the genteel tradition, saying of James that while he was "swaddled" in that tradition he managed to give it a "rude shock" by developing his philosophy, chiefly in controversy against its opposite which he called intellectualism [which was] as he conceived it, pure pedantry; it impoverished and verbalized everything, and tied nature up in red tape. Ideas and rules that may have been occasionally useful it put in the place of the full-blooded irrational movement of life which had called them into being; and these abstractions, so soon obsolete, it strove to fix and to worship forever [but for James] the universe is an experiment; it is unfinished [it is] perpetual hazard.[5]

The rejection of "verbalism" and "intellectualism" Santayana attributes to James was part of James's refusal of the idealism that dominated Harvard philosophy, in the neo-Kantianism of his friend and colleague Josiah Royce, and at Oxford in the work of neo-Hegelians like F. H. Bradley. Instead of the dogmas of the absolute (a closed universe that might be thought of as consistent with a tradition that found souls either damned or elect), James strove for a description of the universe as "perpetual chance and perpetual experiment"; an insistence on real newness in the cosmos that Santayana, describing James's own intellectual temperament, called an "impassioned empiricism."[6]

Alongside this impassioned empiricism, Santayana thought William's brother Henry, while also swaddled in the genteel tradition, broke from it in a different way. Rather than reject an etiolated verbalism (and its attendant absolutism), Henry, according to Santayana, escaped the genteel tradition by "turning [it], as he turns everything else, into a subject-matter for analysis. For him it was a curious habit of mind, intimately comprehended, to be compared with other habits of mind, also well known to him."[7] Indeed, James conducted this analysis throughout his career, in what is sometimes called his International Theme: Daisy Miller's promiscuity in Rome; Catherine Sloper's agon with her father over the Europeanized merce-nary Morris Townshend; Isabel Archer's disastrous marriage to the exiled antiquar-ian Gilbert Osmond; and the more diffuse moral conundrums of the later novels, especially Maggie Verver's triangular intrigue with her father and the Italian prince Amerigo. James's parochial authority figures, from Dr. Austin Sloper to Henrietta Stackpole, to Mrs. Newsome and Sarah Pocock in *The Ambassadors*, have an air about them of absolutism and predetermination that seems a vestige of the genteel tradition.

At once protracted and pitilessly precise, the late style became a specialized instrument for analyzing the drama of New World innocents enmeshed in Old World ambiguity. In a 1905 letter to his brother, William complained about what he took to be this too-nuanced prose:

> I read your Golden Bowl a month or more ago, and it put me, as most of your recenter long stories have put me, in a very puzzled state of mind. I don't enjoy...the method of narration by interminable suggestive reference [and it] goes against the grain of all my own impulses in writing.[8]

In William's distaste for the "interminable suggestive reference" of his brother's late style, we get a clear sense of the difference Santayana identified in the two brothers' ways of critiquing and escaping the genteel tradition. Their "bursting the bonds" of that tradition would seem to part ways around what James calls "verbalism": the moment the "full-blooded irrational movement of life" (William) runs the risk of becoming obstructed by "interminable suggestive reference" (Henry).

As if to formalize the criticism in the letter to his brother into a full-blown philosophy, William, in his 1908 Oxford lectures, attacked F. H. Bradley's neo-Hegelian idealism in similar terms:

> abstract concepts are but as flowers gathered, they are only moments dipped out from the stream of time, snap-shots taken, as by a kinetoscopic camera, at a life that in its original coming is continuous [for] look where you will, you gather only examples of the same amid the different, and of different relations existing as it were in solution in the same thing...a whole of parts and part of higher whole, all simultaneously and without inference or need of doubling-up its being, so long as we keep to...the point of view in which we follow our sensational life's continuity [for] to understand life by concepts is to arrest its movement, cutting it up into bits as with scissors, and immobilizing these in our logical herbarium where [we can] compare them as dried specimens.[9]

James is after a philosophy that does not reduce the multiform continuousness of life to the discrete cut-out of the concept; that arrests the flux of experience in the "dried specimens" of words. For James this leads to the manipulation of language for the posing of nonexistent problems, which are then "solved" through further manipulations of language. Rather than getting bogged down in verbalism, James wants a philosophy that captures "our sensational life's continuity"; an impassioned empiricism that takes the stream of particulars at face value, rather than packaging them into conceptual specimens.

Given the way the lecture seems a continuation of William's letter of complaint about the prose of *The Golden Bowl*, it is telling that the same year William gives the Oxford lecture, 1908, Henry adds the preface to the New York edition of *The Golden Bowl*, in which he explains the late style's relation to "experience":

> The act of revision, the act of seeing [the novel] again caused whatever I looked at on any page to flower before me as into the only terms that honorably expressed it; and the "revised" element in the present Edition is accordingly these terms...so many close notes, as who should say, on the particular vision of the matter itself that experience had at last made the only possible one...what would be really interesting, and I dare say admirably difficult, to go into would be the very history of this effect of experience.[10]

If for William abstract concepts are "flowers" plucked from the stream of experience ("life's continuity"), ending up as dried specimens in a "logical herbarium," for Henry the process of composition and revision causes new terms to "flower" before him as an "effect of experience." And if William wishes to abandon the dried artifacts of verbalism for an impassioned empiricism (with language itself imagined as a block or obstruction to experience), Henry is interested in the way experience can be thought of as continued in composition itself. If William's pitting experience against a "thin and verbal" intellectualism was his way of giving a "shock" to the genteel tradition, then we might say Henry's treating composition as a model for experience, and the way that lead to the suppleness of the late style, is inseparable from his verbal art of analyzing that tradition. Both of them could then be seen as responding, in their different ways, to the historical inertia of the genteel tradition as a working through the relation of language to experience.

The concern to replace a philosophy that would substitute conceptual and discursive "cut-outs" for the continuity of experience was not for William simply a matter of attacking rationalist first principles, but of formulating an idea of experience that would bypass the rationalism/empiricism dyad altogether. James wanted to do away with the correspondence epistemology that had, in his view, hobbled philosophical investigation since Descartes set inquiry down the path that led to Hume's skepticism and Kant's "Copernican" response to Hume. In offering what he called a "radical" empiricism, James rejected, not only philosophy that seemed a vestige of the genteel tradition, but classical empiricism. If for empiricists like Locke and Hume relations between outer phenomena were contributed by a faculty of inner synthesis (the making of impressions into reflective ideas; the association of ideas), for James relations between phenomena were as real and perceivable as the phenomena themselves; an account James described as the way "relations are external to their terms."[11] This is what James means by the "continuity" of experience: the terms of experience and the means of relating those terms are on a continuum, rather than two columns in need of alignment.[12]

While in the previous chapters I have tried to describe different ways experience and composition can be thought to form a continuity, here I want to show how the James brothers, despite the discrepancies over prose style, offer a still more intimately entwined version of that continuity. Like Emerson's solution to the problem of vocation, which takes the form of a search for a method by which essays are built up from journal entries and lectures; and Poe's conversion of the traveling spectacle of the chess-playing machine into a genre marked by the jump from particular perception to general category; and Melville's hastily adding pages to *Pierre* in which a rejection of unity and verisimilitude takes the form of a reflexive use of allegory, William and Henry work out what it means to understand the continuity of experience as capturable in composition. But in this final chapter, I want to shift the focus from the discrete encounter—Cuvier's cabinets, Maelzel's chess-playing machine; Duyckinck's reviews of *Moby-Dick*—to an imbricated "encounter" between William's late philosophy and Henry's late style, such that *The Ambassadors'* analysis of clashing habits of perception between New England and Paris becomes the formal enactment of William's radical empiricism (despite his exasperated complaints about 'verbalism').

What is it about *The Ambassadors* that shares radical empiricism's basic claim that relations are as real as, and external to, their terms? We might begin with the title, which names that relational dynamic as ambassadorship. Indeed, a list of instances in the novel in which relations understood as equated with and instantiated in ambassadorship might include: the primary relation of Strether's being sent to Paris on behalf of Mrs. Newsome to retrieve her son Chad so that he may return to take over the family business in Woollett; Strether's ongoing reportage on this situation to a woman, Maria Gostrey, he first meets in London; Chad Newsome's ambassadorial relation between Madame de Vionnet and Strether, as he reports to her the details of the plan to get him back to Woollett; the fleeting, provisional ambassadorship set up between Jeanne de Vionnet and Madame Vionnet, which serves to preface Strether's introduction to Madame de Vionnet at Gloriani's garden party; a parallel ambassadorship, at the same party, between Miss Barrace and Strether, as she reports of Waymarsh's doings inside; Madame Vionnet's making of Strether into her ambassador back to Woollett, as she extracts information from him concerning Mrs. Newsome's plan to bring Chad home; the meta-ambassadorship set up between Strether and Maria Gostrey concerning Madame Vionnet's history, who turns out to be an old school friend of Maria's; the backup ambassadorship established between Strether's friend Waymarsh and Mrs. Newsome, which serves as a kind of surveillance report on Strether's doings in Paris; Mrs. Newsome's sending, after reviewing Waymarsh's report, a team of follow-up ambassadors to Paris— Sarah (Newsome, Chad's sister) and her husband Jim Pocock; their daughter Maimie Pocock's brief ambassadorship between Strether and Chad, when Strether is trying to decide if Mrs. Newsome is aware of how Chad has "changed"; Chad's becoming Strether's temporary (epistolary) ambassador back to Woollett, in writing the letter to his mother that is to serve as Strether's response to her request for a progress report; and Maris Gostrey's ambassadorship, late in the novel, between Strether and Madame de Vionnet, after the truth of her relationship with Chad has been revealed to Strether. In each instance, the novel's privileging of relations between characters—its being more about relations than fixed terms—is the way *The Ambassadors* embodies and animates radical empiricism.[13]

What I call the "ambassador effect," then, is the way what appears to be a discrepancy in the thinking of the James brothers around the relation of experience to language is in fact the point where they are most in unison. That *The Ambassadors* takes as its formal organizing principle the basic tenet of radical empiricism—externality of relations enacted formally in a novel *about* relations (ambassadors)—shows a crucial point of overlap in the James brothers' different ways of breaking with, and analyzing, the genteel tradition. But I want here to make the further claim that this same affinity affords us an opportunity to reconsider the meaning of the term "cosmopolitanism." In first looking at another instance of ambassadorship—the mutual influence of William James and Henri Bergson, and at precisely the time of the composition and publication of *The Ambassadors*—I find a crossing over into the new and foreign which is the basic predicament confronting Strether in Paris, and a posing of the question of cosmopolitanism as a matter of reconciling local loyalties with a common, or universal, humanity.[14] Looking at some of the correspondence between William James and Bergson, I move on to describe how *The Ambassadors* formally enacts James's and Bergson's shared ideas about radical empiricism, with specific emphasis on William's notion of "pure experience" and Bergson's notion of *durée* [duration]. I then turn to a series of close readings of the novel through the lens of this shared empiricism, showing how it allows us to think of cosmopolitanism as a pragmatic, bottom-up reconciliation of the particular and the universal in place of a *sensus communis* arising from reflective judgments. Cosmopolitanism here is indissociable from the way ambassadors shuttle between what James calls the "Woollett scale" and the "vast bright Babylon" of Paris; a process continued in the supple elasticity of the late style.

TWO TYPES OF RADICAL EMPIRICISM

As Henry James prepared the manuscript of *The Ambassadors* for serial publication in the *North American Review* in the fall of 1902, his brother William acknowledged receipt of a book sent to him four years earlier by a young French philosopher. The book has had a major impact on him:

> I read the copy of your Matiere et Mouvement [*sic*] which you so kindly sent me, immediately on receiving it four years ago or more ... it is a work of exquisite genius. It makes a sort of Copernican revolution as much as Berkeley's Principles or Kant's Critique did, and will probably, as it gets better & better known, open up a new era of philosophical discussion. It fills *my* mind with all sorts of new questions and hypotheses.... How good it is sometimes simply to *break away* from all old categories, deny old worn out beliefs, and restate things ab intitio making the lines of division fall into entirely new places.[15]

Henri Bergson did not take long to reply, writing to James in early January 1903, initiating roughly a decade of steady correspondence.[16] After receiving Bergson's telegram specifying when he would be in Paris and hoping they might meet, James wrote back:

> I think there must be great portions of your philosophy which you have not yet published, & I want to see how well they combine with mine. Writing is too long and laborious a process ... so I will still wait in the hope of a personal interview [upon my arrival in Paris]. I am convinced that a philosophy of pure experience such as I conceive yours to be, can be made to work, and will reconcile many of the old inveterate oppositions of the schools.[17]

The rigidity of the "schools"—by which we must assume James means everything from the neo-Aristotelianism of Aquinas, to the Calvinist metaphysics that lingered obliquely in the Harvard Philosophy Department, and which had been, as Santayana put it, "grafted onto" the genteel tradition, and up to factional quarrels among British neo-Hegelians like F. H. Bradley[18]—is to be "broken away" from into the fresh newness of the empiricism James finds echoed in a philosophy coming from across the Atlantic.[19] The new empiricism is to be an antidote to "old inveterate oppositions" of entrenched philosophical habits.

In June of 1907, James responded, again ecstatically, to his receipt of Bergson's new book, *L'évolution Créatrice*:

> O my Bergson you are a magician, and your book is a marvel, a real wonder in the history of philosophy ... the vital achievement of the book is that it inflicts an irrecoverable death wound upon Intellectualism. ... You will be receiving my own little "pragmatism" book simultaneously with this letter ... it is so congruent with parts of your system and fits so well into interstices thereof, that you will easily understand why I am so enthusiastic. I feel at bottom that we are fighting the same fight. ... The position we are rescuing is "tychism" and a really growing world. But whereas I have hitherto found no better way of defending tychism than by affirming the spontaneous addition of *discrete* elements of being (or their subtraction), thereby playing the game with intellectual weapons, you set things straight at a single stroke by your fundamental conception of the continuously creative nature of reality.[20]

Here James explicitly acknowledges his identification with Bergson's philosophy as part of what he takes to be a battle between "intellectualism" and "tychism."[21] A term first used by Charles Peirce in an 1892 essay, "tychism" designates the belief in chance and contingency as really existing in the universe, as opposed to metaphysical doctrines arguing for prearrangement (which might be found in everything from Calvinist predetermination to the possible worlds of Gottfried Leibniz's *La Monadologie*).[22] For James, the battle between intellectualism and tychism is one between an ontology that would begin from an idea of an absolute to a belief in real contingency; what Santayana characterized as James's conviction that the universe is "unfinished," is "perpetual hazard" and "perpetual experiment," and is an "open" structure, without blueprint or telos.[23]

To this declaration of a shared belief in a tychistic universe, we have Bergson's full reply, in the form of an equally admiring review of *Pragmatism*, which James had included with his letter of praise for *L'évolution créatrice*:

> Thank you, Professor James, for this beautiful and profound study which will no doubt help a great deal in making your philosophy better understood. It seems to me that this time you have adopted a more radical means of warding off misunderstanding: you have *situated* your doctrine in relation to traditional philosophical positions and commonly received ideas. ... Your position vis-à-vis realism is [now] much clearer. The contrast between pragmatism and positivism (an intellectualist system in the worst sense of the word, where I see only an old static metaphysics in disguised form) is also clearly laid

out...one sees in pragmatism a new conception of the relation between the abstract and the concrete, and of the universal and the individual. As far as I am concerned, I have never had a better sense of the affinity between our two modes of thought. At the very least we have the same adversaries and, as you put it in a letter to me some months ago, "we are fighting the same fight."[24]

In this two-way transatlantic admiration between *L'évolution créatrice* and *Pragmatism* we find that the "common adversary" is intellectualism understood as the reinstatement of metaphysical dogmas in the form of "positivism"; and of predetermination at the level of logic and possible world that would preclude the arrival of anything new in the universe. But the affinity between *L'évolution créatrice* and *Pragmatism* nevertheless rests on an important discrepancy: that between Jamesian "discrete-ness" and Bergsonian "continuousness." When James says that he had "hitherto found no better way of defending tychism than by affirming the spontaneous addition of *discrete* elements of being," Bergson "set things straight at a single stroke by [his] fundamental conception of the continuously creative nature of reality." Bergson in turn seems eager to acknowledge this same distinction when he remarks on James's treatment of the "relation between the abstract and the concrete" and "the universal and the individual." Again, for James these distinctions arise from his conviction that discrete parts come before wholes, which are collections or concatenations of parts (individuals before universals), and in which universals are inductive derivations from collections of individuals, and so are in some basic way never "finished." Still, their shared desire to avoid the reinstatement of philosophical dogmas seems deeper than the discrepancy around the discrete and the continuous.

James's and Bergson's shared radical empiricism is developed further in James's next letter, from Oxford (May 8, 1908), where he is about to give the lectures that will later be collected as *A Pluralistic Universe*.

> You will be surprised at seeing where I am. I got here [Harris Manchester College, Oxford] last Monday and am giving a course of seven (or eight?) "Hibbert lectures" on "the present situation in philosophy"—it amounts practically to a critique of intellectualism, and a vindication of the immediately *vécu* flux, in short, to Bergsonism.[25]

The next communication between them is James's July 19 letter, from his brother's East Sussex Rye ("Lamb House") address, where William is considering a trip to Switzerland to relax his nerves:

> I naturally still wish to see you, and since in my own case nothing is fixed irrevocably, I now write to ask you if your own plans are fixed, & whether you are to be in England before August....On the whole I should rather avoid Paris just now; but if you yourself were going to the country in France, I might possibly join you, and even more easily if you were going to Switzerland....Meanwhile I am sending you an uncorrected proof of my lecture on [Bergson] since this book [*A Pluralistic Universe*] will not appear

until next April. . . . You see that I suppress almost all of your philosophy for the sake of emphasizing all the more your critique of intellectualism.[26]

And while Bergson's interim letter of July 23 is fragmented to the point of illegibility (we can discern "soon" and "I could easily meet"), we do have James's full response of July 28:

> Dear Bergson (can't we cease "Professor"-ing each other?—that title establishes a "disjunctive" relation between man & man, and our relation should be "endosmotic" socially as well as intellectually, I think) . . . meanwhile let me say how delighted your letter made me. There are many points in your philosophy which I don't yet grasp, but I have seemed to myself to understand your anti-intellectualistic campaign very clearly, and that I have really done it so well in your opinion makes me proud.[27]

If we infer from this response that Bergson's previous letter was full of praise for James's Oxford lecture on his philosophy, then it is fitting that in lieu of a face-to-face encounter, James wants to clear away some of the formalities, suggesting they replace a 'disjunctive' 'Professor-ing' with a more 'endosmotic' exchange. The medical adjective "endosmotic" is a throwback to James's own earlier psychological research, and is linked to the meanings of "osmotic" and "osmosis" as the passing of a solvent through a semipermeable membrane. James uses it again in his essay "Bradley or Bergson?," a sort of addendum to the Oxford lectures. In it, Bradleyan absolutism—which James paraphrases as the presumption of a "supra-relational being"—is contrasted with the empiricism James finds in Bergson's "affirming the 'endosmosis' of adjacent parts of 'lived' experience [and] treating the minimum of feeling as an immediately intuited much at once."[28] Here, endosmosis marks the way the parts of lived experience are not cleanly demarcated units, but rather bleed into one another forming a smooth continuity. Thus, James suggests, the disjunctive rigidity of the formal address is to be replaced with a more fluid, permeable exchange, as if enacting the attack on static intellectualism in the rhythms of fluid itinerancy—England, Paris, Switzerland, Sussex, Cambridge—and as part of the protocols of correspondence itself. It is as if James were modifying his earlier understanding of particular to particular, finding in the very rituals of letter writing an opportunity to argue for the turning of atomistic empiricism into something more "endosmotic."

While James and Bergson continued their correspondence nearly up to James's death in August 1910, I want now to turn from their letters and look more closely at some of the arguments put forth in two important papers James published in the *Journal of Philosophy, Psychology and Scientific Methods*, and the lecture on "Bergson and Intellectualism" from *A Pluralistic Universe* (1908), and see how they square with Bergson's own writing from the same time. Specifically, I want to look closely at their differing accounts of the relation of the discrete to the continuous, and how this bears upon the thinking of relations in their different empiricisms.

Much of the commentary comparing the philosophies of James and Bergson is quick to point out that while there was real admiration and productive exchange between the them, and genuine affinity in their ways of thinking, their differences are finally more striking than their similarities.[29] While James, like Bergson, "called the monist's attention to the world's diversity [and] the pluralist to its unity,"[30] there is nevertheless an important discrepancy between James's empiricism and Bergson's notion of *durée*.

In James's radical empiricism—as put forth in *A Pluralistic Universe* (1908), but also in the 1904 essays "Does 'Consciousness' Exist?" and "A World of Pure Experience" and the final completed book *The Meaning of Truth* (1909)—the flow of experience is to be taken on its own terms, such that the relations that connect the parts of experience are themselves real and experienceable. This means that one need not refer the stream of particulars to some "higher" category that would make relation-as-such possible. In his introduction to the French edition of *Pragmatism*, Bergson accurately described this aspect of James's radical empiricism:

> At the same time [that our experience] presents us with things and facts it shows us relationships between the things and connections between the facts: these relations are as real, as directly observable, for William James, as the things and facts themselves. But the relations are fluctuating and the things fluid.[31]

In James's empiricism, the world is to be made and composed; it is open and tychistic; it is an experiment. Accordingly, an all-inclusive master connector as the guarantor of the possibility of relations is replaced with a notion that relations are as immediately available to experience as the terms they relate. We can say then that for James the composition of the world arises from the concatenating of external relations into ever-newer arrangements. Such relations are "fluctuating and fluid," as Bergson puts it, because their reality renders them both perceivable as part of the world and the means by which the world is composed.[32]

The upshot of this idea is made explicit in a pair of essays that appeared in consecutive issues of *The Journal of Philosophy, Psychology and Scientific Methods* in September 1904, just prior to James's Oxford lectures. The first, "Does 'Consciousness' Exist" involves nothing less than an attempt to "expel neo-Kantian epistemology" in entirely doing away with correspondence:

> My thesis is that if we start with the supposition that there is only one primal stuff or material in the world, a stuff of which everything is composed, and if we call that stuff "pure experience" then knowing can easily be explained as a particular sort of relation.... The relation is itself a part of pure experience; one of its 'terms' becomes the knower... the other becomes the object known.[33]

Instead of treating the relation of knower to known as a chasm that must be leapt, or a correspondence that must be secured, James says we should treat the knowing of the thing and the thing known as different features of the same stretch of experience.[34] The philosophical tradition, at least since Descartes, imagines consciousness as a special kind of mental equipment (*res cogitans*; unity of apperception), which must then be argued into connection with the world of external phenomena (whether those external phenomena are understood as "extension" or "appearance"). But for James there is no need to refer to an entity called "consciousness," if by consciousness we mean either a form of nonextended substance that, through meditation on clear and distinct ideas, allows us to arrive at a rational justification of its relation to a second kind of (extended) substance; nor as a repository of a priori faculties that transcendental argumentation can reveal to us as the condition of possibility for external objects to become intelligible at all.[35] These are forms of what James calls verbalism or intellectualism; the replacing of the reality of experience with terms of philosophical dispute going back to the schoolmen. Rather, what we are in the habit of calling "consciousness" is for James just another stretch of relations. As David Lapoujade puts it, pure experience is a "plane" that

> precedes all the traditional psychological or philosophical categories [such that] these categories, far from being constitutive of this plane, must on the contrary be constituted from it. The subject, the object, matter, thought, etc. are all described, not as *a priori* givens, but as processes that are made.... To liberate the movement of that which is in the making [*en train de se faire*] implies a critique of the customary forms by which one divides up the flux of life [and so] consciousness is not...revealed, but rather co-extensive with [a] transcendental field. One cannot yet establish any distinctions within it; neither subject nor object [and thus] the peculiarity of our experiences, that they not only are, but are known, which their "conscious" quality is invoked to explain...is better explained by their relations—these relations themselves being experiences—to one another.[36]

Again, instead of thinking of consciousness as required for bringing an organizing principle into a chaotic sensory manifold so as to make it intelligible in conceptual synthesis, consciousness is just one more of the *products* of experience; another of the relations in a transcendental field, open and in the making, in which relations are external to, and as real as, their terms.

The next essay in which James urges the abandonment of the false gap posited by epistemology is "A World of Pure Experience." Again, the argument is made through an appeal to the idea that relations are as real as the terms they relate, and are as such themselves part of experience:

> To be a radical empiricist means to hold fast to...conjunctive relation[s]...for this is the strategic point, the position through which, if a hole be made, all the corruptions of

dialectics and all the metaphysical fictions pour into our philosophy. The holding fast to...relation[s] means taking [them] at face value, neither less nor more.[37]

Showing the influence of Bergson's *Matiere et mémoire,* James argues for the reality of relations through a description of succession:

What I feel...when a later moment of my experience succeeds an earlier one is that though they are two moments, the transition from the one to the other is *continuous.* Continuity here is a definite sort of experience [and has] real empirical content.[38]

Instead of a dualist epistemology we have an attention to the stream of experienced relations, such that relations—here called "continuity"—themselves bestow real empirical content. Rather than conjure through logic an occult power of connection in order to solve a nonexistent problem (the chasm between mind and world), James tells us that in succession we "feel" relations, and are thus given, in the experience of continuity, the means for organizing the discrete terms of perception.

Here, then, is how James finally characterizes his radically empiricist critique of epistemology, in the introduction to *The Meaning of Truth* (1909):

the relations between things, conjunctive as well as disjunctive, are just as much matters of direct particular experience...as the things themselves [and from this the generalized conclusion follows that] the parts of experience hold together from next to next by relations that are themselves part of experience. The directly apprehended universe needs, in short, no extraneous trans-empirical connective support, but possesses in its own right a concatenated or continuous structure.[39]

If the traditional epistemologist requires that there be some "trans-empirical connective" to account for relations between experienced particulars, James tells us that even such relations are part of the "concatenated structure" of the universe. And in response to the argument that a *regressus ad infinitum* results from a thinking of relations without such a trans-empirical connective (a problem "solved" in the positing a super category in which all relations are though to inhere, thus avoiding a Zeno-like infinity of subrelations), James sees a form of "vicious intellectualism"; a merely verbal solution to a merely verbal problem.[40]

What does it mean to say that relations are as real as the terms they relate? Aren't relations by definition dependent on terms? James rehearses a version of this objection in *The Meaning of Truth,* telling of an encounter with one of T. H. Green's "disciples," who responds to James's notion that relations are themselves a part of experience in the following way: "'Yes, *terms* may indeed be possibly sensational [experienced]; but *relations,* what are they but pure acts of the intellect coming upon the sensations from above, and of a higher nature.'"[41] James directs this interlocutor to a passage from his earlier *Principles of Psychology* in which an incipient version of the externality of relations thesis informs his discussion of space. In accord with the description, in *The Meaning of Truth*, of relations as "homogeneous with the terms, between which they are mediated [such that] the terms are spaces and the relations... other intervening spaces."[42] In volume 2 of the *Principles*, James writes:

> a relation, for a certain Platonizing school... is an energy of pure thought, and, as such, quite incommensurable with the data of sensibility between which it may be perceived to obtain. We may consequently imagine a disciple of this school to say to us at this point: "Suppose you *have* made a separate specific sensation of each line and each angle, what boots it? You have still the order of directions and distances to account for; you still have the relative magnitudes of all these felt figures to state; you have their respective positions to define before you can be said to have brought order into your space. And not one of these determinations can be effected except through an act of relating thought, so that your attempt to give an account of space in terms of pure sensibility breaks down almost at the very outset." But "relation" is a very slippery word... most relations are feelings of an entirely different order from the terms they relate [but just as] the relation between two numbers is another number, so in the field of space the relations are facts of the same order with the facts they relate.[43]

Here James is already on the path to radical empiricism; already thinking of relations as themselves as much a "fact" as the terms they put into connection. Rather than a "pure act of the intellect"—a Platonic "higher nature" that would bring connectives to the myriad facts of experience—James makes relations of the "same order as the facts they relate." If the organizing principles of experience are of the same order as the facts they relate, then they are not in need of a deduction from higher categories. For James, the organizing principles are in the world, not in the head.

In partial contrast, then, with James's radical empiricism, Bergson calls "true empiricism" the notion that experienced particulars are themselves the fluid elements of duration [*durée*], which is an absolute, qualitative, and indivisible continuity. For Bergson,

> an empiricism worthy of the name... is obliged for each new object that it studies to make an absolutely fresh effort [*un effort absolument nouveau*]. It cuts out for the object a concept which is appropriate to that object alone, a concept which can as yet hardly be called a concept, since it applies to this thing alone.[44]

In fashioning fresh units of measure for every new object, Bergson imagines an empiricism that would forgo entirely the dimensions of the concept and get right down into the strange particularity of the object (a profoundly anti-Kantian idea, insofar as Kant thinks there can be no awareness of "objects" at all without conceptual articulation). But while Bergson's empiricism is particularist (in the Jamesian sense), it also amounts to a new kind of absolutism. If *durée* is different from the sort of absolute that would find empirical particulars becoming intelligible only as they are brought under a higher categorical unity, it does amount to something like an ontological foundation and so also an ultimate check to tychism. Like James's radical empiricism, Bergson's *durée* gives us a new way of understanding the transcendental; what could be called transcendental empiricism.[45] Like "radical" empiricism, transcendental empiricism finds the condition of possibility for relating experienced particulars in the world, rather than in mental faculties. Again, the old epistemological problem of bridging the chasm between mind and world is replaced with an idea of experience in which the relation of knower to known is itself just one more of the products of a transcendental field of relations. So Bergson's empiricism, like James's, finds the conditions for the possibility of experience in worldly particulars rather than in the higher tribunal of a priori faculties. The important difference here is that, whereas James is genuinely tychistic in his conception of an open cosmos, full of contingency and always in the making, *durée* names a new kind of totality. While Bergson and James are both radical (or transcendental) empiricists, there is then an important difference in their philosophies of experience: James treats experience as a concatenation of particulars in which the whole is an ever-mutating, never-finished, improvised collection, while Bergson, who comparably thinks of experience as a transcendental field of external relations, nevertheless finds the absolute in the fluid whole he calls *durée*.

THE WOOLLETT SCALE

If radical empiricism is about the way ordering principles for experience—relations—are as available in perception as the terms to be ordered, Henry James makes this into the formal design of *The Ambassadors*. In the preface he added to his earlier novel *Roderick Hudson* James indicates that he was thinking of composition explicitly as a matter of relations. "Really, universally," he writes in a well-known passage from that preface, "relations stop nowhere, and the exquisite problem of the artist is eternally but to draw, by a geometry of his own, the circle within in which they will happily appear to do so."[46] If it is through the artist's "own geometry" that the open-ended proliferation of relations is to be composed into a work, then this same dynamic—experience as the endless composability of relations—is what *The Ambassadors* is in some fundamental way about. Arising from the idea that Chad Newsome has fallen in with a woman of ill repute in Paris and that he must be rescued and returned to Woollett, the terms of Lambert Strether's ambassadorship are deduced from what James calls the "Woollett scale."[47] And the series of ambassadorial relations that follow from this presumption (an overview of which I offered above) seems designed both to show what happens when Woollettian habits of perception are refracted through the "bright Babylon" of Paris, and to dramatize the way the novel's central reflector, Strether, is not so much a fixed center of experience as he is more and more absorbed into the ramifying of relations. In what follows, I want to show both how

James demonstrates at the level of form how the Woollett scale is made to undergo revision and how this is his way of enacting his brother's radical empiricism (itself developed out of his "ambassadorship" with Bergson). While this will be for Henry a way of analyzing, as Santayana put it, the genteel tradition (the clash of Woollett with Paris), it also makes vivid the way *The Ambassadors* is concerned to examine how patterns of seeing and thinking are split into multiple significances when immersed in foreign surroundings; the way tidy, provincial categories are atomized in a swirl of new impressions. While the prose of *The Ambassadors*—an exemplary instance of the "interminable suggestive reference" about which William complained—is itself a challenge to the rigidity of the Woollett scale, it is also a tool for dramatizing the way the novel's central reflector is at all points made to merge, as if through an endosmotic membrane, with a world of relations that really stop nowhere.

Even before Strether makes it across the channel he is struck by the strangeness of his London surroundings. That the novel opens with his waiting at a hotel for his companion Waymarsh, and that Waymarsh remains his quasi-confident throughout the first third of the novel, throws immediately into relief Strether's attunement to the limits of the Woollett scale. Still seeing his surroundings through Woollett criteria, Strether reflects on the appearance of a woman he has met while staying at a London hotel, and with whom he is having dinner:

> [Maria Gostrey's] dress was "cut down," as he believed the term to be, in respect to shoulders and bosom, in a manner quite other than Mrs. Newsome's, and who wore around her throat a broad red velvet band with an antique jewel—he was rather complacently sure it was antique—attached to it in front.... It would have been absurd of him to trace into ramifications the effect of the ribbon from which Miss Gostrey's trinket depended, had he not for the hour, at the best, been so given over to uncontrolled perceptions. What was it but an uncontrolled perception that his friend's velvet band somehow added, to her appearance, to the value of every other item [and] he had taken [the band] as a starting-point for fresh backward, fresh forward, fresh lateral flights. The manner in which Mrs. Newsome's throat *was* encircled suddenly represented for him, in an alien order, almost as many things as the manner in which Miss Gostrey's was.[48]

It would have been "absurd to trace into ramifications" the effect of the cut of Miss Gostrey's dress (or the jewels around her neck) because indulgently giving oneself over to speculation about the meaning of different fashions would be an absurd thing to do under Woollettian habits of thought. Because the novelty of Strether's London surroundings has "given over to uncontrolled perceptions," he seems willing to follow these particular perceptions as far as they will go. To call this willingness to give oneself over to "uncontrolled perception" a "tracing into ramification" is not only to describe the way peripheral perceptions grow and reverberate as one moves into a foreign environment, but to prefigure the way ambassadorial relations will split and concatenate in the novel. Here in London, in what is a kind of antechamber to the larger ambassadorial mission to Paris, we find that the dress and the red velvet band, in serving as "starting-points for fresh backward, fresh forward, fresh lateral flights," are an entry point onto the "alien order" Strether will soon have to navigate; the "lateral flights" of perception that will render his ambassadorial mission as a lattice of faceted refractions, and that will (almost) entirely dissolve the principles he's brought with him from Woollett.[49]

Some days after the London dinner, and after crossing over to Paris, Strether undergoes another series of uncontrolled perceptions while strolling the boulevards; what James calls a "process of feeling the general stirred life of connexions" full of "short gusts of speculation."[50] Like the dress that is "cut down" and made legible against the criterion of Woollett dresses, Strether recognizes a typically Parisian object—new novels on display in a librarie window—in what James describes as a "hungry gaze through clear plates behind which lemon-coloured volumes were as fresh as fruit on the tree."[51] This image of fresh, uncut volumes sends Strether on a "backward flight" to an earlier moment in his life, when as a young man he had made a visit to Paris and returned to New England,

with lemon-coloured volumes in general on the brain as well as with a dozen—selected for his wife too—in his trunk... nothing had at the moment shown more confidence than this invocation of the finer taste. They were still somewhere at home, the dozen—stale and soiled and never sent to the binder; but what had become of the sharp initiation they represented? They represented now the mere sallow paint on the door of the temple of taste that he had dreamed of raising up... he perfectly now saw, he had ceased even to measure his meagerness [in abandoning this dream], a meagerness that sprawled, in this retrospect, vague and comprehensive, stretching back like some unmapped Hinterland from a rough coast-settlement. His conscience had been amusing itself for the forty-eight hours [since he'd arrived in Paris] by forbidding him the purchase of a book; he held off from that, held off from everything [but] on this evidence, however, of the way they actually affected him [as] he glared at the lemon-coloured volumes... the green covers [of the journal he edited] at home comprised, by the law of their purpose, no tribute to letters; it was of a mere rich kernel of economics, politics, ethics that, glazed and, as Mrs. Newsome maintained rather against *his* view, pleasant to touch, they formed a precious shell.[52]

Like the cut of a dress, or an antique jewel suspended from a velvet band, the chance perception of "lemon-coloured volumes" sets off for Strether a flood of associative reflection. Here that reflection is on the difference between Woollett taste and Paris taste, as stretched over the years from Strether's youthful visit (when he hoped an intimate contact with French ideas and literature would give him access to a universal "temple of taste"), to his current midlife ambassadorial obligation to get another young man to return to New England. That he edits, at Woollett, a journal that is a "mere rich kernel of economics, politics, ethics," makes still more explicit the way the volumes of French literature stand for an alternate kind of intellectual labor, as if each "lemon-coloured rectangle" were itself a "temple" in tribute to the life of the mind.[53] If, as James puts it, the Woollett review pays no tribute to letters "by the law of its purpose," then it is a law deduced from the Woollett scale, here made perceptually concrete in the different hues of the covers of the objects themselves, as emblems of different habits of thought.[54] Here James shows the way experience is a function, not of getting a fix on the discrete terms of perception, but of how the terms themselves change when "in the presence of new measures, other standards, [and] different scale[s] of relations."[55] As with the difference between Maria's and Mrs. Newsome's fashion sense, the difference between the journal edited at Woollett and the volumes of French fiction glimpsed through a librarie window shows how relations in the novel become perceivable.[56] This making relations real and perceivable takes on a number of different forms in the passage: "paint on the door of the temple of taste"; a "rough coast settlement"; a "kernel"; a "precious shell." At such moments, the late style's luxuriance of analogy becomes a vehicle for the bodying out of relations; as if from out of the differential between the Woollett journal and the "lemon-coloured volumes" there spilled a wealth of freshly imagined likenesses, relations themselves becoming so many "temples," "settlements," "kernels," and "shells."[57]

Shortly after the "uncontrolled perceptions" at dinner, and the flood of new relations set off by the volumes glimpsed in the window, we get a more explicit challenge to the Woollett scale, brought on by the city itself:

> [Strether's] greatest uneasiness seemed to peep at him out of the imminent impression that almost any acceptance of Paris might give one's authority away. [Paris] hung before him this morning, that vast bright Babylon, like some huge iridescent object, a jewel brilliant and hard, in which parts were not to be discriminated nor differences comfortably marked. It twinkled and trembled and melted together, and what seemed all surface one moment, seemed all depth the next.[58]

Unlike his companion Waymarsh, who is at all times unequivocally uncomfortable, Strether worries that any demonstration of an "acceptance" of Paris will compromise the moral authority required for the success of his ambassadorial mission. Since, by the measure of the Woollett scale, Chad is supposed to have been corrupted by the city, any perception of Strether's being charmed, delighted, intoxicated by the "vast bright Babylon" could lead Chad to lose confidence in Strether's ability to enforce that scale. All of this amounts for Strether to a flashing up of new relations which generate "uneasiness" insofar as they threaten to "twinkle and tremble and melt together" he and Chad within a "huge iridescent object." This is a "melting" Strether cannot, in principle, afford to let happen, given the requirements of his ambassadorship—namely, that he preserve a gradient of difference, a perceptible relation, between he and Chad, out of which something like a law or necessity will lead Chad to return to Massachusetts to run the family business. If the "huge iridescent...jewel" of Paris is, on the one hand, a network of faceted refractions scrambling perceptual coordinates (and perhaps also the monstrous ramification of Maria's suspended jewel), it is then this very allure that threatens to undermine Mrs. Newsome's authority. As her controlling agency is broken up into the "new measures" of Parisian experience, ambassadorship becomes less a matter of enforcing the laws of Woollett, and more a fluidity of "parts not discriminated nor differences comfortably marked." Again, all of this amounts to a making relations real and perceivable, such that Strether's interiority (though this is now becoming the wrong word) is shown to be on a continuum with the city. "Relations" now name a stream of experience dissolving the grid of the Woollett scale in a tissue of fresh impressions. With Chad and Strether meeting on this iridescent spectrum, Paris itself begins to undermine the moral authority of the Woollett scale.[59]

The disorienting play of light appears again when Strether meets the sculptor Gloriani. At a moment in the novel when the pressures of his mission are reaching a crisis, James tells us of how the "deep expertness in Gloriani's charming smile—oh the terrible life behind it!—was flashed upon [Strether] as a test of his stuff."[60] Not long after Gloriani makes this "flashing" impression, at once charming and terrible, Strether succumbs to a kind of vertigo amid the guests in the garden, remarking of their faces: "Were they charming or were they only strange?"[61] Discovering himself at the point where the charming is both "terrible" (threateningly unknowable) and "strange" (foreign), Strether finds the "bright Babylon" of Paris compressed into a single term (Gloriani's "flashing" smile), another surface giving way to uncontrolled perceptions. But the strangeness of the garden, of the smile, is, at this relatively early stage of the mission, instinctively snapped back to the grid of the Woollett scale. If the woman for whom Strether functions as an appendage, and to whom he must regularly report on his progress is a "veritable fortress against difference", surprise, alteration,"[62] then Strether still carries with him some of that fortresslike rigidity. Naming the new impressions in the garden "terrible" and "strange," Strether, however conflictedly, still brings the logic of the Woollett scale to a city and smile he sees as a "test of his stuff."

But what marks the scene as decisive is the way it shows that scale beginning to buckle. Immediately after he is struck by Gloriani's "terrible...flashing life," Strether puts forth his own philosophy of life. In a conversation with Chad's friend, the young American artist Little Bilham, he says: "Live all you can.... If you haven't had that what have you had?"[63] "Living" for Strether, at this stage, in part means being in the midst of uncontrolled perceptions without any irritable grasping after certainty, or giving in to the impulse to slot impressions into ready-made molds.[64] Like Maria's dress, the "lemon-coloured volumes," and the way the disorientations of Paris seem uncannily compressed into Gloriani's smile, uncontrolled perceptions give way to the Woollett scale's counter-principle: living all one can. If the encounter in the garden leads Strether to share with Bilham his philosophy of life, the scene also directs us to Gloriani's previous appearance in James's *Roderick Hudson*, and the lines from the preface he added to the novel about "drawing a circle" in a field of relations that "really stop nowhere." The compositional problem as it is sketched in the preface to *Roderick Hudson* is precisely the problem confronting Strether, directly informing the assonant run "live all you can.... If you haven't had that what have you had."[65] As the "a"s echo through the individual words, relations themselves are made as perceivable as the terms they relate. The scene's importance as a transition point in Strether's mission is thus also a key to seeing how the presumed irreconcilability between William's assault on philosophical verbalism and what he called "interminable suggestive reference" is resolved in the late style. The very diffuseness William complained of is the stylistic analogue of radical empiricism, here in its efficacy for beginning to see all that is "false to the Woollett scale and the Woollett humanity."[66] And that analysis in prose (which Santayana thought of as Henry's counterpart to William's "impassioned empiricism") marks a shift in Strether's taking the measure of relations that really stop nowhere, turning him from a dutiful foot soldier carrying out the commandments of Woollett to the improviser of a conspicuously assonant philosophy of life. If the moment in the garden leads Strether to reflect on the poverty of Woollettian habits of perception, it is also the point at which his rescue mission is irreversibly compromised. A single ambassador with orders to recover a young man presumed to have descended into libertinage will, from here on out, become a reticulated series of ambassadorial relations which, rather than executing the prearranged plan, split into finer and finer facets.

Rightly assuming Strether has been diverted in his plan to retrieve Chad, or has himself succumbed to the temptations of Paris, Mrs. Newsome sends a team of follow-up ambassadors from Woollett to Paris: Chad's sister Sarah, her husband Jim Pocock, and their daughter Mamie. While Strether has been gradually learning how to gauge the limits of the Woollett scale, and to compensate for its distortions, Sarah Pocock struggles obstinately with the shifts in scale and proportion, now suspecting Strether to be himself among the corrupting influences working upon Chad.

The tension between first- and second-wave ambassadors comes to a head in a scene at Chad's apartment, in which Sarah and Strether have it out on the topic of the difference between Chad's obligations to Woollett, and those he may believe he has to a *femme du monde*:

"Is it your idea then," she returned, "that I shall keep on meeting you only to be exposed to fresh humiliation?"

He fixed her a longer time. "Are your instructions from Mrs. Newsome that you shall, even at the worst, absolutely and irretrievably break with me?"

"My instructions from Mrs. Newsome are, if you please, my affair. You know perfectly what your own were, and you can judge for yourself of what it can do for you to have made what you have of them.... what is your conduct," she broke out as if to explain—"what is your conduct but an outrage to women like *us*? I mean your acting as if there can be a doubt—as between us and such another—of his duty?"

He thought a moment. It was rather much to deal with at once; not only the question itself, but the sore abysses it revealed. "Of course they're totally different kinds of duty."

"And do you pretend that he has any at all—to such another?"

"Do you mean Madame de Vionnet?" He uttered the name not to affront her, but yet again to gain time.... Everything Mrs. Pocock had failed to give a sign of recognizing in Chad as a particular part of a transformation...affected him as gathered into a large loose bundle and thrown, in her words, into his face. The missile made him to that extent catch his breath; which however he presently recovered. "Why when a woman's at once so charming and so beneficent—"

"You can sacrifice mothers and sisters to her without a blush, and can make them cross the ocean on purpose to feel the more, and take from you the straighter, *how* do you do it?"

Yes, she had taken him up as short, and as sharply as that; but he tried not to flounder in her grasp. "I don't think there's anything I've done in any such calculated way as you describe. Everything has come as a sort of indistinguishable part of everything else. Your coming out belonged closely to my having come before you, and my having come was result of our general state of mind. Our general state of mind has proceeded on its side from out of queer ignorance or queer misconception and confusions—from which since then, an inexorable tide of light seems to have floated us into our perhaps still queerer knowledge. Don't you *like* your brother as he is?" he went on, "and haven't you given your mother an intelligible account of all that that comes to?"[67]

The delay between one ambassadorial mission and another—the way the *relation* between individual ambassadors is given *form* in this exchange—takes Strether "up short" because of the transformation he's undergone since arriving in Paris. Again, if relations themselves are made perceivable in the passage (as it was with the marking of the difference between London dresses and Woollett dresses, and between the journal Strether edits at Woollett and the "lemon-coloured volumes" seen in a Paris storefront), then the fecundity of the late style again spills forth a cluster of analogies giving form to relation as such. Specifically, the difference between Sarah's taking the measure of things (her "failure to give a sign of recognizing"), and Strether's awareness of this failure, materializes in their exchange as a "large loose bundle" that is "thrown into [Strether's] face." The manifestation of this "bundle" Strether explicitly attributes to the delay between their two ambassadorships, and of how it has turned his own way of seeing things into an "inexorable tide of light" that has "floated" him into "queer knowledge." Now confronted with a fresh delegation from Woollett, characterized by what Strether will call, in a later conversation with Maria Gostrey, Sarah's having "no room left; no margin...for any alternation...filled as full, packed as tight, as she'll hold,"[68] the late style again takes the measure of a difference in the scale of relations. Like the "large loose bundle" that gives analogical form to the relation separating one ambassadorial mission and another, here Strether's own recourse to analogy causes to appear a difference in scale in the image of a container "packed tight"; the rigidity of the Woollett scale as a structure filled to capacity, with no room to accommodate new knowledge.

Strether's exchange with Sarah Pocock is placed in the novel at the point where tight containments give way to relations that really stop nowhere. This precarious, compromised, but also strangely privileged perspective is what Robert Pippin calls Strether's "double consciousness": his ongoing sense of an obligation to, and a growing awareness of the limits of, the Woollett scale's fortress of certainties.[69] Given the way, in the scene above, we see a confrontation arising from a perceived "abjuring of local allegiance and partiality in the name of a vast abstraction,"[70] *The Ambassadors* can be thought of as a story of how a man, set adrift somewhere between the stern moralism of Woollett and the bright Babylon of Paris, must "assimilate new events to the categories [he] uses to structure and organize...experience." Given Strether's predicament, I want to consider what the novel might contribute to an understanding of "cosmopolitanism." Specifically, I want to suggest that we think of Strether—with his "double consciousness" straining between local allegiance and foreign newness—as an aspirant to the status of "world citizen." But before going on to look at the scene in the novel in which the truth of Chad's relation to Madame de Vionnet is revealed—which is, I want to claim, the most vivid instance in the novel of Strether's cosmopolitanism—I want to consider in some detail what is, or has been, meant by the term.

The cosmopolitan is on the most literal construal a citizen of the world. A citizen of the world is one who is able to transcend local loyalties in favor of identifying with the larger allegiance of humankind as a whole. The categorical identification with humanity as a whole, though, involves the basic problem of thinking together the universal and the particular. Ross Posnock says of this aspect of cosmopolitanism that it "reconfigures [the relation of] universal and particular as imbricated and entwined rather than as rivals to be chosen, one over the other."[71] Echoing Posnock's description, Gregg Crane describes such imbrication as arising from the

> importance of diverse experience to the faculty of judgment, which, in Hannah Arendt's words, "adopts the position of Kant's world citizen." Through judgment, according to sections 40 and 41 of Kant's *Critique of Judgment*, we assimilate new events to the categories we use to structure and organize our experience. One result of the interplay between particular experience and [universal] category is that our categories change [since Kantian] judgment...begins with an experience that does not conform to our habitual ways of looking at the world. In its most elemental form...judgment depends on a new experience.[72]

If we follow the references to Arendt and Kant, we get a sense of the importance of the role of "judgment" in the cosmopolitan's effort to bring about the "entwining" of the universal and the particular. Here there is more to judgment than the standard Kantian account of subsuming empirical particulars under general categories, since we often encounter particulars for which we have no ready-made categories. Appealing to Kant's distinction between different kinds of judgment Arendt considers the situation in which one encounters a particular for which there are no universals. If, according to Arendt, judgment is for Kant "the faculty of mysteriously combining the particular and the general," then this is "relatively easy if the general is given—as a rule, a principle, a law—so that the judgment merely subsumes the particular under the general."[73] Indeed, we make judgments like this all the time, simply navigating through the spatio-temporal world around us. But what about empirical intuitions for which there are no universals under which to subsume them? Here Arendt points to a distinction Kant makes between "determining" and "reflecting" judgments. In the *Critique of the Power of Judgement* Kant writes that a determining judgment occurs when "the universal (the rule, the principle, the law) is given," such that the making of a judgment is a matter of "subsuming the particular under it."[74] But, Kant goes on, if "only the particular is given, for which the universal is to be found, then the power of judgment is merely reflecting."[75] Arendt elaborates upon this distinction: "the difficulty [in judging] becomes great if only the particular be given for which the general has to be found. For the standard cannot be borrowed from experience and cannot be derived from outside. I cannot judge one particular by another particular."[76] Kant offers a solution to this difficulty through an appeal to regulative ideas on which one may reflect when confronted with a particular for which there is no ready category. The first is "the idea of an original compact of mankind as a whole [*sensus communis*]"[77]; the second, an idea of "purposiveness," such that, as Arendt explains, "every object...as a particular, needing and containing the ground of its actuality in itself, has a purpose [such that] purposiveness is an idea by which to regulate one's reflections in one's reflective judgments."[78]

The basic distinction to keep in mind when thinking about the difference between reflecting and determining judgments, then, is that "while previously [in the *Critique of Pure Reason*] Kant had recognized the ordinary function of judgment as that of subsuming a particular under a universal that is antecedently given to us [the *Critique of the Power of Judgment*] now calls that function a 'determining judgment' in order to distinguish it from the quite different case of the 'reflecting judgment' in which we are not given a concept under which to subsume a particular but are instead given a particular for which we must seek to *find* a universal."[79] This for Arendt stems from the need to "deal with particulars in their particularity...without subsuming them under a pre-given universal, but actively searching out the universal in the particular...a capacity to ascend from the particular to the universal without the mediation of determinate concepts given in advance."[80] As judgments about purposive particulars for which there are no ready-made categorical universals, reflecting judgments become necessary when the "individual does not point to an abstract universal stand[ing] behind it, but is this universal itself."[81] Given Arendt's desire to adapt Kant's critical aesthetics for a discussion of the world citizen, reflecting judgments are for her part of an understanding of persons as at once particular and universal. Persons both demand categorical respect for their particularity—in all their strangeness and idiosyncracy—while at the same time bearing a relation to universals like *sensus communis* and "purposiveness," by which a shared community of recognition, agreement, and disagreement becomes possible (rather than an atomized collection of private affects).

The Ambassadors, as we have seen, offers a number of examples of encounters with particulars for which there are no ready-made universals. Sarah Pocock's exasperation and incredulity at Strether's ability to see Chad's situation from more than one angle—an exasperation that is the result of the unsuitability of the Woollett scale for making sense of a *femme du monde*—has been the latest such example. Given the way the novel is concerned to dramatize the incommensurability between different scales of measure for experience, it does not seem right to say that those committed to the Woollett scale, even if equipped as persons with faculties for rational reflection, would arrive through judgment at an adequate appraisal of the situation (indeed, Sarah Newsome is simply incapable of perceiving that Chad has been "improved"; that he is, as Henry put it in the preface to *The Ambassadors*, "disobligingly and bewilderingly not lost"[82]). In this way the scene shows the limitations of cosmopolitanism as involving an appeal to reflective judgments; that is, of encountering a particular and, rather than bringing it under a general category, reflect upon principles like *sensus communis* and purposiveness, in such a way that one can judge particulars qua particulars. While such judgments have a shape analogous to that of judgments of taste, they are not, in their consequences for cosmopolitanism, necessarily a matter of judging what is beautiful, but of arriving at the form of universalism Arendt calls the "enlarged mentality" of the human community.

Crane's appeal to Arendt in his account of the relation of cosmopolitanism to "experience," and Arendt's own emphasis on the Kantian distinction between "determining" and "reflecting" judgments, raises unavoidable questions about exactly how the world citizen arises from an entwinement of the general and the particular. Since determining judgments are for Kant constitutive of experience as such—experience [*Erfahrung*] is itself made possible through the judgments that subsume empirical particulars under universal concepts—reflecting judgments, which do not begin with conceptual or categorical universals but rather reflect upon regulative principles, are not, in the Kantian sense, examples of experience. As Kant puts it, the criteria in relation to which the reflecting judgment is made "cannot be borrowed from experience and cannot be derived from outside [since] I cannot judge one particular by another particular." Premised on undetermined principles, purified of all empirical content, reflective judgments "fail to reach a determination," and so are at best *incipient* experience.[83] While designed to make intelligible the particular *as* particular, reflective judgments do so through an appeal to principles separate from the determining judgments that are, for Kant, the conditions of possibility for experience.

But what if we want to hang onto both Arendt's idea of the world citizen as a particular for which there is no ready-made universal *and* an idea of experience that would not be understood in relation to Kant's reflecting judgments? That is, how would we have to modify our understanding of experience to make it compatible with the notion that universals can be found or discovered in particulars? Here I want to propose a version of cosmopolitanism that does not operate through an appeal to the distinction between determining and reflecting judgments. Remembering that other ambassadorship I have been tracking through this chapter—that between William James and Henri Bergson—I want to claim here that their shared radical empiricism, as verbally captured in the late style, gives us the tools for imagining a different kind of cosmopolitanism. We might initially think the idea of experience found in Bergson and James—relations are as real as relata—is a radically empirical version of a "reflecting" judgment. But instead of moving to universals from reflection upon the regulative ideals of either purposiveness or an "original compact of mankind as a whole" (*sensus communis*), a radically empirical cosmopolitanism would move from particular to universal through an appeal to the reality and externality of relations. If the cosmos, as James tells us, is tychistic—an open, chance-laden experiment—then the citizen of such a cosmos (of such a world) should be thought of as working toward universals that are themselves tychistic, without predetermination (categorical or otherwise), and so always in the making. Constellating particular to particular through relations that are external to and as real as the terms they relate might then be thought of as forming the basis for a cosmopolitanism appropriate to a world understood as "perpetual hazard and perpetual experiment." It is just this sort of cosmopolitanism that is described in a novel that takes as its subject the incommensurability between Woollett ways of judging and Parisian ways of judging; a novel that takes the reality of relations— "ambassadors"—as its very organizing principle.

Let's take as a test case for this kind of cosmopolitanism the dénouement of *The Ambassadors*. Having decided "almost at random" to take a solo trip out to the countryside, Strether finds himself in the midst of a fantasy of "French ruralism."[84] The French countryside becomes for Strether a living landscape painting, built up in part from a memory of his having once nearly purchased a "certain small [Emile] Lambinet" in a Boston gallery.[85] The scene is so suffused for him with self-conscious artifice that his experience itself becomes an "oblong gilt frame," with the countryside "falling into [a] composition" of "whiteness, blueness and crookedness, set in coppery green."[86] In the midst of this projection of remembered cultural aspirations (what he called during his reverie before the lemon-coloured volumes, the "raising up" of the "door on the temple of taste" now thread through the memory of the almost-acquired Lambinet), Strether feels he's never been further from the provincial rigidities of Woollett. Luxuriating in the surrounding landscape, he has the imaginative freedom to compose the scene in admixture with his own tastes, preferences, and memories. And then, all at once, a new element is added to the picture:

What he saw was exactly the right thing—a boat advancing round the bend and containing a man who held the paddles and a lady at the stern, with a pink parasol. It was suddenly as if these figures, or something like them, had been wanted in the picture...the air quite thickened at their approach, with further intimations; the intimation that they were expert, familiar, frequent—that this wouldn't at all events be the first time. They knew how to do it, he vaguely felt—and it made them but the more idyllic, though at the very moment of the impression, as happened, their boat seemed to have begun to drift wide, the oarsman letting it go. [Strether] knew the lady whose parasol, shifting as if to hide her face, made so fine a pink point in the shining scene. It was too prodigious, a chance in a million, but, if he knew the lady, the gentleman, who still presenting his back and kept off, the gentleman, the coatless hero of the idyll, who had responded to her start, was, to match the marvel, none other than Chad.[87]

Why does James say the appearance of the boat is "exactly the right thing"? On the one hand, it completes Strether's picture. Already immersed in his fantasy of French ruralism, it is the "right thing" insofar as it is a further retouching of the scene; precisely placed within the "oblong gilt frame" Strether brings to his impressions of the countryside. But it is the right thing also because it is, alas, the revelation of the truth of Chad's relation to Madame de Vionnet. And with this latter meaning of the rightness of the detail, Strether's frame shatters. The dissolution of the picture occurs between Strether's observation that the couple in the boat "knew how to do it" (they were expert and familiar not only with the activity of a leisurely boat ride, but with one another), and his realization, within a few seconds of this first judgment, that he "knew the lady whose parasol...made so fine a pink point upon the shining scene." The hovering indirection of the prose here, far from indulging in what William complained of as the late style's "perfume and simulacrum," enacts very precisely Strether's coming into possession of new knowledge. Specifically, the pink point of the parasol is both precariously part of the picture (a painterly detail contributing to the Lambinet-like composedness of the scene as a whole), and a striking particular flashing out as a new element of perception. The pink point thus ceases to be a mere final addition to Strether's composition, and becomes instead the index of a completely new relation; one Strether, in his otherwise prodigious imaginativeness, has failed to take into account. The revelation triggered by the new relation brings about what James calls a "sharp fantastic crisis" in his perspective on the whole of his ambassadorial mission.[88]

The novel's dénouement makes it clear that cosmopolitanism in *The Ambassadors* is then not simply a matter of pitting a loyalty to the certainties of the Woollett scale against the twinkling ambiguities of Paris. With the river revelation we see how Strether's cosmopolitanism rather emerges from a tension between two kinds of Woollettian habits: those, like Sarah's, that project rigid criteria of rightness onto foreign particulars, and then deduce from them what must be the case (Chad "must" be in the clutches of a low woman); and those, like Strether's, which in their zealous immersion in the "changing proportions" of foreign perceptions, establish their own conditions for arranging particulars (the "oblong gilt frame"). It is as if there were, even at this late stage of Strether's mission, some still undissolved shard of the Woollett scale at work in his setting the relations of the French countryside into a "composition." That the unexpected relations that come to disrupt this picture—the boat, the parasol, the woman holding the parasol, the young man seated across from the woman, their "knowing how to do it"—lead him to become aware of his own continuing reliance on the Woollett scale, then bears fundamentally upon the conditions of his ambassadorship. And this is just what gives James's novel a purchase on the new sort of cosmopolitanism I have been describing. For Strether, finding the universal embedded in the particular is not a matter of a reflection upon a regulative ideal but part of a radical empiricism in which the relations by which one compares and judges are themselves in the world. In the case of the scene on the river, this occurs in the way knowing what is really going on is a matter of moving from the pink point of a parasol (a new item added to a composition in the making), to what James calls the "unprovoked harsh note" that transforms, through the addition of a new relation, the whole of the picture.[89] This transition, crucial for Strether, from a mere decorative element to the becoming perceivable of the relation that undermines the whole of his "gilt framed" conception of what has been going on between Chad and Madame de Vionnet—indeed, of the differing proportions and perspectives of the Woollett scale and the "bright Babylon" of Paris—is a moment of finding the universal embedded in a particular.

Such interpenetration of the universal and the particular was hinted at in the novel's opening where it is said of Strether that "there was detachment in his zeal and curiosity in his indifference."[90] Even at this early stage there was for Strether, behind the relishing of particulars, a generally surveying "detachment"; while inhering in the neutrality of "indifference" there is a drive to seek particulars out of sheer "curiosity." To put this more explicitly in relation to the two kinds of cosmopolitanism I have been considering in this section: the reflecting judgment that Arendt takes from Kant, and which Kant invents so as to account for judgments of taste, is here just what falls short. Strether has, in some way, too perfect taste; he is able to make too complete, too fine, too seamless a picture, too able to arrive at a finished a composition. It is just this facility in making judgments of taste—the skill and imagination with which he is able to compose a fantasy of the French countryside from a combination of memories and the particular details of the scene, including, finally and decisively, the point of the parasol—that renders him blind to the only relation that ought to matter, given the terms of his ambassadorship. That he turns out to be a radical empiricist—that he is open to the way a single new relation can break open the outer edges of the composition in a "sharp fantastic crisis"—is what makes him a world citizen in the second sense I have been describing. Strether doesn't just see through the Woollett scale; he sees all the way around it. This new perspective (the culmination of what Pippin calls Strether's "double consciousness") ends in the novel's crowning irony that, in some basic way, the Woollett scale has been "right" all along. But this rightness is closer to what Pippin later describes as the way the "Woollett view of Chad is factually true," but nevertheless "will not allow…many other things to be noted and pursued."[91]

It is thus no accident that in the awkward minutes following the mutual recognition between the couple in the boat and the man watching from the riverbank, Madame de Vionnet goes "wholly into French," rather than the "charming, slightly strange English" by which Strether knew her.[92] This sudden anxious zeal to communicate exclusively in French is marked by what Strether takes to be

> an unprecedented command of idiomatic turns, but in which she got, as he might have said, somewhat away from him, taking all at once little brilliant jumps that he could but lamely match. The question of his own French had never come up for them; it was the one thing she wouldn't have permitted—it belonged, for a person who had been through much, to mere boredom; but the present result was odd, fairly veiling her identity, shifting her back into a mere voluble class or race to the intense audibility of which he was by this time inured.[93]

Madame de Vionnet's swerve into the "little brilliant jumps" of idiomatic French become for Strether a certain kind of obstacle. Up until this moment, before Strether had known the truth about Chad and Madame de Vionnet, the easy traversal through a language not one's own, and the generous openness across that boundary in both directions, is now the barrier of a local idiom. All of which then serves to shift Madame de Vionnet, as James puts it, "back into a mere voluble class or race to the intense audibility of which he was by this time inured."[94] The *femme du monde* reduced to a "mere class or race"! In the minutes following the revelation of the "right" relation on the river, Madame de Vionnet has been reduced to a "voluble," murmuring loquaciousness, a din of idioms to which Strether has become "inured," as if this description were a matter of both recognizing its particularity as a "class" or "race" and its place in a larger schema of ways of being and talking in the world (compare this with Sarah Pocock's earlier announcement that she "*knows* Paris," as if having deduced a certainty that no amount of accident or experiment could dislodge). This process has led to a new, truly cosmopolitan perspective, neither exclusively loyal to the rigid deductions of Woollett moralizing, nor to the iridescent fluidities of Paris. All of this is signaled in the defensive switch into French idioms incongruous with the easy-going "abstract" English that up until the river revelation (the "harsh note" of the parasol's point), had been the shared tone between Strether and Madame de Vionnet.

Strether's radically empirical cosmopolitanism is thus not a matter of reflecting on universal principles, but of being open to, and freely "composing," particulars qua particulars. The empirical attunement to particulars opens onto a kind of universalism in which the absorption of new relations into the composition allows Strether to see "exactly the right thing," and from two perspectives at once: the "rightness" of the texture and quality of perception that a certain kind of taste finds in the saturating brilliances of the French countryside (things the Woollett scale might not, to use Pippin's phrase, "allow to be noted") and the ultimate "rightness" of the Woollett scale's conclusions about Chad.

This chapter began with a catalogue of the ambassadorships holding the novel together, and I want to conclude by looking at another series running through the novel, at the level of a single phrase. What is nowhere commented on in the vast scholarly literature on *The Ambassadors* is that its famous last line—Strether's "Then there we are!"—is the concluding note in a motivic development which James uses to mark moments of tension between local particularities and imagined or emergent universals. While Henry's late style is often characterized by its protracted indirection, I want in this concluding section to uncover a series of variations on four monosyllabic words that seem to contain the whole of what the novel has to tell us.

In an exchange full of portent for the discovery Strether will make in the last chapters of the novel, Miss Barrace says to Little Bilham at Gloriani's party that he's come "over [to Paris] to convert the savages—for I know you verily did, I remember you—and the savages simply convert you.' 'Not even! The young man woefully confessed: "they haven't gone through that form. They've simply—the cannibals!—eaten me; converted me if you like, but converted me into food. I'm but the bleached bones of a Christian.' 'Well then there we are!'"[95] In the grisly conceit we find literalized the tribal "race or class" (here cannibals and Christians), mutually repellent particulars reconciled in a moment of accord or agreement—"Well then there we are!"—in a piece of party chatter.[96]

Later, Strether and Maria Gostrey are discussing the surprising news that Madame de Vionnet's daughter Jeanne is to be in an arranged marriage with a Monsieur Montbron; a practice that strikes the Americans as almost incomprehensibly foreign. Gostrey tells Strether she's already heard: "'It reached me yesterday—roundabout and accidental, but by a person who had it from one of the young man's own people…' 'You thought Chad wouldn't have told me?' She hesitated. 'Well, if he hasn't' 'He hasn't. And yet the thing appears to have been practically his doing. So there we are.' 'There we are!' Maria candidly echoed.'"[97] The New World assessment of an Old World practice (an arranged marriage) is framed in the language of the "young man's own people," as if irreconcilable group differences were marked, and again briefly appeased, with the phrase "there we are." Not long after this, again in conversation with Gostrey about the complicating lines of communication running back to Woollett, Mrs. Newsome's commands are split through the separate channels of Waymarsh, Sarah Pocock, and Jim Pocock, this last now standing "with his little legs apart, at the door of [the] tent" of the family business. Maria thinks his wife Sarah "shouldn't have brought him [because] she doesn't appreciate him"; a thought which Strether completes (as is often the case in the uncannily attuned conversations between Strether and Maria) that she "doesn't know, you mean, how bad he is?"[98] The two then play a game to see who in the camp from Woollett is able to "appreciate" Jim, ruling out Waymarsh, with Strether offering Mamie—Jim's sister—as somehow sensitive to the shortcomings of the Woollett scale. To this Maria replies "'His own sister?' Oddly enough it but let her down. 'What good will that do?' to which Strether replies " 'None perhaps. But there—as usual—we are!'" After a chapter break, James's third-person narration echoes the final phrase: "There they were again."[99] Here we get something like the inversion of the reaction to the arranged marriage in Jim, the novel's most overt figure for the side of Woollett that is all commercial materialism (the element of the American temperament that Santayana said was "leaping down a sort of Niagra rapids of [practical] industry"). Here, though, the novel's pattern of marking moments of tension between the local and the worldly with the phrase "then there we are" is itself remarked upon, in Strether's "as usual" and in third-person echo ("there they were again").

The series continues, again in relation to the question of local loyalties, when Strether and Bilham discuss Chad's taking "what he has picked up" in Paris and "mov[ing] the whole thing over" to Woollett.[100] Bilham says of Woollett that, while it will be "better" for Chad's bringing his changed self back there, the people there are nevertheless "just as good," to which Strether replies, "'Just as good as you and these others? Ah that may be. But such an occasion as this, whether or no,' Strether said 'isn't the people. It's what has made the people possible.' 'Well then,' his friend replied 'there you are.'"[101] And this conversation, about what the new and improved Chad will or will not bring back to Woollett, is continued in another conversation shortly after, between Chad and Strether, in which they discuss the possibility that Mrs. Newsome, and her latest ambassador, Sarah, "hates," not only Chad's "good friend" (by which he appears to mean Madame de Vionnet), but Strether himself for succumbing to the temptations of Paris, to the detriment of his mission. When Strether says he wants to see Sarah again, Chad replies "Ah then there you are!"

The next time he and Maria meet, their conversation anticipates the last lines of the novel, as Maria reassures Strether that she will grant any of his wishes. He says "I'll express fifty," and Maria says "Ah there you are!" A few pages later, after Maria has assured Strether that his "quantity" is keenly felt, Strether replies somewhat perplexedly, that this is "what Chad thinks," to which Maria says "There *you* are then."[102]

During their first discussion after the scene on the river, Maria and Strether consider the extent to which Madame de Vionnet feels herself "judged" by the Americans around her. After Strether states the paradox of his happening upon the river revelation as a problem of "business"—that what had been transpiring between Chad and Marie was "none of my business .. as I saw my business"[103]— Maria says, "I wish she could hear you." There then ensues a moment of ambiguity as to whether "she" here refers to Mrs. Newsome or Madame de Vionnet. That the true topic of their conversation is Madame de Vionnet comes down to a tension between Strether's discrete disclosure that he thinks it "none of his business" and Madame de Vionnet's conviction that Strether has "judged" her. Maria then tells Strether that in fact she had come to think that Strether "believed in her sublimity...until the accident of the other day opened [Strether's] eyes," to which Strether says, "She can't help...being aware? No," he mused "I suppose she thinks of that even yet." To which Maria then replies "Then they *were* closed? There you are!"[104]

The last of the variations on this phrase—"then there we are"—which winds through the novel like an illuminated thread, ciphering the imbrication of the universal with the particular, is the novel's last line, as we realize that Strether will return to Woollett with a new way of thinking and seeing, but without Maria Gostrey:

"There's nothing, you know, I wouldn't do for you."

"Oh yes—I know."

"There's nothing," she repeated "in all the world."

"I know, I know. But all the same, I must go." He had got it at last. "To be right."

"To be right?"

She had echoed it in vague deprecation, but he felt it already clear for her. "That, you see, is my only logic. Not, out of the whole affair to have gotten anything for myself."

She thought. "But with your wonderful impressions you'll have got a great deal."

"A great deal"—he agreed. "But nothing like *you*. It's you who would make me wrong!"

Honest and fine, she couldn't greatly pretend she didn't see it. Still she could pretend just a little. "But why should you be so dreadfully right?"

"That's the way that—if I must go—you yourself would be the first to want me. And I can't do anything else."

So then she had to take it, though still with her defeated protest. "It isn't so much your *being* 'right'—it's your horrible sharp eye for what makes you so."

"Oh but you're just as bad yourself. You can't resist me when I point that out."

She sighed it at last all comically, all tragically, away. "I can't indeed resist you."

"Then there we are!" said Strether.

The "rightness" of Strether's strange logic is the way the demands of the Woollett scale must be made to square with his not "have gotten anything." Maria correctly insists that, on the contrary, Strether has got "wonderful impressions"; indeed, the very impressions that have given him the perspective on things I have been calling cosmopolitan.[105] But again, part of that cosmopolitanism has been to see the way conclusions drawn from the Woollett scale end up being "right" about Chad; and the way that "rightness" puts Strether into the position of having to reconcile his "wonderful impressions" of Paris with a new relation that shatters his too-tidy construction of Frenchness. In this sense, Strether's "not getting anything" is a consequence of his cosmopolitanism; the way his perceptual gain necessitates a lived loss. For the rightness that names both the addition of a last detail, a last relation, to the countryside picture, is now the rightness of the requirement that the ambassador return to Woollett without Maria. That it is his very shrewdness— his keen and discerning sense of composition, his "horrible sharp eye"—that both attracts Maria to Strether, and provokes her exasperated acceptance of his plan with a sigh, is a perspectival irony to which Strether's "then there we are" is just the right response.

Conclusion

Compatibilism, Genre, Allegory, Cosmopolitanism

Les beaux livres sont écrits dans une sort de langue étrangère.

Marcel Proust

William James said of Emerson that "his truth had to be clad in the right verbal garment [and] the form of the garment was so vital…it is impossible to separate it from the matter."[1] This is one way of saying that Emerson's prose can't be paraphrased; that his meaning and his *way* of meaning are bound, as James put it, like a "chemical combination"; that his thought "culminated in his style."[2] Part of what I have tried to do here is extend that insight to four different writers in whose poetry and prose can be found a move from experience understood as a squaring of inner with outer matters to experience understood as a search for the conditions by which a work becomes shareable; a process I call "experimental writing." In what remains I want to outline how that process is differently acknowledged in four provisional universals. I call these "provisional" because their ways of generalizing, or universalizing, particular stylistic inventions are arrived at through experiment, are in the making, and are revisable.

Emerson's rejection of the choice between empiricism and idealism led to a form of experience inseparable from the process of writing up from journal entries; a method of composition Emerson makes explicit in his compatibilism. Compatibilism is a provisional universal because while *all* persons are constrained in this way—this onward trick of nature is too strong for *us; how might we* keep *our* beautiful limits; *we* are sure though *we* know not how necessity does comport with liberty—each is free to affirm the series in which we find ourselves through what he (and after him Nietzsche) called "Joyous science." Poe imagines what Pierce will later call abduction in the invention of a genre whose identity hinges on the difference between creatures capable of "intelligible syllabification" and those that merely make sounds. Poe thus aligns the "intelligible"—the shareable, the meaningful—with a literary experiment that, while being an individual example, at the same time invents the general category of which it is an instance. Melville, in rejecting the linked antebellum criteria of unity and verisimilitude, arrives at an irreverent allegory of literary technique in two novels, *Moby-Dick* and *Pierre*. Whether as an emblem through which all particular perceptions become universalized—*all* that most maddens and torments; *all* that stirs up the lees of things; *all* that cracks the sinews and cakes the brain; *all* were personified and made practically assailable in Moby Dick—or as the accretions of a style registering a "climb up Parnassus with a pile of folios on [one's] back," Melville's most ambitious novels find in allegory a way of giving form to the general as such. And despite his brother's impatience with his late style, Henry James takes the basic thesis of radical empiricism—relations are external to their terms—as the organizing principle for *The Ambassadors*. For James, the novel built upon external relations both leads to a form of cosmopolitanism generalized to the scale of a cosmos understood as "perpetual hazard and perpetual experiment" (as Santayana described William's empiricism) and crystalizes in a single decisive relation that dissolves at once two different provincialisms. In each case, a particular instance of writing requires, for its meanings to become sharable, the discovery in composition of a provisional universal: compatibilism, genre, allegory, cosmopolitanism.

The span of time I call "Emerson to the Jameses" does not so much culminate in cosmopolitanism, as cosmopolitanism has been its running backstory. Emerson's epiphany in Cuvier's *Jardin* and the Divinity School Address, thought to traffic in Continental ideas and so judged a threat to clerical authority, led to his becoming an "Exemplar" for one of the most influential thinkers of late modernity, Friedrich Nietzsche. After witnessing the Bavarian chess android (fresh off of its success in Vienna, Paris, and London), Poe invents, from an apartment in Philadelphia, a genre that now thrives globally—a quick Google search calls up French, German, African, Turkish, Chinese, Greek, Israeli, Vietnamese, Argentinian, Arabic, Russian, and Japanese detective stories and novels. For Melville, literary experiment meant rejecting a narrowly nationalist aesthetics in favor of an abstract allegory of his "thwarted career"; a thwarting due largely to reviewers' indifference toward his previous novel—*Moby-Dick*—which, while itself a novel *about* radical cosmopolitanism ("Better sleep with a sober cannibal than a drunken Christian," says Ishmael as Queequeg beckons him into bed at the Spouter Inn), has also become one of the unequivocal universals of world literature. For Henry James, his career-long preoccupation with the "international theme" culminates in a novel that takes the clash of the local with the worldly as the criterion within which the late style becomes an instrument of analysis.

So there has been, on the one hand, a movement toward greater and greater generality: from Emerson's and Poe's first-hand encounters (Cuvier, Maelzel), to Melville's agon with an entire literary-critical program (Duyckinck and *The Literary World*), to the James brothers breaking with and analyzing the diffuse historical formation Santayana called the "genteel tradition." At the same time, there has been a movement toward greater and greater particularity: twenty-five years of Emerson's development as a writer; a decade of Poe's essays, tales, poems, and criticism; two years of Melville's career as a novelist; and a single novel, and even single phrase—"Then there we are!"—which distills a series of efforts in *The Ambassadors* at finding the general embedded in the particular (the indexical specificity of "there" flush against the universal "we"). This simultaneous zooming out and zeroing in is part of my effort to enact the entwinement of the general and the particular. The search for the universal embedded in the most recalcitrant and idiosyncratic particulars is characteristic of both the problem of cosmopolitanism, and defines the move from experience thought of as an affective encounter to experience as conditioned by public criteria.

The works I've looked at here have not then been about representing the local affiliations of New England or Richmond or Philadelphia or New York, or abstractions like "Young America," but of discovering ways of going on within a common linguistic inheritance. Emerson's search for a vocation begins with his experiments in the sermon form. Poe's wrests from the periodical culture of his time, its forms and genres borrowed from magazines like *Blackwood's* and the *London Magazine*, not just the analytic detective story, but the essay of inductive debunking, the tale of cryptography, the science-fiction fantasy, the horror story, the essay of literary theory, and the fake news hoax. Melville pushes the formal and thematic conventions of the sea adventure and the sentimental romance toward the extreme, often strange, prose of *Moby-Dick* and *Pierre*. Henry James takes the formal resources of the realist novel and, in the sinuous circuits of the late style, starts to experiment with what we would now call the "art novel." The version of experimental writing that comes into focus here might thus be called "modernist," not as the back-dating of a period term, nor as a roster of techniques, but as a certain kind of problem germane to composition itself: the need to find the criteria by which a given set of works might be recognized as that emergent and precarious thing, American literature.

I began with a passage from James's prefaces in which he claimed that the "act of seeing [*The Golden Bowl*] again caused whatever I looked at on any page to flower before me…as who should say, on the particular vision of the matter itself that experience had at last made the only possible one."[3] Like Emerson's search for "beautiful limits" in a method of composition, James finds a "beautiful law" at work in the way revision arrives at the "only terms that honorably express" his novel.[4] Can we call this law style? Would style be the way we gain access to the norms a work invents for itself, so that its specific linguistic inventions may become public and sharable? Would style then be a kind of justification? If justification is a misleading word here (as "knowledge" must also be), can we at least say that style is the law in a work on which its intelligibility depends? Law, in this sense, would be the effect one hears in language issuing from the obligation to make something of, to experiment with, the words we are given in common. In a state of wonder before the flowering of this law, James called it "experience."

NOTES

INTRODUCTION

1. Henry James, *Literary Criticism: European Writers, Prefaces to the New York Edition*, ed. Leon Edel and Mark Wilson, vol. 2 (New York: Library of America, 1984), 1332–33.
2. Richard Poirier, "Why Do Pragmatists Want to Be Like Poets?" in *The Revival of Pragmatism: New Essays on Social Thought, Law and Culture*, ed. Morris Dickstein (Durham, N.C.: Duke University Press, 1999), 353. Two recent studies that take their cue from Poirier's genealogy from Emerson to Stevens to Stein are Jonathan Levin, *The Poetics of Transition: Emerson, Pragmatism, and American Literary Modernism* (Durham, N.C.: Duke University Press, 1999); and Joan Richardson, *A Natural History of Pragmatism: The Fact of Feeling from Jonathan Edwards to Gertrude Stein* (Cambridge: Cambridge University Press, 2007).
3. Richard Poirier, *Poetry and Pragmatism* (Cambridge, Mass.: Harvard University Press, 1992). James's attunement to the relation of experience and composition directly informed his sense of Emerson as a precursor. Reviewing James Eliot Cabot's biography of Emerson for *Macmillan's Magazine* in 1887, James wrote of how he was struck by the way "letters were the very texture" of a life that "stretched itself out in enviable quiet…in which we hear the jotting of the pencil in the notebook…the very life of literature," and his "search for a fashion and a manner on which he was always engaged [and] which never came to a conclusion." Henry James, "Ralph Waldo Emerson," in *Literary Criticism: Essays on Literature, American Writers and English Writers*, ed. Leon Edel and Mark Wilson, vol. 1 (New York: Library of America, 1984), 250, 271.
4. James was equivocal about the importance of Poe for his own writing, mentioning him regularly in reviews, often disparagingly, but also referring to him as a "great genius" in a review of Charles Baudelaire's *Fleurs du mal*, and including a prolonged allusion to *The Narrative of Arthur Gordon Pym* at a decisive moment in *The Golden Bowl*. See Henry James, *Literary Criticism: European Writers, Prefaces to the New York Edition*, 2:154; Henry James, *Novels 1903–1911* (New York: Library of America, 2010), 470. For an account of James's treatment of Poe in his book reviews of the 1870s, and of the allusion to *Pym* in *The Golden Bowl*, see my "*Pym*, Poe and "The Golden Bowl,'" *The Henry James Review* 29, no. 3 (2008): 229–35. While there is barely a word about Melville in all of James's criticism (and while James's beloved Nathaniel Hawthorne might seem a more obvious precursor), Melville forms a strand in the history I am tracking here in the way the winding sentences of *Moby-Dick* and *Pierre* seem an anticipation of the protracted indirection of James's late style. Arthur Johnson makes the connection in his centennial essay on Melville, saying that Melville's *Pierre* and late James "involve devices and idiosyncrasies grotesquely alike…one queries if there isn't something about the convolutions of both that savors of philosophers' painstakingness." Arthur Johnson, "A Comparison of Manners," *New Republic* 20 (August 27, 1919): 114.

5. My thinking about the relation of experience to composition is in certain ways comparable to Steven Meyer's work on Gertrude Stein, which "attempts to demonstrate the ways [Stein] developed a more radical empiricism than [William] James was able to, owing to her great concentration on her compositional practices"; practices that are described as "experimental." For Meyer, Stein's language is made to function in "another register than ordinary communication with its idea of transparency" such that a kind of "radical empiricism [is] extended to the words on the page." Steven Meyer, *Irresistible Dictation* (Stanford: Stanford University Press, 2000), xi. While I am sympathetic to Meyer's alignment of experience (as radical empiricism) with composition, I turn here to figures *prior* to the development of James's empiricism (or at least contemporary, in the case of his brother Henry). On Emerson as a "modernist" writer, see also Richard Deming, *Listening on All Sides: Toward an Emersonian Ethics of Reading* (Stanford: Stanford University Press, 2007), 86–90. Recent works of literary scholarship taking their cue from the pragmatist tradition that deemphasize experience in favor of "transition" include Jonathan Levin, *The Poetics of Transition* and Michael Magee, *Emancipating Pragmatism* (Tuscaloosa: University of Alabama Press, 2004); or place process and experiment on the side of verification (methods for finding out what is true), rather than thinking about what experience *itself* means for pragmatism. On this point I agree with Andrew Epstein that pragmatism "posits that truth is created in the course of experience and [is] not found [and] is a process more than an entity." Andrew Epstein, *Beautiful Enemies* (New York: Oxford University Press, 2006), 56. But, again, rather than invoke experience to explain ways of arriving at truth (consonant with the aims of classical pragmatism as far as it goes), I want rather to look at what the pragmatists *meant* by experience (as distinct from, say, British empiricist and transcendental idealist accounts of experience). In the same way, the claim the literary works I discuss here comprise an experimental literature fills what I take to be a lacuna in the scholarship on experimental American writing. A recent example of this is R. M. Berry's generally excellent essay on "Experimental Writing," in the *Oxford Handbook of Philosophy and Literature*, which goes from German Romanticism to Gertrude Stein and Samuel Beckett, without any mention of writers such as Emerson, Thoreau, Poe, Melville, Whitman, Dickinson, or James (let alone Baudelaire, Rimbaud, or Lautréamont). Some exceptions to the tendency to exclude major nineteenth-century American writers from the category of "experimental writing" are D. H. Lawrence, *Studies in Classic American Literature* (Cambridge: Cambridge University Press, [1923] 2003); Charles Olson, *Call Me Ishmael* (New York: Grove Press, 1954); Stanley Cavell, *Senses of Walden: An Expanded Edition* (Chicago: University of Chicago Press, [1972] 1981); and Susan Howe, *My Emily Dickinson* (New York: New Directions, 1985).

6. See George Santayana, "The Genteel Tradition in American Philosophy," in *The Genteel Tradition and Character and Opinion in the United States*, ed. James Seaton (New Haven: Yale University Press, 2009), 6–7.

7. Stanley Cavell, *Philosophy the Day after Tomorrow* (Cambridge, Mass.: Belknap Press of Harvard University), 93.

8. Poirier, *Poetry and Pragmatism*. One of the few books to look in detail at the relation of Poirier to Cavell is Deming, *Listening on All Sides*.

9. Poirier, *Poetry and Pragmatism*, 29.

10. Ibid., 198n6.

11. Cavell, *Senses of Walden*, 33.

12. Stanley Cavell, "Reflections on Wallace Stevens at Mount Holyoke," in *Artists, Intellectuals and World War II: 1942–1944*, ed. Christopher Benfey (Amherst: University of Massachusetts Press, 2006), 76.

13. For an excellent discussion of how both Locke's empiricism and Kant's effort at securing conditions for the possibility of experience are each in their different ways bound up

with representation, see Richard Rorty, *Philosophy and the Mirror of Nature* (Princeton: Princeton University Press, 1979), 129–209. For a thorough discussion of how Kant's transcendental deduction works in relation to Cavell's reading of Emerson's essays "Self-Reliance" and "Experience," see David Greenham, "The Skeptical Deduction: Reading Kant and Cavell in Emerson's 'Self-Reliance,'" *ESQ* 53, no. 3 (2007), 253–281.

14. Ralph Waldo Emerson, "Experience," in *Essays and Lectures* (New York: Library of America, 1983), 472.

15. Cavell, *The Senses of Walden*, 126.

16. Emerson, "Experience," 472.

17. Immanuel Kant, *Critique of Pure Reason*. "Second Analogy of Experience: Principle of temporal sequence according to the law of causality" [B233–40], trans. and ed., Paul Guyer and Allen Wood (Cambridge: Cambridge University Press, 1998). This section of the First Critique continues the discussion of the necessity of the persistence of substance underlying the succession of inner representations. Both Analogies of Experience set up the "Refutation of Idealism," which Kant added to the 1787 B edition of the *Critique*, and are part of the First Critique's empirical realism. For an account of Kant's argument, in the Second Analogy, about the relation of inner and outer succession, see P. F. Strawson, *The Bounds of Sense: An Essay on Kant's Critique of Pure Reason* (London: Routledge, 1966), 125–40; William Harper, "Kant's Empirical Realism and the Second Analogy of Experience," *Synthese* 47 (1981): 465–80; and Michael Forster, *Kant and Skepticism* (Princeton: Princeton University Press, 2008), 8–9. On Cavell's finding in Emerson's "Experience" an engagement with Kant's Second Analogy, see Anthony Cascardi, "The Logic of Moods," *Studies in Romanticism* 24, no. 2 (summer, 1985): 223–38 and Stephen Mulhall, *Inheritance and Originality* (Oxford UP, 2001) 252–253.

18. Cavell, *Senses of Walden*, 127 (my emphasis). I am grateful to Richard Eldridge and William Day for suggesting I pay closer attention to this "non-tractability."

19. William Day, "Response to Grimstad," Paper delivered at Stanley Cavell and Literary Studies: Consequences of Skepticism, Harvard University, October 16, 2010.

20. Cavell, *Senses of Walden*, 106–7.

21. Ralph Waldo Emerson, "Circles," in *Essays and Lectures*, 472.

22. Here is how Cavell describes the Kantian "settlement" with skepticism: "To settle with skepticism…to assure us that we do know the existence of the world or, rather, that what we understand as knowledge is *of* the world, the price Kant asks us to pay is to cede any claim to know the thing in itself, to grant that human knowledge is not of things as they are in themselves.…You don't—do you?—have to be a romantic to feel sometimes about that settlement: Thanks for nothing." Stanley Cavell, "Emerson, Coleridge, Kant (Terms as Conditions)," in *Emerson's Transcendental Etudes*, ed. David Justin Hodge (Stanford: Stanford University Press, 2003), 63.

23. Cavell, *Senses of Walden*, 127.

24. Ralph Waldo Emerson, *Selected Journals, 1841–1842*, ed. Lawrence Rosenwald (New York: Library of America, 2010), 20.

25. Ralph Waldo Emerson, *Nature, Addresses, and Lectures* (New York: Library of America, 1983), 118.

26. For an account of pragmatist aesthetics organized around the notion of the transitional and the transitive, see Levin, *The Poetics of Transition*. While Levin is good at describing how "method" is relevant to Emerson's writing, he does not explicitly link this word to different accounts of experience (30–31).

27. John Dewey, *Experience and Nature* (London: Dover, 1958), 235

28. Ibid., 25, 358. Dewey's lines pick up on earlier pragmatist insights, as when William James writes "The truth of an idea is not a stagnant property inherent in it. Truth *happens* to an

idea. It *becomes* true, is *made* true by events" (James, *Writings 1902–1910* (New York: Library of America), 574). James meant that, rather than thinking of truth as a matter of correspondence, we should think of it as a function of how our beliefs are born out in the course of perception, action, consequences. James's formulation was itself an echo of an earlier aphorism of Charles Peirce's: "Our idea of anything is our idea of its sensible effects"; what he described in a later lecture on abductive inferences as the way the "elements of every concept enter into logical thought at the gate of perception and make their exit at the gate of purposive action" ("Pragmatism and the Logic of Abduction," in *Essential Peirce*, vol.1, ed. Nathan Houser and Christian Kloesel (Bloomington: Indiana University Press, 1992), 241). For more on Peirce's idea that truth is arrived at through an assessment of the consequences that follow from holding a belief, see Frederich Carpenter, "Charles Sanders Peirce: Pragmatic Transcendentalist," *The New England Quarterly* 14 (1941): 34–48; and John Murphy, *Pragmatism from Peirce to Davidson* (Boulder, Colo.: Westview Press, 1990). On Dewey's rejection of Cartesianism, and epistemology more generally, Cornell West (borrowing language from Emerson) writes: "Dewey associates [such] metaphysical pretensions with the epistemological puzzles of modern philosophy [such that] the 'spectator theory of knowledge [ie, of a privileged subject standing over and above nature] are linked to a paltry notion of experience." Cornell West, *The American Evasion of Philosophy* (Madison: University of Wisconsin Press, 1989), 94. On James's philosophy as being primarily a philosophy of "experimentation," Gérard Deledalle writes, "The principle of pragmatism is the fundamental principle of radical empiricism conceived as a philosophy of experimentation.... Rather than a theoretician, James is really more a philosopher of experimentation." Gérard Deledalle, *La philosophie américaine* (Bruxelle: De Boeck University Press, 1998), 148 (my translation).

29. John Dewey, "Ralph Waldo Emerson," *The Philosophy of John Dewey*, ed. John McDermott (Chicago: University of Chicago Press, 1973), 24–25.

30. Ibid., 25.

31. Ibid., 26. Dewey's phrasing here—of "taking the *way* of truth *as* the truth"—and his linking of that insight to "experience" is part of the reason why I treat the classical pragmatists critique of correspondence as applicable equally to criteria for finding out what is true and to different ways of thinking about the meaning of experience.

32. Ibid., 27.

33. Stanley Cavell, "Music Discomposed," in *Must We Mean What We Say?* (Cambridge: Cambridge University Press, 2002), 197.

34. Ibid., 198.

35. "Experiment" is also a guiding term in Cavell's discussion of Thoreau's *Walden*. See Cavell, *Senses of Walden*, 3–25. On the idea that literature is itself experience, and that composition takes the form of an experimental search, Maurice Blanchot writes, "Poetry is experience... art is experience because it is experimental: because it is a search." Maurice Blanchot, *L'espace littéraire* (Paris: Gallimard, 1955), 107–9. See also Michel Butor, "Le roman comme recherche," in *Essais sur le roman* (Paris: Gallimard, 1960).

36. Cavell, "Thinking of Emerson," in *Senses of Walden*, 134. Sharon Cameron says that in his journals Thoreau is "writing his life so that it actually comes to comprise alternate—natural—phenomena." Sharon Cameron, *Writing Nature: Henry Thoreau's Journal* (Chicago: University of Chicago Press, 1985), 4. For the role of the commonplace book and journal entry as key components in Emerson's compositional process, see Lawrence Buell, *Literary Transcendentalism* (Ithaca, N.Y.: Cornell University Press, 1973); Lawrence Rosenwald, *Emerson and the Art of the Diary* (New York: Oxford University Press, 1988); and Robert Richardson, *First We Read Then We Write* (Iowa City: University of Iowa Press, 2009).

37. As Russell Goodman puts it, "there is a tradition running through the work of Emerson, James and Dewey to Cavell [which amounts to a] response to the epistemological

mind-world relation," and one that is based on the way "Emerson shares an open-ended, experimental attitude with...Dewey"; one operative in the connection between words experience and experiment. Russell Goodman, *American Philosophy and the Romantic Tradition* (Cambridge: Cambridge University Press, 1991), 33, 52. Experience and experiment are in Latin and French the same word, so that to "do an experiment" is also to "have an experience." For an excellent discussion of the relation of *expérience, expérimentation,* and *épreuve* (test), see the entry for "Experiment/Experience," in *Vocabulaire Européen des Philosophies: Dictionnaire des Intraduisibles,* ed. Barbara Cassin (Paris: Seuil, 2004), 437–38.

38. Cavell, *Philosophy the Day after Tomorrow*, 13–14.

39. Stanley Cavell, "What's the Use of Calling Emerson a Pragmatist?" in *The Revival of Pragmatism*, 220.

40. Ibid., 221.

41. The naturalist's "refusal to take the skeptic seriously" is not at all a matter of a "quest for certainty" (to use Dewey's phrase). It is on the contrary a fallibilism, such that any belief can be revised in the course of experience and practice. For an account of pragmatism that treats its emergence specifically as a rejection of "certainty," see Louis Menand, *The Metaphysical Club* (New York: Macmillan, 2002).

42. Cavell, *Emerson's Transcendental Etudes*, 12. For a provocative discussion of Dewey and Cavell as linked by a "tone of...democratic aspiration," see Saudra Laugier, "Emerson Skepticism and Politics," in *The Other Emerson* (Minneapolis: Minnesota University Press, 2010), 206–11.

43. Much literary criticism taking its cue from pragmatism avoids the question of the relation of experience to language raised by the more recent analytic thinkers. While shrewd about the link between Emerson and Dewey, and the relation of experiment to compositional method, Brian Magee gives an account of Emerson's prose as bringing about a "radically democratic relationship between reader and writer," in which it is up to the individual reader to produce "whatever meaning he or she decides is being created." Magee, *Emancipating Pragmatism*, 62–63. My own attention to the critique of classical pragmatism's blurring of cause with justification leads me rather to want to look into the conditions under which meanings can be had at all (as opposed to simply affirming that meanings may be differently had from reader to reader). Thus in contrast to Magee's description of each person's radically private sense of what a given work meant ("whatever meaning she decides is being created"), I want to look into how the work, at its most personal, experimental, idiosyncratic, is always attempting to discover the criteria in relation to which its meanings might become shareable (and so endorsable, rejectable, an occasion for agreement or disagreement, etc.). Elisa New describes what she calls the "literature of experience" as "perceptual rather than conceptual [achieving] not an explanation of its own effects (poetics) but a closer relation with affect itself." Elisa New, *The Line's Eye* (Cambridge, Mass.: Harvard University Press, 1998), 9. While I think New's description captures something of what is going on in Emerson's prose, it nevertheless elides entirely the problem of getting from causal contacts (sensory affection) to language (discursive sayings). New goes on to say that "pragmatism is not a theory but a method [and] the art of experience accordingly is art preserving in its structure the dynamics of the method [such that it is] art distinguished more by its composition than by its other elements [and] gains its power not through mimesis but through composition (ibid., 146). Here I agree entirely, but in this case her description is at odds with her own hard-and-fast division between the perceptual and the conceptual.

44. Robert Brandom, "When Philosophy Paints Its Blue on Gray," *boundary 2* 29 (2002): 2. G. W. F. Hegel, the major common influence linking Dewey and Brandom, also thought of experience as "experimental," and structured as learning. According to Brandom, Hegel

"aims at a conception of experience [*Erfahrung*] that [stresses] the *alternation* and *development* of the content of...concepts [and] conceptual content arises out of the *process* of applying concepts." Robert Brandom, "Some Pragmatist Themes in Hegel's Idealism: Negotiation and Administration in Hegel's Account of the Structure and Content of Conceptual Norms," *European Journal of Philosophy* 7, no. 2 (1999): 166–67. While he was early in his career decisively influenced by Hegel, Dewey shed his rationalism while hanging on to the historicism and processualism. Ken McClelland describes this as Dewey's "move away from the purely ideational processes of Hegel, toward the more naturalistic processes of Darwin." Ken McClelland, "Dewey's Hegel: A Search for Unity in Diversity," *Transactions of the Charles S. Peirce Society* 44, no. 4 (fall 2008): 416. Still, there is much debate about whether Deweyan pragmatism should be read as breaking with Hegelianism, or as harboring what Dewey himself called a "permanent Hegelian deposit." For more on this debate, see James A. Good, *A Search for Unity in Diversity* (Lanham, Md.: Lexington Books, 2006); and *John R. Shook*, preface to *Dewey's Philosophy of Spirit* (New York: Fordham University Press, 2010). On the distinction between *Erfahrung* and *Erlebnis*, and its relation to pragmatism, see also Martin Jay's excellent *Songs of Experience: Modern American and European Variations on a Universal Theme* (Berkeley: University of California Press, 2005).

45. Robert Brandom, *Between Saying and Doing: Toward an Analytic Pragmatism* (New York: Oxford University Press, 2008), 87.

46. Richard Rorty, *Philosophy and Social Hope* (New York: Penguin Books, 1999), xii.

47. In his 2007 Locke lectures "Toward an Analytic Pragmatism," Brandom says Rorty "argued that two central concepts of the philosophical tradition...that have separated themselves from any connection of a practice that could give them the kind of meaning they are assumed to have...are the concepts of experience and of representation. Rorty's suggestion was that the way forward for philosophy was to get rid of those notions as no longer having the kind of meaning that could support real philosophical work [and so] experience is not one of my words." Robert Brandom, "Response to John McDowell," available at www.pitt.edu/~rbrandom/multimedia/. Conversely, John McDowell's *Mind and World* is something like an effort to resuscitate the word "experience," in light of the critique of the myth of the given. In that book, McDowell describes the difference between perception (causal, passive) and expression (conceptual, spontaneous) as the difference between the "realm of law" (nature) and the "space of reasons" (norms), but then goes on to offer an account of experience in which perception is thought to be itself conceptually contentful; what he elsewhere describes as a "conception of perceptual experience as [an] actualization of conceptual capacities in sensory consciousness." John McDowell, *Having the World in View* (Cambridge, Mass.: Harvard University Press, 2009), 185. For recent essays on the problem of the relation of nature to norms, see Mario de Caro and David Macarthur, eds., *Naturalism and Normativity* (New York: Columbia University Press, 2010), especially Peter Godfrey-Smith, "Dewey, Continuity and McDowell."

48. Richard Rorty, "Dewey's Metaphysics," in *Consequences of Pragmatism: Essays 1972–1980*, (Minneapolis: Minnesota University Press, 1982), 81. Rorty extends his critique of Deweyan naturalism in more recent essays. In "Pragmatism and Romanticism," Rorty writes that the "line between mechanism and something categorically distinct from mechanism comes when organisms develop social practices that permit those organisms to consider the relative advantages and disadvantages of alternative descriptions of things. Mechanism stops and freedom begins, at the point where we go metalinguistic—the point at which we can discuss which words best describe a given situation." Richard Rorty, "Pragmatism and Romanticism," in *Philosophical Papers 4: Philosophy and Cultural Politics* (Cambridge: Cambridge University Press, 2007), 114. And in "Cultural Politics and God," Rorty writes that "we should not treat the causal ability of certain events to

produce non-inferential beliefs in suitably programmed organisms as a justification for their holding those beliefs." Rorty, "Cultural Politics and God," in *Philosophical Papers 4: Philosophy and Cultural Politics*, 10–11.

49. Rorty, "Dewey Between Hegel and Darwin," in *Philosophical Papers*, 3:295–96.

50. Ibid., 296. Rorty's quote is from Dewey, *Experience and Nature*, 29–30. See also Richard Rorty, ed., *The Linguistic Turn: Essays in Philosophic Method* (Chicago: University of Chicago Press, 1967).

51. James Kloppenberg, "Pragmatism: An Old Name for Some New Ways of Thinking?" in *The Revival of Pragmatism*, 93.

52. Brandom, "When Philosophy Paints Its Blue on Grey," 25. Both Rorty and Brandom follow Wilfrid Sellars here; see Sellars, *Empiricism and the Philosophy of Mind* (Cambridge, Mass.: Harvard University Press, 1997); especially Rorty's "Introduction" and Brandom's appended "Study Guide," Harvard University Press edition, 1956 [1997]); and Willem A. deVries and Timm Triplett, *Knowledge, Mind and the Given: Reading Wilfrid Sellars's "Empiricism and the Philosophy of Mind"* (Indianapolis: Hackett, 2000), esp. xxx–xxxii, 76–77. Brandom's effort to synthesize Sellarsian insights with insights borrowed from German idealism and American pragmatism leads to his formidable project of "inferentialist semantics." See Robert Brandom, *Making It Explicit: Reasoning Representing and Discursive Commitment* (Cambridge, Mass.: Harvard University Press, 1994; and *Articulating Reasons: An Introduction to Inferentialism* (Cambridge, Mass.: Harvard University Press, 2000). For more on the difference between classical and analytic pragmatism, see Tom Rockmore, *Hegel, Idealism and Analytic Philosophy* (New Haven: Yale University Press, 2005); and Alan Malachowski, *The New Pragmatism* (Ontario: McGill-Queens University Press, 2010).

53. Dewey, *Experience and Nature*, xiii. William James had earlier imagined a version of this continuity, advising that we "ought to say we have a feeling of *and*, a feeling of *if*, a feeling of *but*, and a feeling of *by*, quite as readily as we say a feeling of *blue* or a feeling of *cold*," as if qualifiers, conjunctions, and prepositions were as deserving of their perceptual analogues as the nominal terms they place in syntactic relations. William James, *Principles of Psychology* (New York: Holt, 1890), 238–39. Joan Richardson's *A Natural History of Pragmatism* takes James's lines as central to the problem of what she calls pragmatism's "recognition of the intrinsic connection between perception and language" (99), and imagines the working out of this tension as beginning with the New England Puritans. Her study might be thought of as imagining Henry James's "history of an effect of experience" as beginning in the way the Calvinist notion of experience as "conversion," as it is bound up with typological pattern recognition, continues up to the prose experiments in Emerson, the Jameses, Stevens, and Stein. While Richardson's study also treats in detail Darwin's importance for the development of pragmatism, she barely mentions Dewey, the classical pragmatist most attuned to the philosophical consequences of natural selection, and the one who gives the most philosophically ambitious account of what is at stake in the move, as she nicely puts it describing Emerson, the "scaling continuity of matter and spirit" (99). For more on the influence of Darwin on the classical pragmatists, see also Philip Weiner, *Evolution and the Founders of Pragmatism* (Cambridge, Mass.: Harvard University Press, 1949).

54. For Brandom's unpacking of this Sellarsian point, see *Empiricism and the Philosophy of Mind* (Cambridge, Mass.: Harvard University Press, 1997), 123–30, 139–44. For a helpful account of how Brandom (glossing Sellars) construes the myth of the given as hinging specifically on the move from sense data to noninferential beliefs, see Danielle Macbeth, "Inference, Meaning and Truth in Brandom, Sellars and Frege," in *Reading Brandom: On Making It Explicit*, ed. Berhard Weiss and Jeremy Wanderer (London: Routledge, 2010), 198–201.

55. The iron example is taken from Brandom, *Making It Explicit*, 87–88. The example of the photoelectric cell hitched up to a tape recorder—the point of which is that we "cannot readily imagine continuing a conversation with [such a] gadget"—is from Richard Rorty, *Philosophy and the Mirror of Nature* (Princeton: Princeton University Press, 1979), 189.

56. Cavell, "Music Discomposed," 198.

57. It should be noted that Brandom is not a formalist about inference, taking from Sellars the idea of "material inference." In relations of material implication, mastery of concepts, say "East" and "West," allow one to make a good *material* inference from "Pittsburgh is to the West of Philadelphia" to "Philadelphia is to the East of Pittsburgh"; such that "endorsing these inferences is part of grasping or mastering those concepts, quite apart from any specifically logical competence." Brandom, *Making It Explicit*, 97–98; see also Wilfrid Sellars, "Inference and Meaning," in *In the Space of Reasons* (Cambridge, Mass.: Harvard University Press, 2007), 3–7. In Brandom's pragmatism, the order of explanation moves from inferences of material implication to the making explicit of premises "hidden" in the material inference, in logical vocabulary like the conditional: "*If* Pittsburgh is to the West of Philadelphia, *then* Philadelphia is to the East of Pittsburgh." See Brandom, *Making It Explicit*, 101. In this sense I think there is a genuine difference between what Cavell is saying about justification (as distinct from composition) and what analytic pragmatists like Rorty and Brandom are saying about justification; as that which allows inferences of material implication to become "judgeable, claimable, believable contents, as the contents of potential propositional committements." Brandom, *Making It Explicit*, 101. My thanks to Robert Pippin for stressing the importance of Brandom's distinction between inferences of material implication and formally valid inferences, in his response to my essay "On Going On: Rules, Inferences and Literary Conditions," *nonsite.org*, issue 4. See Robert Pippin, "Response to Izenberg and Grimstad," *nonsite.org*, issue 4.

58. Stanley Cavell, "A Matter of Meaning It," in *Must We Mean What We Say?*, 219. Cavell is talking about painting and sculpture, but I take it such descriptions apply to other kinds of composition (literary or musical); and that these are also places where a "discovering of the limits or essence of procedures" can occur.

59. Ibid. (my emphasis). J. M. Bernstein offers a (very Kantian) description of Cavell's construal of modernism as "the moment in which we no longer have clear criteria for what constitutes a new work of art: neither tradition nor pure reason can determine what a poem or a painting or a sculpture or a musical composition is. But if these things are not known a priori, before we attend to or produce a work, then we also do not know what art is. . . . A modernist work is [then] one that can claim validity or authenticity for itself if and only if its claim is transcendentally valid, that is, if *its* claim to validity is at the same time the lodging and sanctioning of a claim as to what art is. Modernist works risk the very idea of being an artwork in order to establish, make possible again, what art is." J. M. Bernstein, "Aesthetics, Modernism, Literature: Cavell's Transformations of Philosophy," in *Stanley Cavell: Contemporary Philosophy in Focus* (Cambridge: Cambridge University Press, 2003), 177. Cavell returns to this idea in *The Claim of Reason*, saying that modern works do not "have anything to go on . . . that secures the value or the significance of an object apart from one's wanting the thing to be as it is." Stanley Cavell, *The Claim of Reason* (New York: Oxford University Press, 1979), 95.

60. Walter Benn Michaels, *The Shape of the Signifier: 1967 to the End of History* (Princeton: Princeton University Press, 2004), 1–15. For Michaels, one of the historical consequences of mistaking the "seeing" for the "reading" of a work has been the way the focus on the "materiality of the signifier" (the work as physical marks) led to the emergence of identity politics, such that an emphasis on "experience" replaces the meaning of the work (what you believe) with the private affects of the person (what you are).

61. Michael Fried, "Art and Objecthood," originally in *Artforum* (June 1967), in *Art and Objecthood* (Chicago: Chicago University Press, 1998), 150–51. Michaels says the subtitle of his book—*1967 to the End of History*—is in part an acknowledgment of the year of the publication of Fried's essay, which marks (and laments) a turn from high modernism to minimalist theatricality.

62. Fried, *Art and Objecthood*. In a more recent reassessment of "Art and Objecthood," in "An Introduction to My Art Criticism," Fried describes the minimalist emphasis on "heightened perceptual experience" as an "essentially inartistic [and] unmodernist effect." Fried, Art and Objecthood, 40.

63. Ruth Leys, "The Turn to Affect: A Critique," *Critical Inquiry* 451 (2011): 451n31

64. Fried writes: "[it is] not that in the realm of art nothing like experience matters—on the contrary, it is crucial—but under the Minimalist/Literalist paradigm the viewer's (real time, ongoing, incommensurably unique) experience *stands in for* the work of art. And once that happens you get Post-Modernism, subject position, identity politics, performativity, affect theory, difference instead of disagreement, etc., etc., all the mindless bullshit that has encumbered thinking about art (and life) for the past forty years or more." Michael Fried, e-mail message to author, July 23, 2012. See also Fried's questioning of distinctions implicit in Tony Smith's anecdote about the drive on the turnpike, and its relevance to Clement Greenberg's account of modernism (which Fried both inherits and critiques): "Why should any experience that is not an experience of art be taken as laying bare the end of art? Would the experience of a spectacular sunset or a nuclear explosion do as much?...What's wrong with painting, even modernist painting, 'looking pictorial'? And how tenable is the contrast between 'framing' and 'experiencing' on which Smith insists? (There is no more sacred term in Greenberg's lexicon than 'experience')." Michael Fried, "An Introduction to My Art Criticism," in *Art and Objecthood*, 44.

65. Michael Fried, *Four Honest Outlaws: Sala, Ray, Marioni, Gordon* (Hew Haven: Yale University Press, 2011), 6.

66. Ibid., 6–7 (my emphasis).

67. Cavell, "Music Discomposed," 212.

68. Fried, *Art and Objecthood*, 155.

69. John Dewey, *Art as Experience* (New York: Penguin, 1932), 50.

70. Fried, *Art and Objecthood*, 166–67. Fried ends "Art and Objecthood" by linking the idea of presentness to his epigraph from Perry Miller's biography of Jonathan Edwards, saying presentness is the exception to the prosaic literalism of most of our lives, and so "Presentness is grace." Fried, *Art and Objecthood*, 168.

71. Fried, "An Introduction to My Art Criticism," in *Art and Objecthood*, 47.

72. Fried and Cavell have each repeatedly acknowledged their mutual influence on one another. Fried writes that he and Cavell have been "involved in a wide-ranging conversation [which] soon came to explore the question of artistic modernism." Fried, "An Introduction to My Art Criticism, in *Art and Objecthood*, 10. In *Absorption and Theatricality* Fried writes that "between Cavell's work and my own there exists a community of concept and purpose which will be apparent to anyone reading us both." Michael Fried, *Absorption and Theatricality* (Chicago: University of Chicago Press, 1988), 182n13. Cavell, in his book on film, *The World Viewed*, says he "follows [Fried] in speaking of modernist [works] as an acknowledging of its conditions." Stanley Cavell, *The World Viewed* (Cambridge, Mass.: Harvard University Press, 1979), 109. Fried in turn speaks of "acknowledgment" as the word that best captures how modernist works raise the question of the conventions inherent in a given medium, such that "notions of convention and acknowledgment...link my art criticism with the early philosophical writings of Stanley Cavell." Fried, *Four Honest Outlaws*, 9. Recently Cavell recalled his first meeting with Fried, in which they

immediately began talking about the "axes of art and philosophy and the concept of the modern." Stanley Cavell, *Little Did I Know* (Stanford: Stanford University Press, 2010), 406. For Fried's account of this same meeting, see his "Meeting Stanley Cavell," in *Modern Language Notes* 126 (2011): 937–42.

73. That this account of experience has little to do with the private affective states of individual persons is made clear in Dewey's description of experience as a "serial course of affairs with their own characteristic properties [with] nothing personal or subjective about it" and "not some person's [and not] owned by someone." John Dewey, *Experience and Nature*, 231. Echoing Dewey's point about the impersonality of experience, Sharon Cameron notes that in Emerson's prose, experience is not exclusively tied to the person, but to the "public...idiosyncrasies of style," such that Emerson's "life fail[s] to be experienced as his own"; an externalizing of interiority she finds captured in words like "ravishment" and "ecstasy." See Sharon Cameron, *Impersonality* (Chicago: University of Chicago Press, 2007), 107. A recent book that does not treat experience as synonymous with private personal affects, but nevertheless follows Michaels in linking experience to a critique of identity, is Theo Davis, *Formalism, Experience, and the Making of American Literature in the Nineteenth Century* (Cambridge: Cambridge University Press, 2010). While Davis interestingly describes experience as a "projection *out of* certain texts [of nineteenth-century American literature]" such that it is to be "distinguished from subjects [so that] beliefs and meanings are independent of identity [as] inarguable," she nevertheless describes pragmatism as giving an "account of experience as the ever-expanding ground of ever-changing beliefs, which is ultimately to posit what we *are* instead of what we believe." Davis, *Formalism, Experience, and the Making of American Literature in the Nineteenth Century*, 7–9 (my emphasis). But my attention in this introduction to Dewey has been precisely to show how the pragmatist conception of experience does not reduce experience to this sort of identitarianism.

74. Cavell, *Emerson's Transcendental Etudes*, 70.

75. Cavell, *Disowning Knowledge in Seven Plays of Shakespeare* (Cambridge: Cambridge University Press, 1987), 4–5. Cavell, *Must We Mean What We Say?*, 269; James Conant, "An Interview With Cavell," in *The Senses of Stanley Cavell* (Lewisburg, Penn.: Bucknell University Press, 1989).

CHAPTER 1

1. Frederick Henry Hedge, "Coleridge," *The Christian Examiner*, March 1833, 119.

2. Ibid., 120. Barbara Packer attributes Hedge's insouciant tone to his "affecting the witty non-chalance of the *Edinburgh Review*," the Scottish journal that often introduced the latest developments in continental thought to New England readers. Barbara Packer, *The Transcendentalists* (Atlanta: University of Georgia Press, 2007), 28–29.

3. Ibid., 199. Packer says of this review that Hedge "was better qualified than anyone in America to pull off [an elucidation of Kant's critique since] Hedge had spent four years in German preparatory schools...which made him fluent in academic German." Packer, *The Transcendentalists*, 29.

4. Philip Gura, *The Wisdom of Words: Language, Theology, and Literature in the New England Renaissance* (Middletown, Conn.: Wesleyan University Press, 1981), 40.

5. Perry Miller, *The Transcendentalists* (Cambridge, Mass.: Harvard University Press, 1950), 34. Louis Menand describes Marsh's particular intellectual, religious, and philosophical goals as his trying to "resolve the current theological conflicts between American Congregationalists [Calvinists] and Unitarians [in raising] their disagreements to the higher ground of Kantian idealism." Louis Menand, *The Metaphysical Club* (New York: Macmillan, 2002), 245.

6. James Marsh, ed., "Preliminary Essay," in *Aids to Reflection* by Samuel Taylor Coleridge (Vermont: C. Goodrich, 1840), xxix. The premise regarding the "sources of our knowledge" refers to the well-known passage in Book II of Locke's *Essay Concerning Human Understanding*, about the mind being "white Paper void of all characters....Whence has it all the materials of Reason and Knowledge? To this I answer, in one word, from *Experience*,"104.

7. Lawrence Buell, *Literary Transcendentalism* (Ithaca, N.Y.: Cornell University Press, 1973), 75–76.

8. Marsh, "Preliminary Essay," in *Aids to Reflection*, xxxviii–xxxix.

9. Ibid., xxxviii–xxxix. William Paley's *Natural Theology: or Evidences of the Existence and Attributres of the Deity, Collected from the Appearances of Nature*, ed. Frederick Ferré (New York: Bobbs-Merrill, 1963 [1802], an influential book on Unitarian thought, was also concerned with ferreting out the part of the human person that was rational and reflective from that part that was the mere receptacle of causal impingements, and in such a way that reason and revelation could be thought of as compatible, rather than mutually exclusive. For more on Paley's influence on Unitarian intellectual life, see Daniel Walker Howe, *The Unitarian Conscience: Harvard Moral Philosophy 1805–1861* (Middletown, Conn.: Wesleyan University Press, 1988), 70–79.

10. Laura Dassow Walls, *Emerson's Life in Science* (Ithaca, N.Y.: Cornell University Press, 2003), 5–6.

11. Marsh, "Preliminary Essay," in *Aids to Reflection*.

12. See Joseph Warren Beach, *The Concept of Nature in Nineteenth-Century English Poetry* (New York: Russell and Russell, 1966), 330. Philip Gura notes that "between 1820 and 1850 New England witnessed a lively debate over the origin and meaning of language, with roots in the dialogue that began when Immanuel Kant rejected Lockean sensationalism as a satisfactory epistemological model." Philip Gura, *The Crossroads of American History and Literature* (University Park: Pennsylvania State University Press, 1996), 159.

13. Samuel Taylor Coleridge, *Aids to Reflection*, 573.

14. Ibid., 574–75. In fact such descriptions are in perfect accord with "the traditional doctrine of the scale of being," which Coleridge might have found in more orthodox works. See Beach, *The Concept of Nature in Nineteenth Century English Poetry* (New York: Russell & Russell, 1966), 330. For the central importance of the "great chain of being" view to Unitarian scholarship, see especially Henry Ware's *Inquiry into the Foundation, Evidence and Truths of Religion* (Cambridge: Cambridge University Press, 1842).

15. It is something of a commonplace in the scholarship to enumerate the various ways Coleridge (and assorted New England thinkers at the time) got Kant's transcendental idealism wrong. As Barbara Packer puts it, "as many people have noticed, Coleridge's terminology, though translated from Kant (*Vernuft* [Reason]; *Verstanden* [Understanding]) differs in significant ways from its source." Packer, *The Transcendentalists*, 24–25. While Kant "employed [the reason/understanding distinction] to argue that the understanding never escaped entanglement with the sensory but that pure reason yearned to attain super-sensory truths, its efforts inevitably run up against logical conundrums that doomed it to failure. [Kant] was impressed by reason's limits. For Coleridge, however, the distinction suggested a confidence that reason, unlike understanding, could lead the mind beyond the sensory world into a realm of eternal truth." Brooks Holifield, *Theology in America: Christian Thought from the Age of the Puritans to the Civil War* (New Haven, Conn.: Yale University Press), 2003, 436. This confusion leads to a reversal of what Kant called the transcendental/transcendent distinction. Since for Kant, the "objects" about which reason is led to speculate—God, for example—are "transcendent" (and not "transcendental"), this means that they *cannot* be given as objects of possible experience. For more

on Coleridge's idiosyncratic appropriation of German idealism, see Gian N. G. Orsini, *Coleridge and German Idealism: A Study in the History of Philosophy* (Carbondale: Southern Illinois University Press, 1969); Tom MacFarland, *Coleridge and the Pantheist Tradition* (London: Clarendon Press, 1969); and especially Rene Wellek, *Immanuel Kant in England* (Princeton: Princeton University Press, 1931). For an account of Coleridge as a conduit of German idealism in New England, see Rene Wellek, "The Minor Transcendentalists and German Philosophy," in *Confrontations: Studies in the Intellectual and Literary Relations Between Germany, England, and the United States during the Nineteenth Century* (Princeton: Princeton University Press, 1965).

16. Samuel Taylor Coleridge, "Essays on the Principle of Method," in *The Collected Works of Samuel Taylor Coleridge, vol. 4, The Friend* (Princeton: Princeton University Press, 1969), 560.

17. Samuel Taylor Coleridge, "Treatise on Method," in *Encyclopedia Metropolitana* (London: Richard Griffen, 1851), 2. Jerome Christensen describes Coleridge's notion of "method" as the "external development...of relations contemplated within." Jerome Christensen, *Coleridge's Blessed Machine of Language* (Ithaca, N.Y.: Cornell University Press, 1981), 234.

18. Samuel Taylor Coleridge, *Table Talk I* (Princeton: Princeton University Press, 1990), 90.

19. Samuel Taylor Coleridge, "Essays on the Principle of Method," in *The Collected Works of Samuel Taylor Coleridge*, 4:564. "Methodos" is etymologically derived from *hodos* (road; way), ibid., 564.

20. Ibid., 562–63.

21. Ibid., 566.

22. J. R. de J. Jackson gives an example of what he takes Coleridge to mean by "progressive method," asking us to imagine a mosaic whose pieces are "in a state of complete disorder [such that] one might begin by collecting the pieces according to their colours. The red pieces could be put in one pile, the blue in another, and so on. This would be [mere] *arrangement*...the purpose of the exercise, however, would be to put the pieces together again so as to reconstitute the original picture.... This process would be a progressive transition [but] if one had no idea what the picture was originally of [then] there would be no guiding principle to determine which steps to follow." J. Jackson, *Method and Imagination in Coleridge's Criticism* (London: Routledge, 1969), 37–39. Lee Rust Brown says of Coleridge's "method" that it is the "vital principle that organizes and directs a representational system [as it is] found manifested in that system." Lee Rust Brown, *The Emerson Museum: Practical Romanticism and the Pursuit of the Whole* (Cambridge, Mass.: Harvard University Press, 1997), 87.

23. Emerson, Ralph Waldo, *The Letters of Ralph Waldo Emerson Volume One*, ed. Ralph Rusk (New York: Columbia University Press, 1939), 402.

24. Harold Bloom says of Emerson and method that he "rejects Coleridgean metaphysical method because he knows methods are just changes in diction, and that new methods always yield to newer ones." Harold Bloom, *Agon* (New York: Oxford University Press, 1982), 20. This is one way of characterizing Emerson's experimentalism.

25. Emerson, *Selected Journals: 1820–1842*, "France and England," ed. Lawrence Rosenwald. (New York: Library of America), 389–91. For an account of Coleridge's own work as a Unitarian preacher, see David Bromwich, *William Hazlitt: The Mind of a Critic* (New Haven, Conn.: Yale University Press, 1999), 24–25.

26. On the importance of the cabinets for Emerson as a direct eye-witness encounter, see David Robinson, "Emerson's Natural Theology and the Paris Naturalists: Toward a 'Theory of Animated Nature,'" *Journal of the History of Ideas* 41 (1980): 69–98. Cuvier, it should be pointed out, saw the animal kingdom as comprised of "four principle forms, four general plans...in accordance with which all animals seem to have been modeled." It

was against such views that Darwin's descent with modification was offered as an alternative. For a thorough account of the links between Coleridge and Cuvier, see Rust Brown, *The Emerson Museum*. See also James Moore, *The Post-Darwinian Controversies: A Study of the Protestant Struggle to Come to Terms with Darwin in Great Britain and America, 1870–1900* (Cambridge: Cambridge University Press, 1979).

27. In their introduction to the *Selected Lectures* Ronald Bosco and Joel Meyerson tell us that "a significant portion of the lecture was drawn from journals in which he had reported his travels in Europe throughout most of 1833 [and] the experience that most influenced his decision to become a naturalist were the hours he spent examining objects on display in the Cabinet of Natural History... as he studies case after case of specimens preserved in the museum, Emerson achieved the profound insight that would serve as the unifying vision of his philosophy from this day through to the end of his life. Ronald Bosco and Joel Myerson, *The Selected Lectures of Ralph Waldo Emerson* (Athens: The University of Georgia Press, 2005), 1.

28. Emerson, "The Uses of Natural History," in *Selected Lectures of Ralph Waldo Emerson*, 5.

29. Lawrence Buell describes the "characteristic Transcendentalist pattern of composition as... a threefold process of revision from journal to lecture to essay." Buell, *Literary Transcendentalism*, 280. And Lawrence Rosenwald says that Emerson's "transcribing and adapting... passages from the journal for use in the lectures and essays" is "both the most important and the most misleading thing to know about the Emersonian literary system." Lawrence Rosenwald, *Emerson and the Art of the Diary* (New York: Oxford University Press, 1988), 65. It is both important and "misleading" for Rosenwald, because he is concerned to counter the tendency to see the essays as the "finished" product built up from journal entries, since Emerson built not only from the journals, but recycled passages from his own lectures and essays. Thus Rosenwald wants to "unsettle the distinction between raw material and finished product," such that the journals are seen not merely as "ancillary to literary work" but as a literary work in themselves. Rosenwald, *Emerson and the Art of the Diary*, 65. For the journals as a space of "experimentation," and as part of Emerson's search for an original literary form, see Ralph C. Larosa, "Emerson's Search for Literary Form: The Early Journals," *Modern Philology* 69, no. 1 (1971): 25–35; and Glen M. Johnson, "Emerson's Craft of Revision: The Composition of the *Essays*," in *Ralph Waldo Emerson: A Collection of Critical Essays*, ed. Laurence Buell (New York: Longman, 1993).

30. Brown, *The Emerson Museum*, 58.

31. Ibid.

32. Ibid., 59.

33. Ibid.

34. Ibid., 67–69.

35. Ralph Waldo Emerson, *Nature*, in *Emerson's Nature—Origin, Growth, Meaning*, ed. Merton M. Sealts Jr. and Alfred R. Ferguson (New York: Dodd, Mead & Company, 1969), 32–33.

36. Ralph Waldo Emerson, *The Journals and Miscellaneous Notebooks of Ralph Waldo Emerson*, ed. William H. Gilman, Alfred R. Ferguson, Merrell R. Davis, Merton M. Sealts, and Harrison Hayford et al. (Cambridge, Mass.: Harvard University Press, 1960), 4:95; 5:66. Emerson copied this quotation into his journal from Elizabeth Peabody's manuscript translation of G. Oegger's *Le vrai messie* (Paris: n.p., 1829). See also Gura, *The Wisdom of Words*, 86–88.

37. Ralph Waldo Emerson, *Nature*, 15. David Bromwich says of this passage from *Nature* that for Emerson commodity "includes both the thing and what man does to the thing—which is understood as part of the thing itself, its final cause." Bromwich, *A Choice of Inheritance* (Cambridge, Mass.: Harvard University Press, 1989), 141.

38. Emerson, *Nature*, 32.

39. Francis Bowen, "Transcendentalism," *Christian Examiner* 21 (January 1837), in *Emerson and Thoreau: The Contemporary Reviews* (Cambridge: Cambridge University Press, 2009), 5–6.

40. John Locke, *An Essay concerning Human Understanding*, bk. iii, chap. 10, sec. 9, quoted in Bowen, "Transcendentalism," 21.

41. It is something of an intellectual historical irony that Bowen learned his logic at Harvard from Frederick Hedge's father, Levi Hedge.

42. Bowen, "Transcendentalism," 11.

43. Perry Miller says established Unitarian thought treated transcendentalism as "a foreign and un-American fad [whose] adherents [were] arrogant and dogmatic." Miller, *The Transcendentalists*, 173. Barbara Packer calls Bowen's review an "occasion for an attack upon the arrogance and obscurantism of the whole Transcendentalist school." Packer, *The Transcendentalists*, 62. Robert Habich gives a precise description of what would have been meant by a "new school" of religious thought in Boston, 1838, "the four events on everyone's minds as they listened to Emerson's address at Divinity School chapel were as follows: in early June [1838] the students of the Philanthropic Society openly defied the Harvard faculty; a week later the *Western Messenger* published [James Freeman] Clark's attack on the coldness of Unitarian ministers; within another week Abner Kneeland was jailed for blasphemy; and Jones Very, a known 'disciple' of Emerson's, had begun to show signs of madness." Robert Habich, "Emerson's Reluctant Foe: Andrews Norton and the Transcendental Controversy," *New England Quarterly* 65, no. 2 (1992): 223.

44. On the wider consequences of the "American Scholar" address in relation to Emerson's crisis of vocation, see Kenneth Sacks, *Understanding Emerson: The American Scholar and His Struggle for Self-Reliance* (Princeton: Princeton University Press, 2003).

45. Emerson, *Selected Journals 1820–1842*, 633. The preacher in question is thought to have been Barzillai Frost. Wright says of Frost that "like his professors at the Divinity School, [he] believed that Christianity was a divinely inspired religion, attested by the miracles of Christ. The bible is the only source of Christian truth, as distinguished from the truths of natural religion which may be determined by the use of reason alone." Conrad Wright, *The Liberal Christians* (Boston: Beacon Press, 1970), 46. Packer says Emerson "chafed under [Frost's] wretched preaching," and that Frost was a "glaring example of what was wrong with theological instruction at Cambridge. When Emerson visited him at home and inspected his library, the works of historical criticism and proofs of the Christian religion from 'internal and external evidences' made Emerson shiver." Packer, *The Transcendentalists*, 71.

46. Emerson, *Journals and Miscellaneous Notebooks* (Cambridge, Mass.: Harvard University Press, 1969), 7:42; Wright, *The Liberal Christians*, 54.

47. Emerson, *Essays and Lectures*, 84–85.

48. Emerson again put the image to use for his 1847 poem "The Snow-Storm."

49. For an account of nineteenth-century American literature as a unified poetics of the "symbol," see Charles Feidelson, *Symbolism and American Literature* (Chicago: University of Chicago Press, 1953).

50. Ralph Waldo Emerson, *Journals and Miscellaneous Notebooks* (Cambridge, Mass.: Harvard University Press, 1969), 34.

51. Ralph Waldo Emerson, "Divinity School" Address, in *Essays and Lectures* (New York: Library of America, 1983), 80.

52. William Hutchison, *The Transcendentalist Ministers: Church Reform in the New England Renaissance* (New Haven: Yale University Press, 2005), 19–20. Brooks Holifield calls this coupling of empiricism and revelation "evidential Christianity," linking it to "New England theologians [who] expanded their interest in rationality...adopting an understanding of reason [for a] position which consisted of the claim that rational evidence confirmed the...truth of biblical revelation." Brooks E. Holifield, *Theology in America:*

Christian Thought from the Age of the Puritans to the Civil War (New Haven, Conn.: Yale University Press, 2003), 5. In the particular case of Emerson's disparagement of the treatment of miracles as "evidence" of revelation, Holifield writes that Unitarian establishment figures like Norton needed to "defend empiricism [in order to] rest Christianity on the testimony of eyewitnesses who had seen the miracles. To discard empiricism was to imply that their testimony was irrelevant." Holifield, *Theology in America*, 210. In rejecting the idea that there could be anomalous suspensions of natural laws, Emerson was invoking, however obliquely, the argument against miracles in David Hume's *Enquiries*, as well as William Paley's "intuitionist" refutation of Hume. Paley says that it is wrong from the get-go to approach the problem of whether or not there could have been miracles as in need of a "proof." For Paley, since Divine causation is "outside" earthly causation, it makes no sense to try to understand miracles in relation to observable regularities of the natural world. For a discussion of Paley's addressing the challenge of Hume's chapter on miracles in the *Enquiries*, see Habich, "Emerson's Reluctant Foe."

53. Packer, *The Transcendentalists*, 72.

54. Perry Miller tells us that Norton "dominated the theological world of Cambridge," and Sydney Ahlstrom, in his *Religious History of the American People*, calls him "the Unitarian pope." For an essay cautioning against a too-Manichean construal of the event as (good) Emerson versus (evil) Norton, see Habich, "Emerson's Reluctant Foe."

55. Andrews Norton, "The New School in Literature and Religion," in *The Transcendentalists*, 194. Norton's outburst here is odd given his praise for the innovations of German philological criticism. On this aspect of Norton's work see Gura, *The Wisdom of Words*, 28. For evidence of Schleiermacher's influence on the "new school," see George Ripley, "Schleiermacher as Theologian," *The Christian Examiner* 20 (March 1836): 35–36. Ripley says Schleiermacher devoted his life to working through the problem in which a "prevailing Rationalism would not do, and [an] ancient Supernaturalism would do still less"; a line Miller takes to be a "transparent allegory for New England" in which "Supernaturalism" should be translated as "Calvinism" and "Rationalism" as "Unitarianism." For a more recent intellectual historical account of the specific influence of Schleiermacher's "natural religion" on theology and philosophy in the late eighteenth and early nineteenth centuries, see Andrew Dole, *Schleiermacher on Religion and the Natural Order* (New York: Oxford University Press, 2009).

56. Norton, "The New School in Literature and Religion," in *The Transcendentalists*, 195.

57. Ibid., 196; Emerson, "Divinity School Address," *Essays and Lectures*, 78.

58. Norton, "The New School in Literature and Religion," in *The Transcendentalists*, 196. Emerson himself acknowledged that he was indulging in a form of "heresy" in the Divinity School address, in a letter to Henry Ware: "The Discourse was delivered at the request of the class leaving the theological school, &, as I found, offended the faculty a good deal. The Faculty have certainly a right to any strong statement of their disapprobation, as otherwise the title-page of the address would seem to make the College an endorser for the heresy." Emerson, *Collected Letters*, 2:156. The tone and language of the letter suggests that Emerson "acknowledges the right of academic institutions to protect their doctrines from heresy." Richard Grusin, *Transcendentalist Hermeneutics* (Durham, N.C.: Duke University Press, 1990), 58.

59. Norton, "The Latest Form of Infidelity," July 19, 1839, in *The Transcendentalists*, 210.

60. Daniel Walker Howe, *The Unitarian Conscience: Harvard Moral Philosophy, 1805–1861* (Middletown, Conn.: Wesleyan University Press, 1988), 77. The Unitarian view stems from what is sometimes called the "teleological" argument, which was "compatible with the Unitarian conception of God [insofar as it was] an a posteriori induction from empirical evidence. As such, it led to the claim that the existence of God was a scientifically respectable fact, and not a mere definition." Howe, *The Unitarian Conscience*, 79.

61. As David Robinson puts it, "Emerson's eventual departure from [the Unitarian] tradition was due in part to his rejection of the idea that reasoning about nature had to be

supplemented by belief in miracles as revealed in Scripture." David Robinson, "Emerson's Natural Theology and the Paris Naturalists," *Journal of the History of Ideas* 41 (Jan.–Mar. 1980): 69–88.

62. Baruch Spinoza, *Theological-Political Treatise*, ed. Jonathan Israel (Cambridge: Cambridge University Press, 2007), xi.

63. Ibid., 81.

64. Ibid., 82.

65. Ibid.

66. Jonathan Israel, "Introduction," in Spinoza, *Theological-Political Treatise*, xvii. In Spinoza's late seventeenth-century milieu, miracles were "seen as the 'first pillar' of faith, authority, and tradition by theologians at the time [and] Spinoza's rejection of the possibility of miracles seemed to bring all accepted beliefs, the very basis of contemporary culture into question"; and so Spinoza's "purposes in publishing the *Treatise* was to weaken the authority and prestige of the public church." Jonathan Israel, *Radical Enlightenment: Philosophy and the Making of Modernity, 1650–1750* (Oxford: Oxford University Press, 2001), 219. Norton's firm adherence to the idea that miracles be understood as disruptions of the natural order—and Emerson's capacity to offend him on this issue—shows an affinity between the theo-political tensions of Amsterdam circa 1670 and Boston circa 1830.

67. It should be stressed that Spinoza's adoption of the *more geometrico* in his *Ethics* is also a matter of finding a method adequate for his metaphysics. For Spinoza, this was premised on the way *deus sive natura*—divinity as immanent in nature—could be expressed as a series of rational deductions. Emerson's compositional method, as I have been describing it, has a different way of moving through the "progressive arrangement" (even while it is nevertheless also about the immanent link between the natural order and a way of writing). For a detailed account of how Spinoza'a method in the *Ethics* expresses his metaphysics, see Edwin Curley, "Notes on a Neglected Masterpiece (1): Spinoza and the Science of Hermeneutics," in *Spinoza: The Enduring Questions*, ed. Graeme Hunter (Toronto: University of Toronto Press, 1994); and his *Behind the Geometric Method, A Reading of Spinoza's Ethics* (Princeton: Princeton University Press, 1988).

68. Emerson, "Divinity School Address," in *Essays and Lectures*, 75.

69. Ibid.

70. Emerson, "The Method of Nature," in *Essays and Lectures*, 85.

71. Ibid.

72. Emerson, *The Selected Lectures of Ralph Waldo Emerson*, 84.

73. Emerson, *Essays and Lectures*, 456.

74. Thomas Constantinesco offers a vivid description of Emerson's naturalism as it is imagined in "The Method of Nature": "every sign and form gives way to every other sign and form, in accordance with a principle of endless circulation [such that] the study of nature consists in observing a bursting forth of appearances" (Constantinesco, "L'extase et la method," in *Ralph Waldo Emerson: L'Amérique à l'essai* (Paris: Editions rue d'Ulm, 2012), 59 (my translation).

75. Ibid., 282.

76. Ibid., 330–31.

77. Ibid., 285.

78. Ralph Waldo Emerson, *The Correspondence of Emerson and Carlyle*, ed. Joseph Slater (New York: Columbia University Press, 1964), 196.

79. Ralph Waldo Emerson, *Journals and Miscellaneous Notebooks*, July 6, 1841. Emerson's poem "Uriel" is also thought to be "an account [the Divinity School Address] generalized and sublimed." Edward Waldo Emerson, *The Complete Works of Ralph Waldo Emerson*, Centenary Edition (Boston: Houghton, Mifflin and Company, 1903–1994), 9:409.

80. Ralph Waldo Emerson, *The Early Lectures, 1838–1842*, ed. Robert E. Spiller and Wallace Williams, vol. 3 (Cambridge: Belknap Press, 1972), 368.

81. Stanley Cavell, *Emerson's Transcendental Etudes* (Stanford: Stanford University Press, 2003), 214–15. George Stack says that Nietzsche "expands, develops and dramatizes insights that Emerson presents in an almost casual way." George Stack, *Nietzsche and Emerson: An Elective Affinity* (Athens: Ohio University Press, 1993), 51. After a work of (idiosyncratic) classical philology, *The Birth of Tragedy*, Nietzsche began to experiment with his writing voice in *Human, All Too Human, The Gay Science*, and in the parables, Socratic ventriloquism, dream visions and parodic evangelism of *Thus Spoke Zarathustra*. The thought experiment of the eternal return (which becomes a cosmological doctrine in the *Nachlaß*), also begins in *The Gay Science* and *Thus Spoke Zarathustra*.

82. Ralph Bauer, "Against the European Grain: The Emerson-Nietzsche Connection in Europe, 1920–1990," *ESQ: A Journal of the American Renaissance* 43, nos. 1–4 (1997): 69–93. I am grateful to Mason Golden for his translation and commentary upon sections of Nietzshce's *Nachlaß* pertaining to Emerson.

83. Eduard Baumgarten, *Der Pragmatismus. Die geistigen Grundlagen des amerikanischen Gemeinwesens* (Frankfurt am Main: V. Klostermann, 1938).

84. Herman Hummel, "Emerson and Nietzsche," *New England Quarterly* 19, no. 1 (March, 1946): 80.

85. Benedetta Zavatta, "Nietzsche and Emerson on Friendship and Its Ethical Political Implications," in *Nietzsche, Power and Politics: Rethinking Nietzsche's Legacy For Political Thought*, ed. Herman W. Siemens and Vasti Roodt (Berlin: De Gruyter, 2008), 511.

86. Jennifer Ratner-Rosenhagen, *American Nietzsche: A History of an Icon and His Ideas* (Chicago: Chicago University Press, 2012), 20.

87. Friedrich Nietzsche, *Nachlaß 1880–1882: Kritische Studienausgabe. Samtliche Werke, Band 9*, ed. Giorigi Colli and Mazzino Montinari (Berlin: de Gruyter, 1999), 618.

88. Emerson, *Nature, Addresses, Lectures*, 85. The epigraph from Emerson's essay was appended only to the first 1882 edition of *The Gay Science*. George Stack reminds us that Nietzsche drops the word "saint" from Emerson's original; and while it is reused again in *Thus Spoke Zarathustra*, it is there reduced simply to "all days shall be holy to me"; an announcement linked for Zarathustra to "joyful wisdom." Stack, *Nietzsche and Emerson*, 67n68.

89. Emerson, *Nature, Addresses, Lectures*, 89.

90. Section 92 of *The Gay Science* lists Emerson as one of "four very strange and truly poetic human beings in [the nineteenth] century who have attained mastery in prose....Not including Goethe, who may fairly be claimed by the century that produced him, I regard only Giacomo Leopardi, Prosper Mérimée, Ralph Waldo Emerson and Walter Savage Landor."

91. Babette Babich, "Nietzsche's 'Gay' Science," in *A Companion to Nietzsche*, ed. Keith Ansell Pearson (London: Wiley-Blackwell, 2007), 97; and Elizabeth Aubrey, *The Music of the Troubadours* (Bloomington: Indiana University Press, 1996). The term "gaya scienza" comes from the *Leys D'amor* (the laws or art of love) a manual on the art of songwriting. Robert Pippin notes the way both Emerson and Nietzsche refer to "*la gaya scienza* [which goes back to] twelfth-century Provencal lyric poetry, the earlier poetry extant in a modern European language, and of the troubadours' art of the fourteenth century (*Leys d'amours*)." Robert Pippin, *Nietzsche, Psychology and First Philosophy* (Chicago: University of Chicago Press, 2010), 35. Nietzsche was no doubt aware of these style manuals from his work as a philologist, and Emerson perhaps picked up the term "*gai saber*" from his reading in the works of Mistral. For more on Mistral's vast influence on nineteenth-century letters, see Marcel Decremps, *De Herder et de Nietzsche a Mistral* (Toulon: L'astrado, 1974). My thanks to R. Howard Bloch for pointing this out to me.

92. Emerson, *Essays and Lectures*, 307.

93. Friedrich Nietzsche, *Ecce Homo*, "La Gaya Scienza," in *The Anti-Christ, Ecce Homo, Twilght of the Idols, and Other Writings*, ed. Aaron Ridley and Judith Norman (Cambridge:

Cambridge University Press, 2005). In *Beyond Good and Evil* Nietzsche writes that the concept of romantic love is "known to have been invented in the knightly poetry of Provence, by those magnificent, inventive men of the *gai saber*." Friedrich Nietzsche, *Beyond Good and Evil*, ed. Rolf-Peter Horstmann and Judith Norman; trans. Judith Norman (Cambridge: Cambridge University Press, 2002), sec. 260.

94. Richard Poirier, *Poetry and Pragmatism* (Cambridge, Mass.: Harvard University Press, 1992), 156.

95. In drawing attention to Emerson's compatibilism, I am inheriting a central idea in Emerson scholarship, most canonically Stephen Whicher's indispensible *Freedom and Fate: An Inner Life of Ralph Waldo Emerson* (Philadelphia: University of Pennsylvania Press, 1953). Where Whicher sees the tension between freedom and fate as stemming from the way Emerson's life was split into "two distinct personalities, the believer who sees through to the mystical perfections of things, and the detached observer, Mr. Emerson of Concord, who gives their due to the facts." (Whicher, *Freedom and Fate*, 32), I treat Emerson as holding the view that persons are always both free and determined. It is not unlikely that Emerson's ideas about the "determinist" side of his compatibilism were helped along by his enthusiastic reading of Pierre-Simon Laplace, whose *Philosophical Essays on Probabilities* he read in the early 1830s. For Laplace, the importance of probability stemmed from our ignorance of the total situation of matter at any given instant. As he famously put it: "We may regard the present state of the universe as the effect of its past and the cause of its future. An intellect which at a certain moment would know all forces that set nature in motion, and all positions of all items of which nature is composed, if this intellect were also vast enough to submit these data to analysis, it would embrace in a single formula the movements of the greatest bodies of the universe and those of the tiniest atom; for such an intellect nothing would be uncertain and the future just like the past would be present before its eyes." Laplace, *Philosophic Essay on Probability*, 1814; quoted in David J. Chalmers, *Constructing the World* (Oxford: Oxford University Press, 2012), xiii. Laura Dassow Walls links Emerson's interest in Laplace to his claim that Plato's "celestial geometry had anticipated the astronomy of Laplace, such that for Emerson, "many needles were needed to detect true north." Walls, *Emerson's Life in Science*, 188.

96. Friedrich Nietzsche, *The Gay Science*, ed. Bernard Williams; trans. Josefine Nauckhoff (Cambridge: Cambridge University Press, 2001), 253.

97. Ibid., 335.

98. Friedrich Nietzsche, *The Anti-Christ, Ecce Homo, Twilight of the Idols and Other Writings*, ed. Aaron Ridley and Judith Norman (Cambridge: Cambridge University Press, 2005), sec. 11.

99. Kaufmann, Walter, "Introduction," *The Gay Science*, 4.

100. Friedrich Nietzsche, *Ecce Homo*, trans. Walter Kaufmann (New York: Vintage, 1967), 293.

101. George Kateb, *Emerson and Self-Reliance* (New York: Rowman and Littlefield, 2002), 8–9. For an account of Nietzsche's view that one should turn one's life into a "literary unity," as "inherently unstable," "potentially incoherent," and, at the very least, "wildly implausible"—since it would involve arranging into a stylized whole every deed undertaken in the course of one's life—see Robert Pippin, *Nietzsche, Psychology, and First Philosophy* (Chicago: University of Chicago Press, 2010), 109–11.

102. Nietzsche, *The Gay Science*, sec. 109. It is important to stress that Nietzsche's naturalism is *not* a mechanistically reductive one (i.e., that our claiming and acting as persons can be explained by appeal to neuro-physiological states). For a good description of why Nietzsche is not a naturalist in this mechanically reductive sense, see Pippin, *Nietzsche, Psychology, and First Philosophy*, 73–74.

103. Nietzsche, *Beyond Good and Evil*, 110–11.

104. On Nietzsche's idea of a determined freedom, see Brian Leiter, "Who Is the Sovereign Individual? Nietzsche on Freedom," in *Cambridge Critical Guide to Nietzsche's* On the Genealogy of Morality (Cambridge: Cambridge University Press, 2011).

105. Emerson, "Prospects," *The Complete Works of Ralph Waldo Emerson*, centenary edition (Boston: Houghton, Mifflin and Company, 1903–94), 7:37.

106. In Kant's *Groundwork*, this is imagined as our ability to act "spontaneously," outside causal determinations, such that we are free insofar as we act in accordance with the categorical imperative. In this way Kant can be thought of as an "incompatibilist." For a compelling account of how compatibilism's "fatalistic implications" need not preclude the idea that "agents may be held legitimately [morally] responsible in circumstances where they are subject to fate," and such that "the truth of determinism is compatible with the conditions of responsibility," see Paul Russel, "Compatibilist-Fatalism: Finitude, Pessimism and the Limits of Free Will," in *The Philosophy of Free Will: Essential Readings from the Contemporary Debates*, ed. Paul Russell and Oisin Deery (New York: Oxford University Press, 2013).

107. Emerson, "Experience," in *Essays and Lectures*, 473. Nietzsche continued to make specific references to his "exemplar" in the book just after *The Gay Science*, whose opening lines are as follows: "We are unknown to ourselves, we knowers: and with good reason. We have never looked for ourselves—so how are we supposed to *find* ourselves? How right is the saying: 'Where your treasure is, there will your heart be also' *our* treasure is where the hives of our knowledge are. As born winged-insects and intellectual honey-gatherers we are constantly making for them, concerned at heart with only one thing—to bring something home. As far as the rest in concerned, the so-called 'experiences'—who of us ever has enough seriousness for them?" Nietzsche, *Genealogy of Morality*, ed. Keith Ansell-Pearson (Cambridge: Cambridge University Press, 2006 [1887]), 3. This is a good example of what Cavell called Nietzsche's direct "transfiguration" of Emerson's prose.

108. On Emerson's icy treatment of the loss of his five-year-old son Waldo as part of an "impersonal" style which enacts imperviousness to grief as a logic of "dissociation," see Sharon Cameron, "The Way of Life by Abandonment: Emerson's Impersonal," in *Impersonality* (Chicago: University of Chicago Press, 2007).

109. Kateb, *Emerson and Self-Reliance*, 39.

110. Richard Poirier says of this "superfluity" that it is part of Emerson's effort to "refloat the world, to make it less stationary and more transitional," *Poetry and Pragmatism*, 41–43.

111. Emerson, *Essays and Lectures*, 473. Referring to a youthful essay of Nietzsche's "Fate and History" Jennifer Ratner-Rosenhagen says Nietzsche too "wondered what role temperament plays in the individual's freedom to apprehend the world." Jennifer Ratner-Rosenhagen, *American Nietzshce* (Chicago: University of Chicago Press, 2011), 12. See also Nietzsche, "Fate and History," in *The Nietzsche Reader*, ed. Keith Ansell Pearson (London: Wiley, 2006). For an excellent discussion of how Emerson experiments with the word "mood," altering its meaning in relation to "grammatical" moods, see Branka Arsić, *On Leaving* (Cambridge: Harvard University Press, 2009), 135–43, 296–303. For the claim that Emerson's use of the word "temperament" in "Experience" is systematically undercut in his other essays, such that he does not mean that it is the "iron wire" on which our variable moods are strung (but instead thinks temperament is as susceptible to "discontinuities in personal identity" as mood), see Arsić, *On Leaving*, 138–39.

112. Emerson, *Essays and Lectures*, 474–75.

113. Ibid., 474.

114. Ibid., 496–99.

115. An exception to all this is, of course, slavery. In his "Address to the Citizens of Concord on

the Fugitive Slave Law" (1851) Emerson characterizes his own relation to the "ignominy" of this law by saying that it "robs the landscape of its beauty, and takes the sunshine out of every hour"; and "as long as men have bowels, they will disobey" it (*Selected Lectures*, 170–76). Emerson's disgust at slavery in general stemmed from the way it mangled the relation of temperament to character; the way it amounted to a systematic negation of self-reliance. If, for Emerson, all persons are potentially self-reliant (all persons are bound to a deeper cause through temperament and capable of affirming that bond in manifestations of character) then in legally defining some persons as *non*-persons, institutions like slavery run monstrously against nature. George Kateb says about the relation of mental self-reliance to slavery that for Emerson "perhaps a society has no self-reliance anywhere in it if there are slaves anywhere in it." Kateb, *Emerson and Self-Reliance*, 178.

116. Emerson, *Essays and Lectures*, 480.

117. Ibid., 482.

118. Ibid., 484. Emerson also says in this essay that "life itself is a bubble and a skepticism, and a sleep within a sleep" (*Essays and Lectures*, 481), and indeed, "skepticism" is one of the essay's central concerns. While I discussed some differences between skepticism and naturalism in the introduction, this distinction is differently relevant to Emerson's influence on Nietzsche, and to the way both were admirers of Montaigne. As Jessica Berry points out, Nietzsche's philosophy is a "naturalism [in which] human beings are to be understood as continuous with the rest of nature." Jessica Berry, "The Pyrrhonian Revival in Montaigne and Nietzsche," *Journal of the History of Ideas* 65, no. 3 (July 2004): 500. Praising Montaigne in *Untimely Meditations*, Nietzsche used the same terms he reserved for Emerson: "That such a man wrote has truly augmented the joy of living on this earth [for Montaigne possesses] a cheerfulness that really cheers." Friedrich Nietzsche, *Untimely Meditations*, ed. Daniel Breazeale (Cambridge: Cambridge University Press, 1997), 135. And in Emerson's own praise for Montaigne, he seems to literalize the method of nature as the making of prose: "The sincerity and marrow of the man reaches into his sentences...cut these words and they would bleed; they are vascular and alive" (*Essays and Lectures*, 243). For an excellent discussion of Montaigne's and Hume's different versions of skepticism, and their very different roles in Emerson's thought, see Joseph Urbas, "'The Other' and 'the Otherest': The Hidden Figure in Emerson's 'Montaigne; or, the Skeptic,'" *Cahiers Charles V* (special Emerson issue: *Emerson dans ses textes: Rhétorique et Philosophie*), Université de Paris VII—Denis Diderot (2005): 247–86.

119. George Kateb notes that in his characterizations of joyous science Emerson "may theorize harmonization...but [he] does not practice it." Kateb, *Emerson and Self-Reliance*, 9. By this Kateb means that Emerson does not wish to reduce to a tidy unity "all sides of an unstoppable struggle"; a claim with which I agree. When I say joyous science is a matter of searching out a harmony between the "deeper cause journeying always with us" (temperament) and the freedom of a method of expression (composition), I don't mean that this amounts to a bringing of myriad particulars under a unity, but the way Emerson thinks of the relation of freedom to necessity as an affirmation of "all sides of an unstoppable struggle."

120. Cavell, *Emerson's Transcendental Etudes*, 124.

121. Emerson, *Essays and Lectures*, 492.

122. Emerson, *Essays and Lectures*, 943. Steven Meyer links Emerson's "irresistible dictation" to Gertrude Stein's concern in "Composition as Explanation," that the "person" be explained by the "act of composition, and not the other way around." Steven Meyer, *Irresistible Dictation: Gertrude Stein and the Correlations of Writing and Science* (Stanford: Stanford University Press, 2003), 122. On the idea of "taking steps" in Emerson's thought, see also Stanley Cavell, "Finding as Founding: Taking Steps in Emerson's 'Experience,'" in *Emerson's Transcendental Etudes*, 110–40.

123. Emerson, *Essays and Lectures*, 943.

124. Ibid., 306–7, 967–68. Elsewhere in "Spiritual Laws" Emerson returns to this idea in relation to the tension between deeds and natural compulsion.

125. Emerson, *Essays and Lectures*, 967–68.

126. Meyer, *Irresistible Dictation*, 123.

127. Nietzsche, *The Gay Science*, sec. 276.

CHAPTER 2

1. Edgar Allan Poe, *Essays and Reviews* (New York: Library of America, 1984 [1836]), 1253. When he wrote the essay on the chess player, Poe had just become the assistant editor of the *Southern Literary Messenger*. F. O. Mattheissen says that Poe "wrote [all of the *Messenger's*] reviews, an immense number, on the average of nine or ten a month, and generally of essay length," and adds that until the publication of "The Raven" Poe's reputation was based "almost entirely as a magazine critic." F. O. Mattheissen, "Poe," *The Sewanee Review* 54, no. 2 (1946): 175–205. Claude Richard calls Poe "l'inventeur du journalisme à sensation" (Claude Richard, *Edgar Allan Poe: Journaliste et critique* [Paris: C. Klinksieck, 1978], ix), of which "Maelzel's Chess-Player" would certainly be an example. Throughout this chapter, I have relied upon Richard's scrupulous month-by-month chronology of Poe's magazine publications. See also Michael Allan, *Poe and the British Magazine Tradition* (Oxford: Oxford University Press, 1969).

2. Maelzel purchased the chess automaton from the German inventor Baron Wolfgang von Kempelen. After being sold to Maelzel, the chess player made a series of appearances along the eastern seaboard of the United States in the 1820s and 1830s, where it caused a sensation. For a history of the machine, see Charles Michael Carroll, *The Great Chess Automaton* (New York: Dover, 1975); and Tom Standage, *The Turk: The Life and Times of the Famous Eighteenth-Century Chess Playing Machine* (New York: Walker, 2002). For a detailed account of the chess machine's appearance in Richmond, see W. K.Wimsatt, "Poe and the Chess Automaton," *American Literature* 11 (1939): 144–46.

3. Hervey Allen writes that "Maelzel's Chess-Player" was the first of Poe's works to feature the "unerring abstract reasoner [and so] foreshadowed the method he followed later in his detective stories such as the murders in the Rue Morgue." Hervey Allen, *Israfel: The Life and Times of Edgar Allan Poe* (New York: Rinehart, 1949), 323–24. More recently, John Irwin writes: "Critics frequently point to Poe's analysis [of Maelzel's chess player] as a prefiguration of the analytic method of the Dupin stories and a trial run for Dupin's 'voice.'" John Irwin, *The Mystery to a Solution* (Baltimore: Johns Hopkins University Press, 1994), 104. In his history of the chess-playing automaton, Tom Standage writes: "Poe's explanation [of how the chess machine works] has the structure of a short detective story of the sort that he was later to become famous for writing. After a brief prologue, the mystery is introduced, and the evidence, replete with numerous red herrings, is laid out. Once all other investigators have professed themselves baffled, the detective makes a number of observations whose significance is not immediately apparent. He then appears to leap directly to the solution; only at the end of the story does he explain how several steps of reasoning, confirmed by his observations, enabled him to solve the mystery." Standage, *The Turk*, 181.

4. The most obvious and immediate inheritor is of course Arthur Conan Doyle, whose first published Sherlock Holmes mystery, *A Study in Scarlet*, has Watson saying to Holmes: "You remind me [of] Edgar Allan Poe's Dupin—I had no idea such individuals existed outside of stories." Arthur Conan Doyle, *The New Anthology of Sherlock Holmes*, vol. 3, ed. Leslie S. Klinger (New York: Norton, 2006), 42. In the opening paragraph of his analytic detective story "Death and the Compass" ["La muerte la brújula"], Jorge Luis Borges

says his detective, Erik Lönnrot, "believed himself a pure reasoner, an August Dupin." Borges, "Death and the Compass," in *Labyrinths: Selected Stories and Other Writings*, ed. Donald A. Yates and James E. Irby (New York: New Directions, 1962 [1944]). Doyle's version of the "locked room" mystery, "The Adventure of the Speckled Band," set off its own series of imitators, the most extravagant of which are Jacques Futrelle's 1906 story "The Problem of Cell 13," in *The Thinking Machine* (New York: The Modern Library, 2003); and Gaston Leroux's 1907 novel *Le Mystère de la chambre jaune* (Paris: Le Livre de Poche, 1960). For a taxonomy of locked-room tales, see John Dickson Carr's "The Locked Room Lecture," in *Art of the Mystery Story*, ed. Howard Haycraft (New York: Simon and Schuster, 1946), 278. On the soundness of the claim that Poe invented sui generis the detective story, see Howard Haycraft, *Murder for Pleasure: Life and Times of the Detective Story* (London: Appleton-Century, 1941); and Nancy Harrowitz, "The Body of the Detective Model," in *The Sign of Three*, ed. Umberto Eco and Thomas Sebeok (Bloomington: Indiana University Press, 1983). Poe himself downplayed the importance of his tales of ratiocination writing in an 1846 letter to Philip Pendelton Cooke: "I do not mean to say that they are not ingenious—but people think they are more ingenious than they are—on account of their method and *air* of method. Where is the ingenuity of unravelling a web that you yourself have woven for the express purpose of unraveling?" *Collected Works of Edgar Allan Poe: Tales and Sketches 1831–1842*, ed. Thomas Ollive Mabbott (Cambridge, Mass.: Harvard University Press, 1978), 521. Henri Justin has recently written that with "The Murders in the Rue Morgue," "The Purloined Letter," and "The Mystery of Marie Roget" Poe "avait inauguré un nouveau genre: la mécanique [of] le récit policier à énigme se mettait en place" Henri Justin, "Les Racines du mal," *Le Magazine Littéraire: Hors-série* no. 17 (July/August, 2009): 18. Justin also rightly points out that there is "protopolicière" in Poe's writing before "The Murders in the Rue Morgue," in tales like "The Tell-Tale Heart" and "Berenice." See Justin's excellent *Avec Poe jusqu'au bout de la prose* (Paris: Editions Gallimard, 2009), 96–98, 193–205.

5. Charles Peirce, "Pragmatism and the Logic of Abduction," in *The Essential Peirce*, ed. Nathan Houser and Christian Kloesel, vol. 2 (Bloomington: Indiana University Press, 1998), 227; "Illustrations of the Logic of Science: Deduction, Induction, and Hypothesis" in *The Essential Peirce*, vol.1, ed. Nathan Houser and Christian Kloesel (Bloomington: Indiana University Press, 1992), 189. Peirce divides all inference up into analytic and synthetic, placing deduction in the former category and induction and hypothesis (abduction) in the latter. On Peirce's notion of abductive inference, and its distinctness from induction, Cheryl Misak writes "the role played by induction is to test hypotheses. The job of abductive inference is to provide hypotheses for testing." Cheryl Misak, "Charles Sanders Peirce, 1839–1914," in *The Cambridge Companion to Peirce*, ed. Cheryl Misak (New York: Cambridge University Press, 2004), 18. Douglas R. Anderson notes that abduction is the "hypothesizing what an abstract concept and its object [or 'some very curious circumstance'] *might* mean... and testing inductively to see if these consequences are borne out in experience." Douglas Anderson, "Peirce and Pragmatism," in *The Oxford Handbook of American Philosophy*, ed. Cheryl Misak (New York: Oxford University Press, 2008), 47 (my emphasis). Commenting on Peirce's claim that abductive inferences "shade into perceptual judgment," Anderson notes that abductive inference is "where logic discovers the first stage of inference," such that it is "often difficult to distinguish a perceptual judgment from an abductive infer-ence." Douglas Anderson, "Another Radical Empiricism: Peirce 1903," in *Conversations on Peirce: Reals and Ideals*, ed. Douglas R. Anderson and Carl R. Hausman (New York: Fordham, 2012), 103.

6. John Haugeland, *Artificial Intelligence: The Very Idea* (Cambridge, Mass.: MIT Press, 1989), 87. In his book-length polemic against the artificial intelligence (AI) research program

Hubert Dreyfus links his claims that a machine could never simulate human immersion in a form of life to "what Peirce called abduction." Hubert Dreyfus, *What Computers Still Can't Do* (Cambridge, Mass.: MIT Press, 1992), 21. For Dreyfus, "abduction" is crucial to our ability to sort essential from inessential information as starting points for inference; something a computer would have to have fed into it as contextless instructions. The field of AI is usually thought to begin with Alan Turing's idea for a "Universal Machine" (or Turing machine), and his indistinguishability test for intelligence; what is sometimes called the "imitation game," or Turing test. For Turing, if a machine cannot be distinguished from a human being when participating in a conversation (using a tele-printer to record and communicate questions and answers), it can be said to be "intelligent." See Turing, "Computing Machinery and Intelligence," in *The Philosophy of Artificial Intelligence*, ed. Margaret Boden (Oxford: Oxford University Press, 1984). The test's reliance on observable verbal behavior as a criterion for intelligence has more recently been seen as begging the question about what "intelligence" is: should it be understood as the ability to carry out what John Searle calls "computational operations on formally specified elements," or just everyday skillful coping in the world? AI research premised on the former is sometimes called "strong" AI. In a recent lecture, Robert Brandom describes the strong AI thesis as the slogan: "mind is to brain as software it to hardware [so that if] computing is manipulating symbols according to definite rules...then reasoning *is* manipulating symbols according to definite rules." Robert Brandom, "Artificial Intelligence and Analytic Pragmatism," in *Between Saying and Doing* (Oxford: Oxford University Press, 2008), 72. In contrast to strong AI functionalism, Brandom elaborates his own pragmatically mediated version of AI (though he does not acknowledge Peirce's writings on abduction or logic machines). For critiques of strong AI, see Dreyfus, *What Computers Still Can't Do*; and John Searle, "Minds, Brains and Programs," in *The Philosophy of Artificial Intelligence*. For defenses of the strong AI thesis, see John Haugeland, *Artificial Intelligence: The Very Idea* (Cambridge, Mass.: MIT Press, 1989); and Daniel Dennett, *Brainchildren: Essays in Designing Minds* (Cambridge, Mass.: MIT Press, 1998). For more on Turing's own skepticism about the possibility of there being genuine machine intelligence, see note 30 below.

7. Shawn Rosenheim, *The Cryptographic Imagination: Secret Writing from Edgar Allan Poe to the Internet* (Baltimore: Johns Hopkins University Press, 1997), 100–101.

8. Charles Peirce, "A Neglected Argument for the Existence of God," in *The Essential Peirce*, 2:437. What Peirce calls in this essay the "Play of Musement" is linked in important ways to abduction, which he says comes to one in a "flash." See "Pragmatism and the Logic of Abduction," in *The Essential Peirce*, 2:226.

9. Poe, "Maelzel's Chess-Player," in *Essays and Reviews*, 1253.

10. Charles Babbage was a British mathematician and the inventor of the first programmable calculating machine. For more on Babbage's place in the history of the computer, see Doron Swade, *Difference Engine: Charles Babbage and the Quest to Build the First Computer* (New York: Viking, 2001); Martin Davis, *The Universal Computer: The Road from Leibniz to Turing* (New York: Norton, 2000); Herman Goldstine, *The Computer from Pascal to von Neumann* (Princeton: Princeton University Press, 1972); David Leavitt, *The Man Who Knew Too Much: Alan Turing and the Invention of the Computer* (New York: W. W. Norton, 2006); and James Gleick, *The Information: A History, A Theory, A Flood* (New York: Random House, 2011).

11. Poe, *Essays and Reviews*, 1256. Denis Marion (pseudonym of Marcel Defosse) nicely summarizes Poe's discussion of mechanism, determinism, and chess. For Poe, "il est impossible qu'une machine joue aux échecs, alors qu'elle peut fort bien marcher, parler, calculer, trier, tous ses mouvements étant rigoureusement determines à l'avance. Aucune prevision, aucune loi generale, ne peut choisir le coup qui constitue la meilleure—ou meme une bonne—riposte à un coup quelconque au cours d'une partie d'échecs. L'éfficacité d'une

stratégie qu'on supposerait mécaniquement determinée sera continuellement mise en question par les coups de l'adversaire que l'automate ne peut ni prévoir, ni meme enregistrer (du moins sous la forme qu'il avait en 1835)." Denis Marion, *La methode intellectuelle d'Edgar Poe* (Paris: Les Editions de Minuit, 1952), 70–71.

12. Much of Poe's knowledge of the history and workings of the chess automaton is taken, at times verbatim, from reprint pamphlet copies of David Brewster's *Letters on Natural Magic*. For a detailed publication history of how Brewster's writings about the chess machine reached North American periodicals, see W. K. Wimsatt, "Poe and the Chess Automaton," *American Literature* 11 (March 1939–January 1940): 138–51. For a view that does not treat Poe as having simply cribbed the material, but rather extracted and embellished it to suit his argument in "Maelzel's Chess-Player," see Régis Messac, *Le Detective Novel et l'influence de la pensée scientifique* (Geneva: Slatkin Reprints, 1975). For more on Poe and the antebellum milieu of reprinting, see Meredith McGill, *American Literature and the Culture of Reprinting: 1834–1853* (University Park, University of Pennsylvania Press, 2003).

13. The difference between genuine machine intelligence and what *appears* to be machine intelligence animates more recent discussions. Describing the match in 1996 between IBM's Deep Blue computer and Russian grandmaster and world chess champion Gary Kasparov, John Searle writes: "When it was first announced that Deep Blue had beaten Gary Kasparov...I suspect that the attitude of the general public was that what was going on inside Deep Blue was much the same sort of thing as what was going on inside Kasparov [but] none of this whatever happened inside Deep Blue." In contrast with the description of what Kasparov was doing when he was playing chess, this is how Searle describes what the IMB is doing: "Imagine that a man who does not know how to play chess is locked inside a room, and there he is given a set of, to him, meaningless symbols. Unknown to him, these represent positions on a chessboard. He looks up in a book what he is supposed to do, and he passes back more meaningless symbols. We can suppose that if the rule book, i.e., the program, is skillfully written, he will win chess games. People outside the room will say, 'This man understands chess, and in fact he is a good chess player because he wins.' They will be totally mistaken. The man understands nothing of chess, he is just a computer. The point of the parable is this: if the man does not understand chess on the basis of running the chess-playing program, neither does any other computer solely on that basis." John Searle, "I Married a Computer," *New York Review of Books*, April 8, 1999; and John Searle, "Minds, Brains and Programs." For more on Kasparov's later matches against computers, see David Shenk, *The Immortal Game: A History of Chess* (New York: Doubleday, 2006), 199–221. See also the memoire by Deep Blue system architect and chip designer Feng-hsiung Hsu, *Behind Deep Blue: Building the Computer That Defeated the World Chess Champion* (Princeton: Princeton University Press, 2002).

14. James Berkley calls this Poe's "taking up and usurping the sublime theatricality that had previously belonged to [the exhibition of] Maelzel's Chess Player." James Berkley, "Post-human Mimesis and the Debunked Machine," *Comparative Literature Studies* 41, no. 3 (2004): 369.

15. Charles Peirce, "Logical Machines," *American Journal of Psychology* 1 (1887): 165–67. Peirce was himself familiar with Babbage's work and wrote Babbage's obituary for the *Nation* in 1871. In it he acknowledged the important distinction between Babbage's "Difference Engine #1" and his later plans for an "analytical" engine. The former was initially designed to make the computation of logarithmic tables more efficient. Babbage imagined doing this by reducing all calculation to relations of simple addition (what he called the "calculus of finite differences": hence his calling the machine a "difference engine"), then implementing those relations in cogwheels of his own design. But with the analytic engine, inspired by Babbage's discussions with Lord Byron's daughter Ada

Lovelace and his interest in Joseph-Marie Jacquard's punch-card operated loom, the cogs and wheels stand not just for numbers but for functions and variables, allowing for more complex kinds of computation. On the distinction between the difference engine and the analytical engine, see Charles Babbage, *Passages from the Life of a Philosopher*, chaps. 5 and 8, in *Charles Babbage and His Calculating Engines*, ed. Philip Morrison and Emily Morrison (New York: Dover, 1961); Doron Swade, *The Immortal Game*, 9–87, 155–71; and James Gleick, *The Information* (New York: Knopf Doubleday, 2011), 88–108. For a compelling fictional imagining of a Victorian London in which Babbage's inventions set off a steam-powered information age, see William Gibson and Bruce Sterling, *The Difference Engine* (New York: Bantam Books, 1991).

16. Peter Skagestad, "Peirce's Semeiotic Model of the Mind," in *The Cambridge Companion to Peirce*, 254–55.

17. Peirce, "Logical Machines," 169. It is telling that both Poe and Peirce use the word "ratiocination" repeatedly to describe, respectively, the class of tales featuring a character who will dramatize the process of reasoning, and the theory of the process of reasoning. Nancy Harrowitz says that Poe "relied heavily on [the word 'ratiocination'] to place emphasis on the 'how' of reasoning." Nancy Harrowitz, "The Body of the Detective Model," in *The Sign of Three*, 185. The word "ratiocination" entered the French language in 1495, from the Latin *ratiocination*; it was, in 1836 or 1896, a rare word in English (see Le Robert's *Dictionnaire Historique de la langue francais*, 3098).

18. In his *Prior Analytics*, Aristotle defines a "syllogism" as "a discourse in which, certain things being stated, something other than what is stated follows of necessity from their being so." Richard McKeon, *The Basic Works of Aristotle* (New York: Random, 1941), 66.

19. Allan Marquand, "A New Logical Machine," in *Proceedings of the American Academy of Arts of Sciences* 21 (1886): 303–7.

20. Stanley Jevons, "On the Mechanical Performance of Logical Inference," in *Philosophical Transactrions of the Royal Society of London,* vol. 160, pt. 2 (London: Taylor and Francis, 1870. For an account of the Peirce/Marquand relationship, see Kenneth Laine Ketner "The Early History of Computer Design: Charles Sanders Peirce and Marquand's Logical Machines," *The Princeton University Library Chronicle* 45 (1984): 187–211. Ketner conjectures that Peirce provided Marquand with a circuit diagram, explaining in a letter how a logical machine might be electrically powered, and so laying the theoretical groundwork for an electronic computing machine. This would make Peirce the inventor of a "general-purpose, truth-functional, logical computer." Ketner, "The Early History of Computer Design," 204. For further evidence that Peirce designed such a circuit for Marquand, see James Mark Baldwin, *Dictionary of Philosophy and Psychology* (New York: Macmillan, 1902), 2:28–30. For a dissenting view, see Alice Burks and Arthur Burks, *The First Electronic Computer: The Atanasoff Story* (Ann Arbor: University of Michigan Press, 1989), in which the authors acknowledge the importance of Peirce in the history of computing, but dispute the claim that Peirce drew the circuit diagram in the letter to Marquand.

21. Charles Peirce, "Logical Machine," in *The Century Dictionary and Cyclopedia*, ed. William D. Whitney (New York: The Century Company, 1889).

22. Claudine Tiercelin notes that, while Peirce was interested in the practical uses to which machines such as Babbage's might be put, his interest in the essay on "Logical Machines" is more theoretical: "It is rather remarkable that [in the essay "Logical Machines"] what mostly captures Peirce's attention is not—as can be seen by looking over his commentaries on Jevons, Marquand and Babbage—the practical importance of these sorts of machines...but their *philosophical* implications. Studying such machines is useful, Peirce writes, because their study 'cannot fail to throw needed light on the reasoning process' [Peirce, 'Logical Machines,' 187] [that is] the importance of this sort of study rests on the

way it sheds light, not on processes of *thought,* but on processes of *reasoning.*" Claudine Tiercelin, *La pensée-signe: Études sur C.S. Peirce* (Nîmes: Éditions Jacqueline Chambon, 1993), 224 (my translation).

23. Ketner, "The Early History of Computer Design," 208.
24. Charles Peirce, Letter to J. M. Hantz, "Manuscript Letter to J.M. Hantz," Northwestern Univeristy, Watertown Wisconsin, March 29, 1987 [1887].
25. Kenneth Ketner, "Peirce and Turing; Comparisons and Conjectures, *Semiotica* 68 (1988): 44.
26. Charles Peirce, "Our Senses Are Reasoning Machines," unpublished ms., 1900.
27. Ketner, "Peirce and Turing," 46.
28. Ibid., 49. Peirce's switch from formal logic to his logic of relations is linked to the development of his diagrammatic logic and existential graphs. Since I am focusing on how the work on logical machines informs the development of his idea of the "abductive" inference, I do not here go into detail on how this relates to Peirce's graph theory. For a thorough account of this aspect of Peirce's thought, see Ketner, "Peirce and Turing," and especially Don Roberts, *The Existential Graphs of Charles S. Peirce* (The Hague: Mouton & Co., 1973). For excellent discussions of how George Boole's logical algebra was fundamental for Peirce's logic of relations, see Hilary Putnam, "Peirce the Logician," in *Realism with a Human Face,* ed. James Conant (Cambridge, Mass.: Harvard University Press, 1990); and I. Grattan-Guinness, *The Search for Mathematical Roots 1870–1940* (Princeton: Princeton University Press, 2000), 140–54.
29. Ketner, "Peirce and Turing," 53. Turing sounds remarkably like Peirce when he says: "What we want is a machine that can learn from experience...the possibility of letting the machine alter its own instructions." Alan Turing, Public lecture in London 1947, available at www.alanturing.net. Ketner, "Peirce and Turing," 50. Ketner argues that nondeterministic Peirce machines are genuine prototypes of Alan Turing's "universal" machines, described in his 1936 paper "On Computable Numbers with an Application to the Entscheidungsproblem." *Proceedings of the London Mathematical Society,* 2d series, 42 (1936). Inspired by David Hilbert's work on the Entscheidungsproblem, or "decision problem," Turing began to think about what in principle a machine would need to be able to do in order to carry out programlike instructions. For more on how Turing's idea for a Universal machine grew out of his engagement with Hilbert's decision problem, see Jack Copeland, "Computable Numbers: A Guide," in *The Essential Turing: The Ideas That Gave Birth to the Computer Age* (Oxford: Oxford University Press, 2004), 5–54; Andrew Hodges, *Turing: The Enigma* (Princeton: Princeton University Press, 2012 [1987]), 90–4; James Gleick, *The Information: A History, A Theory, A Flood,* 204–14; George Dyson, *Turing's Cathedral: The Origins of the Digital Universe* (New York: Random House, 2012).
30. Peirce's claim that reasoning is not deterministic does not mean Peirce is "denying...that there could be nondeterministic machines." See Peter Skagestad, "Peirce's Semeiotic Model of the Mind," in *The Cambridge Companion to Peirce,* 255–56.
31. Peirce, "Pragmatism as the Logic of Abduction," in *Essential Peirce,* 2:227. For more on how Peirce's writing on logical machines informed his invention of the "abductive" inference, see Arthur Burks, "Peirce's Theory of Abduction," *Philosophy of Science* 13, no. 4 (October, 1946): 304–5.
32. For consideration of the apparent paradox in the idea that there could be a "logic" of discovery, see Arthur Burks, "Peirce's Theory of Abduction," 301. For outright skepticism about this idea, see Harry G. Frankfurt, "Peirce's Notion of Abduction," *Journal of Philosophy* 55, no. 14 (1958): 593–97.
33. According to Umberto Eco, what makes an abductive inference a genuinely "new" thought is its capacity for introducing, in addition to a new middle term, an entirely new rule: "[For Peirce] the real problem is not whether to find first the case or the rule, but rather how to figure out both the rule and the case *at the same time,* since they are inversely

related...where the middle term is the keystone of all inferential movement [in abduction] the law must be *invented ex novo.*" Eco, "Horns, Hooves, Insteps: Some Hypotheses on Three Types of Abduction," in *The Sign of Three,* 206–7. Nancy Harrowitz describes this as "the process [by which] a subject, in order to explain [some state of affairs], needs to *come up with* a law....Abduction is the instinctive perceptual jump which allows the subject to guess an origin." Harrowitz, "The Body of the Detective Model," in *The Sign of Three,* 193.

34. Poe, "The Murders in the Rue Morgue," Mabbott, 1:527–28.

35. Ibid., 1:527. This paragraph was part of the text that appeared in *Graham's Magazine* in April 1841, but omitted from the further printings of the tale in *Prose Romances* (1843) and *Tales* (1845).

36. Poe, "The Murders in the Rue Morgue," Mabbott, 1:533. John Irwin points out that Poe's West Point curriculum, based in part on that of the École Polytechnique, led him to fashion Dupin's opponent (and double), the Minister D. as both "poet and mathematician," in the third of the tales of ratiocination "The Purloined Letter." John Irwin, *The Mystery to a Solution,* 344–345; and Thomas O. Mabbott, 2:986 (the tale originally appeared in *The Gift* [annual] in 1844).

37. Poe, "The Murders in the Rue Morgue," Mabbott, 1:528. When Poe discusses, in the opening paragraph of "The Murders in the Rue Morgue," the "lively enjoyment" derived from disentangling enigmas, he might be describing his own interest in cryptography, put to use in his tale "The Gold Bug" and in the newspaper contests in which he invited readers to submit ciphers that he would then (almost always successfully) solve. Poe's interest in cryptography forms another parallel with Peirce; and according to Yvan Beaulieu, "cryptanalysis...is mainly an abductive process." Yvan Beaulieu, "Peirce's Contribution to American Cryptography," *Transactions of the Charles Peirce Society* 44, no. 2 (2008): 282. For more on Poe's skill as a cryptographer, see Terrance Whalen, "The Code for Gold: Poe and Cryptography," in *Edgar Allan Poe and the Masses* (Princeton: Princeton University Press, 1999). For a wide-ranging essay on Poe's role in the larger French-American intellectual history of cryptography, the development of binary code, and cybernetics, see Lydia H. Liu, "The Cybernetic Unconscious," *Critical Inquiry* 36 (winter, 2010).

38. Poe, "The Murders in the Rue Morgue," Mabbott, 1978, 1:528–29.

39. Ibid., 1:528.

40. Ibid., 1:529. Whist is something like contract bridge.

41. Ibid., 1:529–30.

42. Ibid., 1:548.

43. Ibid., 1:534.

44. Ibid.

45. Ibid., 1:536

46. Ibid.

47. Some of the hypothesized rules Dupin creates in order to make sense of the narrator's expressions are, as Burton Pollin puts it, "brilliant [but] faulty." Burton Pollin, "Poe's 'Murders in the Rue Morgue: An Ingenious Web Unravelled," *Studies in the American Renaissance* 1 (1997): 289. For an excellent schematic rendering of Dupin's chain of abductions, see Harrowitz, "The Body of the Detective Model," in *The Sign of Three,* 189–90.

48. Ibid., 189.

49. Ibid. Poe altered specifically this segment of Dupin's reasoning in later printings of the story after the initial appearance in *Graham's Magazine.* The April 1841 *Graham's Magazine* version and the 1843 version, included in *Prose Romances,* has "stereotomic," while in the 1845 version included in Wiley and Putnam's *Tales* Poe has changed "stereotomic" to "stereotomy" and has added: "very affectedly applied to this species of pavement." Pollin says Poe did this to remedy an "Associative step which too readily assumed the reader's

knowledge of the rare word 'stereotomy'...the science of shaping and cutting blocks of wood or stone for building material." Pollin, "Poe's 'Murders in the Rue Morgue,'" 239. Pollin further surmises that it was Poe's "Southern pronunciation of vowels may have been the cause" of his thinking that the word "stereotomy" formed a phonetic link "atomies." Pollin, "Poe's 'Murders in the Rue Morgue,'" 239.

50. Blakey Vermeule calls this the "double operation" in which Dupin "runs a chain of inferences," in an "exercise in pure rationality [arising from his] knowing what inferences his friend will form. Once he figures out the formula, all he needs to do is plug in the first association and the whole chain runs like an algorithm [that is] attached to the mental processes of somebody else." Blakey Vermeule, *Why Do We Care about Literary Characters?* (Baltimore: Johns Hopkins University Press, 2010), 87. My argument here is exactly the reverse. In making a series of inductive tests of abducted hypotheses, Dupin reasons in tandem with external perceptions, such that the rules for getting at the narrator's thought are custom fit to each discrete perception. Vermeule's language of "pure rationality" and of "algorithms" suggests the kind of necessary determinations both Poe and Peirce reject as constitutive of reasoning. At a later point in this chapter I discuss in detail how Poe creates the *effect* of having composed his poem "The Raven" in accordance with something like an algorithm, in his essay "The Philosophy of Composition."

51. Poe, "The Murders in the Rue Morgue," Mabbott, 1978, 1:537.

52. Mabbott tells us that Mademoiselle L'Espanaye "was found with the head downwards because Poe wanted to make it obvious that she did not herself attempt to escape by climbing into the chimney." Mabbott, 1978, 1:571n25.

53. Poe, "The Murders in the Rue Morgue," Mabbott, 1978, 1:538–39. Mabbott reminds us that "métal d'Alger" is an "inexpensive alloy of lead, tin, and antimony, used in place of silver." And a "napoleon" is a "twenty-franc gold piece." Mabbot, 1978, 1: 571n23.

54. Ibid., 1:538–44.

55. Ibid., 1:556.

56. Harrowitz, "The Body of the Detective Model," in *The Sign of Three*, 194.

57. Poe, "The Murders in the Rue Morgue," Mabbott, 1978, 1:556–57.

58. Ibid., 1:558.

59. Ibid., 1:559.

60. Shawn Rosenheim, "Detective Fiction, Psychoanalysis, and the Analytic Sublime," in *The American Face of Edgar Allan Poe* (Baltimore: Johns Hopkins University Press, 1998), 161.

61. Poe liked this word, and used it again in his mesmeric hoax "The Facts in the Case of M. Valdemar," in which the narrator says of the (briefly) undead Valdemar that his voice was "one of distinct—of even wonderfully, thrillingly distinct—syllabification." Edgar Allan Poe, "The Facts in the Case of M. Valdemar," in Mabbott, 1978, 2:1240. In some ways this tale takes the idea of "intelligible syllabification" further, as Valdemar's eerie utterances from beyond the grave—*I say to you that I am dead!*—arise as literally unarticulated syllables, since his "thrillingly distinct" speech issues from an inert tongue.

62. Rosenheim attempts to clarify the discussions of the Ourang-Outang and human language, appealing to James's Burnet's *The Origin and Progress of Language*, pointing out how for Burnet the "ourang-outang is actually a species of humankind" (Rosenheim, "Detective Fiction," 159). Rosenheim also makes explicit the affinities between Dupin and Cuvier, finding in Cuvier's "ability to reconstruct an animal's anatomy from fragmentary paleontological remains" an analogy with Dupin's ability to get from particulars to the general categories (from parts to wholes) (Rosenheim, "Detective Fiction," 160). Lawrence Frank also reads the logic of species against a capacity for intelligible speech, writing that in "destroying the women's organs of speech, the [ape] blindly denies their status as human beings." Lawrence Frank, "'The Murders in the Rue Morgue': Edgar Allan Poe's Evolutionary

Reverie," *Nineteenth Century Literature* 50, no. 2 (September 1995): 39. But this leaves open the question as to whether the distinction between a language-using creature and a non-language-using creature is a legitimate criterion for making the distinction between motivelessness and agency.

63. Poe, Headnote to "The Murders in the Rue Morgue," Mabbott, 1978, 1:521.

64. I take "The Murders in the Rue Morgue" to be an example of what Stanley Cavell describes, in his essay "A Matter of Meaning It," as an artwork that "find[s] the limits [or] essence of [his] own procedures" as the invention of a genre that imagines this discovery in its dénouement. Stanley Cavell, "A Matter of Meaning It," in *Must We Mean What We Say?*(Cambridge: Cambridge University Press, 2002), 219. In a later essay on Poe's tale "The Imp of the Perverse," Cavell speaks of the "idea of a criterion [as] a way of counting something as something." Stanley Cavell, "Being Odd, Getting Even," in *Emerson's Transcendental Etudes*, ed. David Justin Hodge (Stanford: Stanford University Press, 2003), 106. Again, I take it this discussion might be extended, without too much trouble, to the notion of what it means for a given piece of writing to "count" as an example of, say, "detective fiction," and hence Poe's literary experiment of inventing the rules by which his own tale becomes intelligible as an instance of a new generic category.

65. Edgar Allan Poe, "The Philosophy of Composition," in *Critical Theory: The Major Documents*, eds. Stuart Levine and Susan Levine (Chicago: Illinois University Press, 2009), 63.

66. Walter Benn Michaels writes in a recent essay that, "the fact that ["Nevermore"] is the sound the Raven makes (in the meter the Raven makes them in) rather than the words he utters has its own importance. The emergence of 'form' out of 'nevermore' [is] the form that gives the sound or the marks their meaning, that connects the same marks to two different things, or different marks to the same thing." Walter Benn Michaels, "The Death of a Beautiful Woman, available at http://www.cipa.ulg.ac.be/intervalles4/54_michaels.pdf. This is a version of the argument Michaels makes, with Steven Knapp, in his essay "Against Theory," in which a stanza of Wordsworth found washed up a beach, if produced by a non-intentional process like erosion, is not a poem at all, but merely *resembles* one. See "Against Theory," *Critical Inquiry* 8 (summer 1982): 723–42. The analogy here is with my claim that the raven's uttered sound "nevermore" merely resembles the spoken word "nevermore."

67. Edgar Allan Poe, "The Raven," in *Complete Poems*, ed. Thomas Ollive Mabbott (Urbana: University of Illinois Press, 1969), 365. Poe liked this figure—the narrator or central figure abnormally sensitive to sound—and variations on it can be found in his tales "Berenice," "Morella," "Ligeia," "The Fall of the House of Usher," "The Tell-Tale Heart," and "The Facts in the Case of M. Valdemar."

68. Ibid., 366.

69. Ibid.

70. In his strange treatise on prosody, "The Rationale of Verse" (1848), Poe, perhaps cribbing from Goold Brown's *The institutes of English grammar*, writes, "When a syllable is wanted, the verse is said to be *catalectic*; when the measure is exact, the line is *acatalectic*." Poe is concerned in this essay with questions like whether the sound *elais ea*—isolated from the sequence *in Rab | elais ea | sy chair*—is heard as either an anepest or an iamb such that the difference between triplicate and duple meter becomes an explicit concern with the relation of sound to meaning. Edgar Allan Poe, *Essays and Reviews*, ed. G. R. Thompson (New York: Library of America, 1848), 43.

71. My account of the poem's toggling between the merely phonetic and the genuinely intelligible is different from Richard Godden's account of what he calls the "anti-semantic." Richard Godden, "Poe and the Poetics of Opacity: Or, Another Way of Looking at That Blackbird," *English Literary History* 4 (winter, 2000): 994. For Godden, in order to think about what it would mean to "read" the anti-semantic, he says we should "consider the degree to which a particular linguistic opacity articulates or denies access to the

originating event against which it provides a preliminary psychic defense." Godden, "Poe and the Poetics of Opacity," 994. But if we are calling what is allegedly "anti-semantic" (whether through "articulation," "denial," "deformation," or "opacity") an "access to [an] originating event," then we are back to the semantic, since the "nonsemantic" opacity *means,* for Godden, its "originating event." In my own attention to the way the poem continually blurs the line between rational discourse and a meaningless sound, I am closer to Roman Jacobson's account of the poem's refrain as an "utterance [which] lacks both cognitive and emotive information." For Jacobson, the absence of "cognitive and emotive information" in the raven's utterance "nevermore" means the narrator's assigning of intent to it amounts to a form of "verbal hallucination." Roman Jacobson, "Language in Operation," in *Language in Literature,* ed. Krystyna Pomorska and Stephen Rudy (Cambridge, Mass.: Harvard University Press, 1987), 52–53. For an ingenious reading of the relation of sound to sense in Poe's tale "The Cask of Amontillado" and his poem "The Bells," see Tom Cohen, "Poe's *Foot D'Or*: Ruinous Rhyme and Nietzschean Recurrence (sound)" in *Anti-Mimesis From Plato to Hitchcock* (Cambridge: Cambridge University Press, 1994), 105–25.

72. Poe, "The Raven," in *Complete Poems,* 366.

73. Ibid., 365–66 (my emphasis).

74. Jakobson, "Language in Operation," 59. Jakobson goes further, saying that the word "never" should be heard (and read) as an anagrammatic inversion of "raven"; a lexical cell reiterated throughout the poem. Jakobson, "Language in Operation," 54.

75. Poe, "The Raven," in *Complete Poems,* 367.

76. Ibid., 368.

77. Poe, "The Philosophy of Composition," in *Critical Theory: The Major Documents,* 69.

78. Poe, "The Murders in the Rue Morgue," Mabbott, 1978, 1: 558.

79. Poe, "The Philosophy of Composition," in *Critical Theory: The Major Documents,* 60.

80. Ibid., 65, 69. Eliza Richards also notes that "The Philosophy of Composition" "rode the wave of ['The Raven's'] success." Eliza Richards, *Gender and the Poetics of Reception in Poe's Circle* (Cambridge: Cambridge University Press, 2004), 53.

81. Poe, "The Philosophy of Composition," in *Critical Theory: The Major Documents,* 61. After Charles Baudelaire made, between 1856 and 1861, translations into French of nearly all of Poe's published work, the theory of effects has had a lasting influence on French poetics and literary theory (indeed, the symbolist movement could be said to begin with Baudelaire's translations of Poe). Poe's literary theory was taken up with particular care and thoroughness in the work of Paul Valéry. In an 1889 article, "Sur la technique littéraire," Valéry wrote, "La littéraire est l'art de se jouer de l'âme des autres…un effet entièment calculé par l'artiste." Later in this essay Valéry speaks of "la Poétique si originale d'Edgar Poe," who Valéry describes, somewhat exaggeratedly, as a "mathématicien, philosophe et grand écrivain, dans son curious opuscule *La Genèse d'un poème*" (Baudelaire's translation of "The Philosophy of Composition"). In a later lecture at the Collège de France in 1937, Valéry discusses Poe's emphasis on "l'effet qui sera produit et de ses consequences pour le producteur." Paul Valéry, "Première Leçon du Cours Poétique," in *Œuvres,* ed. Jean Hytier (Paris: *NRF* Gallimard), 1960. For more on how Valéry developed an entire critical program from Poe's essays of literary theory, see Edmund Wilson, "Poe at Home and Abroad" in *The Shores of Light* (Boston: Northeastern University Press, 1985 [1952]), and *Axel's Castle* in *Literary Essays and Reviews of the 1920s and 30s* (New York: Library of America, 2007); T. S. Eliot, "From Poe to Valéry," in *To Criticize the Critic and Other Essays* (Lincoln: University of Nebraska Press, 1965); and Lois Davis Vines, *Valéry and Poe: A Literary Legacy* (New York: New York University Press, 1992).

82. Poe, "The Philosophy of Composition," in *Critical Theory: The Major Documents,* 64.

83. Ibid.

84. As Daniel Hoffman notes, Poe "compares the composing of a poem to the management of theatrical props and machinery." Daniel Hoffman, *Poe Poe Poe Poe Poe Poe Poe* (Baton Rouge: Louisianna State University Press, 1972), 81. John Tresch says that the "open-handed demonstration of the *modus operandi* of 'The Raven'...places Poe in a position directly analogous to that of the exhibitor of the chess-play[er] [and so] "The Philosophy of Composition" can thus be seen as Poe's attempt...by presenting himself explicitly as a poetry automaton." John Tresch, "The Potent Magic of Verisimilitude," *The British Journal for the History of Science* 30 (1997): 275–90.

85. Edgar Allan Poe, "Lenore," *The Pioneer*, February 1843. This was for Poe a career-long practice, often taking the form of inserting previously published poems in the text of newly published tales. To give just two examples: the fourth 1845 printing of "Ligeia" in the *New World* included a reprinting of the poem "The Conqueror Worm," which had previously appeared in *Graham's* in 1843; and "The Fall of the House of Usher," first published in *Burton's Gentleman's Magazine* in September 1839, included Roderick Usher's performance of the song "The Haunted Palace," the text of which first appeared as the poem of that title six months earlier, in the *American Museum of Science, Literature and the Arts*.

86. Haugeland, *Artificial Intelligence*, 65. "Algorithms" are named for the Arab mathematician al-Khwarizimi who made a number of major innovations in logic and mathematics in the eighth and ninth centuries. For more on the history and function of algorithms, see Philippe Breton, *Une histoire de l'informatique* (Paris: Seuil, 1990); David Berlinski, *The Advent of the Algorithm* (New York: Mariner Books, 2000).

87. Poe, "Maelzel's Chess-Player," in *Essays and Reviews*, 1257.

88. Poe, "The Philosophy of Composition," in *Critical Theory: The Major Documents*, 64.

89. Ibid., 62–68. On how an incremental series "lurks" behind the sensational effects of Poe's essay, Pierre Macherey writes: "As a merely technical secret ["The Raven"] is by no means what it appears; it lurks, deceptively, *behind* its real meaning. Through this confession, the author leads us back to that initial reality which is the source and truth of all its remote and ulterior manifestations." Pierre Macherey, *A Theory of Literary Production* (New York: Routledge, 2006), 22. The "technical secret" that is lurking behind "The Raven" is not, I would argue, the algorithm Poe offers in Maelzelian fashion as a sensational effect, but the series of magazine experiments he attempts to conceal through the *effect* of having composed the poem in accordance with a series of predetermined steps.

90. Another important affinity between pragmatism and Poe's emphasis of "effects" is what Peirce called, in an 1878 magazine article, the pragmatic "maxim": "Our idea of anything *is* our idea of its sensible effects; and if we fancy that we have any other we deceive ourselves, and mistake a mere sensation accompanying the thought for a part of the thought itself." Charles Peirce, "How to Make Our Ideas Clear," in *The Essential Peirce*, 1:132. It was this maxim that William James sought to generalize in his lecture "What Pragmatism Means," where he writes: "to attain perfect clearness in our thoughts of an object...we need only consider...what sensations we are to expect from it, and what reactions we must prepare. Our conceptions of these effects, whether immediate or remote, is then for us the whole of our conception of the object, so far as that conception has positive significance at all. This is the principle of Peirce, the principle of pragmatism." William James, "What Pragmatism Means," in *Pragmatism and Other Writings*, ed. Giles Gunn (New York: Penguin, 2000 [1907]), 25. For an account of how these central claims of classical pragmatism inform both Poe's writing and the emergence of probability theory, see Maurice S. Lee, "Probably Poe," *American Literature* 81, no. 2 (2009): 225–52.

CHAPTER 3

1. Edgar Allan Poe, *Essays and Reviews* (New York: Library of America, 1984), 1161–62.

2. Ibid.

3. Poe's distancing himself from Evert Duyckinck stemmed from his distaste for the cliquish-ness of what he called the "Mutual Admiration Society" of the Young America movement, and a reviewing style that required the "practice of puffing works into reputation." Sidney P. Moss, *Poe's Literary Battles* (Carbondale: Southern Illinois University Press, 1969), 46. Poe's professed distaste for such practices did not, however, prevent him from writing such reviews, and for many of the books released in Duyckinck's Library of American Books series. For a detailed chronicle of Duyckinck's relation to Poe as publisher, see Moss, *Poe's Literary Battles*, 42–62; Perry Miller, *The Raven and the Whale* (Baltimore: Johns Hopkins University Press, 1997), 135–53; Claude Richard, *Poe: Journaliste et Critique* (Paris: Librairie C. Klincksieck, 1979), 155–83; and Kevin Hayes, *Poe and the Printed Word* (Cambridge: Cambridge University Press, 2000), 45–57.

4. Evert Duyckinck to Nathaniel Hawthorne, March 13, 1846, Duyckinck Collection, Mss. Division, New York Public Library. As Edward Widmer points out in his book *Young America: The Flowering of Democracy in New York City*, "It is surprising in retrospect to see Duyckinck complaining about Melville's lack of philosophy, since that is precisely the aspect of his thought that most annoyed him in later works such as *Mardi* and *Moby-Dick*." Edward Widmer, *Young America: The Flowering of Democracy in New York City* (New York: Oxford University Press, 2000), 240.

5 William Spengeman indentifies the period's dominant literary critical categories as "formal coherence, verisimilitude, plausibility and stylistic naturalness." William Spengeman, "Introduction," in *Pierre; or, the Ambiguities* by Herman Melville (Boston: Northwestern University Press, 1971 [1852]), vii. Examples of the centrality, in 1846, of the evaluative criterion of "verisimilitude," can be found in unsigned reviews of *Typee*, which praise Melville's prose descriptions as "doubtless transcriptions of the facts" (*Graham's Magazine*, May 1846) and for "scenes of peculiar animation and vivacity [which are] without doubt faithfully sketched" (*United States Magazine and Democratic Review*, May 1846).

6. Cataloguing some typifying instances of *Mardi*'s critical reception Nina Baym writes that *Mardi* "promised to be a romance but was not one, because it pertained to no genre at all. It was described as wavering confusingly among pleasantry, allegory, romance, and prose poem." Nina Baym, "Melville's Quarrel With the Fiction," *PMLA* 94 (October, 1979): 913. Critical attacks on Melville's "mixed form" novel *Mardi* were enough send him back to the generic formula of the sea adventure, and he wrote *Redburn* (1849) and *White-Jacket* (1850) in just under a year, returning him to the favor of critics eager to praise the novels' "literal truthfulness," their "daguerreotype-like naturalness of description," and "evident truthfulness and accuracy of personal and individual delineation." Lewis Gaylord Clark, review of *White-Jacket*, in *Melville: The Critical Heritage*, ed. Watson G. Branch (London: Routledge, 1974), 236. On antebellum disputes about the mixed form of the metaphysical novel versus those loyal to "literal truthfulness", see Sheila Post-Lauria, *Correspondent Colorings* (Amherst: University of Massachusetts Press, 1996), 120–35. A representative sample of *Pierre*'s general reception can be found in the first sentence of George Washington Peck's review of the novel in 1852 for the *American Whig Review*: "A bad book!" Branch, *Melville: The Critical Heritage*, 316.

7. Melville, *Pierre; or, The Ambiguities*, 244–45.

8. For a full account of the critical reception of *Pierre*, see Branch, *Melville: The Critical Heritage*, 294–320.

9. Brian Higgins and Hershel Parker, *Reading Melville's* Pierre, or the Ambiguities (Baton Rouge: Louisianna University Press, 2007), 153.

10. Hershel Parker, *Herman Melville: A Biography, vol. 2: 1851–1891* (Baltimore: Johns Hopkins University Press, 2002), 22.

11. Evert Duyckinck, "Unsigned review of *Moby-Dick*,"in *Melville: The Critical Heritage*, 265. David Bromwich says that the clique of littérateurs around Duyckinck had "set themselves up as New York's rivals to Concord in the search for a native literature. . . . But when, from within their precincts, *Moby-Dick* emerged, they were unequipped to appreciate it." David Bromwich, *A Choice of Inheritance* (Cambridge, Mass.: Harvard University Press, 1989), 148.

12. Branch, *Melville: The Critical Heritage*, 268. Of this review Perry Miller writes: "What . . . disturb[ed] critics was the mixture of forms and types, so that they could not put it in any category. . . . The English reviews, with phrases about 'ill compound mixture' 'Bedlam literature' 'wordmongering' had an effect in America, and warned Duyckinck that if he was still to keep his few forces intact, these were the charges he had to repel. Miller, *Raven and the Whale*, 298. This partially explains Duyckinck's "reluctant" critique of *Moby-Dick*, and his pulling back at the conclusion to praise what he still recognized as its "acuteness."

13. Already with *Mardi* reviewers began to complain of Melville's propensity for allegory. The novel was described in periodicals of the time as "a heap of fanciful speculations, vivid descriptions, satirical insinuations, and allegorical typifications"; a "bizarre work, commencing as a novel, turning into a fairy tale, and availing itself of allegory to reach the satirical after passing through the elegy, the drama, and the burlesque novel." Nina Baym, "Melville's Quarrel With Fiction," 6. Reviews are from Henry Fothergill Chorley, *Athenæum* (March 24, 1849); Unsigned review, *Examiner* (March 31, 1849); Unsigned review, *Bentley's Miscellany* (April 1849); Charles Gordon Greene, *Boston Post* (April 18, 1849); and George Ripley, *New York Tribune* (May 10, 1849).

14. Herman Melville, "Letter to Sophia Hawthorne, 8 January 1852," *Correspondence*, Northwestern-Newberry ed. (Evanston: Northwestern University Press, 1993), 219. The letter from Hawthorne to which Melville here refers has not been located, but it seems to have reached Melville during the second week of November 1851. See Melville, *Correspondence*, 210–11.

15. In chapter 45 of *Moby-Dick*, Melville brings up allegory in a way that suggests he is aware of its status as a term of reproach in the literary criticism of his time, writing that for those who have not themselves been out on a whaler the story of a White Whale might seem "a monstrous fable, or still worse and more detestable, a hideous and intolerable allegory." Herman Melville, *Moby-Dick: The Northwestern-Newberry Edition*, in *The Writings of Herman Melville, vol. 6*, ed. Harrison Hayford, Hershel Parker, and G. Thomas Tanselle (Evanston, Ill.: Northwestern University Press, 1988 [1851]), 205. Melville's ironic tone here ("still worse") is picked up later by Jorge Luis Borges, who glossed this passage as Melville's parrying "the usual connotation of the word *allegory* [which] seems to have confused the critics [since] they all prefer[red] to limit themselves to a moral interpretation of [*Moby-Dick*]." Jorge Luis Borges, *Selected Non-Fictions*, ed. Eliot Weinberger (New York: Penguin, 1999), 245.

16. The same year Duyckinck brought out Melville's *Typee* in his Wiley and Putnam series, Poe was also theorizing about the relation of unity and verisimilitude to allegory. In a review of Nathaniel Hawthorne's *Twice Told Tales* Poe wrote: "there is not one respectable thing to be said about [allegory] under the best circumstances, it must always interfere with that unity of effect which, to the artist is worth all the allegory in the world. Its vital injury however, is rendering to the most vitally important point in fiction—that of . . . verisimilitude." Poe, *Essays and Reviews*, 582–83. Despite the superficial resemblances, Poe's critique of allegory, and praise of "unity of effect" and verisimilitude, is very different from Duyckinck's, as my previous chapter ought to make clear.

17. Richard Poirier, "Melville's Vanity of Failure," in *Trying It Out in America* (New York: Farrar, Straus and Giroux, 1999), 276, 261–62, 268. Poirier's notion of "foregrounding" is

of course borrowed from Viktor Shklovsky, who spoke of "laying bare the devices" of literature. See Viktor Shklovsky, "Art as Device" and "The Novel as Parody," in *Theory of Prose* (Dalkey Archive, 2009 [1925]). While Poirier does not include Melville in his group of "poet-pragmatists," there are, in his reading of *Pierre*, consistencies with the more explicitly "pragmatist" points he makes about writers like Emerson, William James, Robert Frost, and Gertrude Stein. I have specifically in mind his claim that what poet-pragmatists are concerned with is "writing itself as an activity [as] a dramatization of how life may be created out of words"; a phrase that sounds close to what Poirier calls Melville's attention to "the activity of the writer [as a] direct foregrounding of literary technique." Richard Poirier, "Why Do Pragmatists Want to Be Like Poets?" in *The Revival of Pragmatism: New Essays on Social Thought, Law and Culture*, ed. Morris Dickstein (Durham, N.C.: Duke University Press, 1999), 353.

18. Philippe Jaworksi, *Préface à Pierre ou les Ambiguïtés* (Paris: Gallimard-Bibliothèque de la Pléiade, 2006), x (my translation). In his earlier book on Melville, Jaworksi says that in *Pierre* the reader is "held captive by [their] own attention to... [and made] to feel a strange opacity in words." Phillipe Jaworski, *Melville: Le désert & l'empire* (Paris: Presses de l'Ecole Normale Supérieure, 1986), 326 (my translation).

19. Richard Brodhead acknowledges this aspect of *Pierre's* form and style when he notes that "the novel's world seems perpetually out of focus" and that its "mode of representation and style... is marked by a persistent quality of distortion." Richard Brodhead, *Hawthorne, Melville, and the Novel* (Chicago: University of Chicago Press, 1973), 163–64. Brodhead's characterization of *Pierre's* style as "out of focus" and "distorted" captures the way the novel bucks against aesthetic criteria premised on verisimilitude, faithful portraiture, and descriptive accuracy.

20. Angus Fletcher, *Allegory: The Theory of a Symbolic Mode* (Ithaca, N.Y.: Cornell University Press, 1964), 2. Fletcher gives the etymology of "allegory": "*allegory:* from *allos + agoreuein* (*other + speak openly; speak in the market*). Fletcher also points to Coleridge's well-known description of allegory as a "mechanic" form, such that "on any given material we impress a predetermined form, not necessarily arising out of the properties of the material [while organic form] is innate; it shapes, as it develops from within." Samuel Taylor Coleridge, *The Statesman's Manual* (Burlington, Vt.: C. Goodrich, 1932), 46. Paul de Man says of Coleridge's construal of allegory that it treats it as "an abstraction whose original meaning is even more devoid of substance than its 'phantom proxy,' the allegorical representatives." Paul de Man, "The Rhetoric of Temporality," in *Blindness and Insight* (Minneapolis: University of Minnesota Press, 1983), 193. But de Man pushes it further, describing allegory as a "relationship between signs [which] necessarily contains a constitutive temporal element [such that] the allegorical sign refers to another sign which precedes it [and so] the meaning constituted by [it] can consist only in the *repetition*... of a previous sign with which it can never coincide, since it is of the essence of this previous sign to be pure anteriority." de Man, "The Rhetoric of Temporality," in *Blindness and Insight*, 207. In a discussion of Mallarmé's poetics, de Man sees in allegory a move toward the "nonrepresentational," such that it names a "process by which the literary text moves from a phenomenal, world-oriented to a grammatical, language-oriented direction." Paul de Man, "Lyric and Modernity," in *Blindness and Insight*, 175–76. De Man is here adapting Walter Benjamin's use of the word "allegory," which involves a far-reaching intellectual history from German counterreformation drama to Charles Baudelaire. See Walter Benjamin, *Origin of German Tragic Drama* (London: Verso, 1998), 159–235; and, Benjamin, *The Writer Of Modern Life: Essays on Charles Baudelaire*, ed. Michael W. Jennings (Cambridge: Harvard UP, 2006).

21. John Huizinga, *The Waning of the Middle Ages* (quoted in Angus Fletcher, *Allegory* [Ithaca, N.Y.: Cornell University Press, 1964], 17).

22. Eric Auerbach, "*Figura*," in *Scenes from the Drama of European Literature: Six Essays* (Minneapolis: University of Minnesota Press, 1984), 13. In Auerbach's philological account of *figura*, the term is most directly linked to allegory in the context of a discussion of biblical typology.

23. Sacvan Berkovich, *Rites of Assent* (New York: Routledge, 1993), 275, 265, 250, 264.

24. Melville did have actual rock formations around him as he worked on the novel. Hershel Parker reminds us that when Melville "planned *Pierre*... the mountains surrounding him (the Catskills far to the west, the Taconics to the west and south, Greylock to the north) still formed a magic circle containing the disparate fragments of his life from childhood to the present." Hershel Parker, *Herman Melville: A Biography*, 2:58.

25. Poirier, "Melville's Vanity of Failure," in *Trying It Out in America*, 262.

26. Walker Percy, *Signposts in a Strange Land*, ed. Patrick Samway (New York: Picador, 2000), 201.

27. Melville, "April 1852 Letter to Richard Bentley," in Melville, *Correspondence*, 226.

28. Charles Olson says of the relation between Melville's reading and his habits of composition that "Melville's reading is a gauge of him," and that he "read to write." Charles Olson, *Collected Prose*, ed. Donald Allen and Benjamin Friedlander (Berkeley: University of California Press, 1997), 39.

29. In an 1849 letter to Duyckinck, Melville mentions reading in the seven-volume 1837 edition (Boston: Hilliard, Gray and Company) of Shakespeare's works in "an edition in glorious great type, every letter whereof is a soldier." Melville, *Correspondence*, 119.

30. Melville bought an edition of Thomas De Quincey's *Confessions of an English Opium Eater* during a trip to England in 1849, excitedly reporting of a "most wondrous book" in a December 22 journal entry of that year. At a slightly later point in his trip Melville writes, "Cabbed it to London Docks & put my luggage aboard to go round to Portsmouth. Ship Sailed at 3 P.M. to day. Thence to Davidson's to see about my money. While waiting for him, ran out, & at last got a hold of "The Opium Eater" & began it in the office. A wonderful thing, that book." Herman Melville, *Journals*, ed. Howard Horsford with Lynn Horth (Boston: Northwestern University Press, 1989), 46.

31. Graham Foley, "Herman Melville and the Example of Sir Thomas Browne," *Modern Philology* 81, no. 3 (1984): 265. Widmer writes: "Duyckinck allowed Melville free access to his large library, where Melville was able to pillage Sir Thomas Browne." Widmer, *Young America*, 95. F. O. Mattheissen says of Browne's influence on Melville at the time of *Moby-Dick* that "Browne's resources of sound...exercised a powerful spell over him," characterizing the sonic aspects of Browne's prose in a description I think could equally be applied to Melville's: "Browne's stately elevation is kept from being vitiated into the merely learned...by the inclusion of monosyllabic Germanic elements in his prose. F. O. Mattheissen, *American Renaissance* (New York: Oxford University Press, 1968), 121. In his essay "Rhetoric and Style," de Quincey himself praises Browne as one of the masters of English prose: "If not absolutely the foremost in the accomplishments of art, [Browne] was, undoubtedly the richest, most dazzling, and, with reference to their matter, the most captivating of all rhetoricians [in whom] the opposite forces of eloquent passion and rhetorical fancy [are] brought into an exquisite equilibrium, approaching, receding, attracting, repelling—blending, separating—chasing and chased, as in a fugue, and again lost in a delightful interfusion, so as to create a middle species of composition, more various and stimulating to the understanding than pure eloquence...more gratifying to the affections than naked rhetoric...Sir Thomas Browne, deep, tranquil, and majestic as Milton, silently premeditating, and disclosing his golden couplets, as under some genial instinct of incubation." Thomas de Quincey, *Style and Rhetoric and Other Papers*, in *De Quincey's Works*, vol. 10 (Edinburgh: Adam and Charles Black, 1862), 44.

32. Foley, "Herman Melville and the Example of Sir Thomas Browne," 266.

33. To point to just one example of how Melville's bibliophilia directly informed the sty-
    listic experiments of the earlier novel, *Moby-Dick*'s chapter 32, "Cetology" imagines a
    taxonomy of whales as modeled on bound, printed books ("Folio Whale, Octavo Whale,
    Duodecimal Whale," *Moby-Dick*, 149), and links this taxonomic blending of whales and
    books to the "great Cuvier." Like Emerson's discovery that he might treat his journal
    entries as so many "specimens" to be rearranged into larger compositions, and Poe's con-
    cern to relate species and genre in the dénouement of the first detective story, Melville's
    likening of whales and books around a logic of types tests out what the sea adventure
    can handle in the way of formal invention. Melville's bookishness is well-documented
    in Hershel Parker's *Herman Melville: A Biography*; and Merton M. Sealts, ed., *Melville's
    Reading: A Check-List of Books Owned and Borrowed* (Cambridge, Mass.: Harvard
    University Press, 1948).
34. Paul Lyons says Melville's experiments with style around 1851–52 "invokes a *kind* of rhet-
    oric, rather than any specific text...in which rhetoric reinforces a type of physical strug-
    gle that poses metaphysical questions"; a bond between rhetoric and metaphysics that
    Lyons likens to Renaissance tragedy. Paul Lyons, "Melville and His Precursors: Styles and
    Metastyle and Allusion," *American Literature* 62, no. 3 (September, 1990): 452–53.
35. Melville, *Pierre; or, The Ambiguities*, 67.
36. For a detailed discussion of the figure of the "heart" in sentimental romance, Melville's
    parodic deployment of it, and its relation to moral philosophy, see Samuel Otter, *Melville's
    Anatomies* (Berkeley: University of California Press, 1999), 172–254. For an interesting
    account of the role of "broken hearts" in *Pierre*, see Branka Arsić, *Passive Constitutions
    7½ Times Bartleby* (Stanford: Stanford University Press, 2007), 65–66. For a reading of
    Pierre's acid parody of the sentimental romance as arising from Melville's sexual and mari-
    tal frustrations, see Andrew Delbanco, *Melville: His World and Work* (New York: Vintage,
    2005), 181–86.
37. Melville, *Pierre; or, The Ambiguities*, 68.
38. In a recent book on Poe, Melville, and baroque emblems William Engel claims there is
    "buried in *Pierre* an allegory about the disastrous consequences of the refusal of allegory,"
    but does not say anything more about how allegory functions in the novel. See William
    Engel, *Early Modern Poetics in Melville and Poe* (Farnam: Ashgate, 2012), 75.
39. Melville, *Pierre; or, The Ambiguities*, 68.
40. Another, perhaps better known, moment of ekphrasis in Melville's writing around this
    time, is the "Boggy soggy squishy picture" Ishmael sees, puzzles over, and attempts to
    interpret. See *Moby-Dick*, chapter 3: The Spouter Inn.
41. Melville, *Pierre; or, The Ambiguities*, 68.
42. Ibid., 69.
43. These terms are of course not entirely synonymous. As Jeremy Tambling notes, the "intri-
    cate metaphor" of conceit shares its basic features with allegory, primarily the extension in
    time of a metaphorical transposition. See Jeremy Tambling, *Allegory* (London: Routledge,
    2010), 174. For a radicalization of the relation of allegory to time, see Paul de Man, "The
    Rhetoric of Temporality," in *Blindness and Insight*, 187–228.
44. Melville, *Pierre; or, The Ambiguities*, 69.
45. This is what Paul Lyons refers to as the novel's "word compoundings." See Lyons, "Melville's
    Styles," 455. It was just such infelicities of usage that Peck objected to in his November
    1852 review of *Pierre* in the *American Whig Review*, going so far as to make a chart listing
    them with page numbers. Jaworski says that Melville's experimentation with the substan-
    tive in *Pierre*—his example is the difference between "beautiful" and "beautifulness"—is a
    matter of the making "visible the operation of agglutination" around a word, causing it to
    "be perceived materially and physically." Jaworski, *Melville: Le désert & l'empire*, 326 (my
    translation). I take Jaworski to be describing a clustering of prefixes and suffixes around a

word so that it becomes impacted and, not so much emptied of meaning, as freighted with meaning (or such that that meanings become "distorted," to use Brodhead's word). For an interesting account of how constative language (subject to criteria of truth and falsity) is displaced by the performative effects of the novel's "extraordinary accumlations of words, syllables and clauses," see Elizabeth Duquette, "*Pierre's* Nominal Conversions," in *Melville and Aesthetics*, ed. Samuel Otter and Geoffrey Sanborn (New York: Palgrave, 2011), 117. The distinction between constative utterances and performative utterances is taken from J. L. Austin, *How to Do Things with Words* (Cambridge, Mass.: Harvard Univeristy Press, 1962).

46. Melville, *Pierre; or, The Ambiguities*, 133.

47. Melville, *Pierre; or, The Ambiguities*, 134. Hieroglyphic rock formations appear also in the huge geologic inscriptions that form part of the climax of Poe's *The Narrative of Arthur Gordon Pym of Nantucket*, a literal fusion of letters with rock formations. For more on Melville, Poe, and "hieroglyphics," see John Irwin, *American Hieroglyphics: The Symbol of the Egyptian Hieroglyphics in the American Renaissance* (Baltimore: Johns Hopkins University Press, 1983).

48. For a compelling reading of the Memnon Stone as a "ponderous yet teetering...symbol...for a superabundance of mythic patriarchs," such that an "explicit congruency is established between [it] and the massive rock formation to which Melville dedicates his novel (Mt. Greylock)," see Sianne Ngai, *Ugly Feelings* (Cambridge, Mass.: Harvard University Press, 2007), 239–41.

49. Melville, *Pierre; or, The Ambiguities*, 205.

50. Ibid.

51. Ibid., 210.

52. Ibid., 211.

53. Some have considered Emerson to be a model for Plinlimmon. In that case, Melville's ridicule would refocus his irreverence toward Duyckinck's literary-critical doctrine, since part of the *Moby-Dick* reviews involved Duyckinck's accusing Melville's of "run-a-muck" Emersonianism; what he called an "indifferent conceitedness." In aping Emerson's more mystical-sounding pronouncements in the Plinlimmon pamphlet, it is as if Melville, in denying his link to Emerson through mockery, further defies Duyckinck's appraisal of *Moby-Dick*. For more on Melville's complicated relation to Emerson, see his later novel *The Confidence Man* (1857), in which the character Mark Winsome is unambiguously modeled on Emerson.

54. Parker and Higgins, *Reading Melville's Pierre*, 114.

55. Melville, *Pierre; or, The Ambiguities*, 211.

56. Ibid., 212.

57. Ibid.

58. Evert Duyckinck, Review of *Moby-Dick*, in *The Literary World*, in *Melville: The Critical Heritage*, 267.

59. Parker, *Herman Melville: A Biography*, 2:34.

60. Newton Arvin cited in "Historical Note," in Melville, *Pierre; or, The Ambiguities*, 406. In his biography, Parker makes the suggestion that Melville, "persistently aggrieved at...Boston and New York Unitarians" was in the pamphlet venting "disgust toward English Unitarians; judging them by Jesus' standards for what one had to do to become one of his followers." Parker, *Herman Melville: A Biography*, 2:68.

61. Parker, "Historical Note," in Melville, *Pierre; or, The Ambiguities*, 406.

62. Ibid., 206.

63. Ibid., 212.

64. Berkovich, *Rites of Assent*, 278.

65. Parker, "Historical Note," in Melville, *Pierre; or, The Ambiguities*, 406.

66. Parker, *Herman Melville: A Biography*, 2:78.
67. Parker and Higgins, *Reading Melville's* Pierre, 146–47.
68. Ibid., 147.
69. Melville, *Pierre; or, The Ambiguities*, 245.
70. Ibid.
71. Ibid.
72. Higgins and Parker, *Reading Melville's* Pierre, 151. For a more complete list of the appropriations Melville made of the language of the reviews of *Moby-Dick* in the fictional account of Pierre's literary accolades, see Parker, *Reading Melville's* Pierre, 150–51.
73. Duyckinck's original letter to Melville is lost. Lynn Horth tells us that Evert and his brother George Duyckinck "were scheduled to become editors of *Holden's* beginning with the April [1851] issue [and they were] planning to do a series of articles on contemporary authors with portraits." Lynn Horth, ed., *The Writings of Herman Melville: Correspondence* (Chicago: Northwestern University Press, 1993), 178. Laura Rigal notes that at the time of this letter the word "mug" had connotations (as a noun) of "dupe, fool, sucker" and (as a verb) of "assault, attack, and rob"; such that Melville seems to suggest that "anybody with a face (a mug to be mugged) could be assaulted by means of the camera and chemicals that had opportunistically seized the moment." Rigal, "Pulled by the Line: Speed and Photography in *Moby-Dick*," in *Melville and Aesthetics*, 113.
74. Ibid., 180.
75. Melville, *Pierre; or, The Ambiguities*, 254.
76. John Evelev suggests Melville's turning *Holden's* into the "Captain Kidd Monthly," is an allusion to "piracy" as "a term for the editorial practice of republishing uncopyrighted British and American writings without recompensing authors." But since the passage is clearly transposed from the earlier correspondence with Duyckinck, and seems to have been altered in accord with Melville's more recent meeting with him it seems unlikely that this is an allusion to "piracy" in the sense of reprinting. See John Evelev, *Tolerable Entertainments: Herman Melville and Professionalism in Antebellum New York* (Amherst: University of Massachusetts Press, 2006), 153. Michael J. Everton suggests, interestingly, that the *Captain Kidd Monthly* is not only a version of *Holden's* but "also a fictional *Harper's New Monthly Magazine* [which is part of Melville's] pervasive ironically expansive condemnation of Duyckinck and Harpers" and in which Melville attacks the "dogmatic insensitivity to the interests of the author with an energetic pursuit of profit." Michael J. Everton, *The Grand Chorus of Complaint: Authors and the Business Ethics of American Publishing* (New York: Oxford University Press, 2011), 131. While I agree with Everton's take on Melville's "pervasively ironic…condemnation" of the "dogmas" of antebellum publishing world (as personified in Duyckinck), I find them more specifically at work in Melville's direct appropriation of some of the terms informing Duyckinck's critical theory.
77. Alan Trachenberg stresses how responses to the new technology regularly invoked the figure of the "mirror" and stood "unambiguously for exactitude." Alan Trachtenberg, "Mirror in the Marketplace: American Responses to the Daguerreotype, 1839–1851," in *The Daguerreotype, A Sesquincenternnial Celebration*, ed. John Wood (London: University of Iowa Press, 1989), 60. More relevant to Melville's reluctance to have his daguerreotype taken would likely have been what Trachtenberg calls the "danger of appearing in public as a caricature of oneself." Trachtenberg, "Mirror in the Marketplace," 62. Complicating the "mirror" analogy, Tranchtenberg also points out the public anxiety specific to the daguerreotype: that of fixing or fastening what is typically fluid and animate; an anxiety reflected in Melville's description of daguerreotype as "oblivionating." Trachtenberg, "Mirror in the Marketplace," 62. On the relation of this logic of "mirroring" to nationalist critical program of "Young America," Pricilla Wald describes Duyckinck's essay "Nationality in Literature"

as "simultaneously advocat[ing] a mirroring and a generating role for literature," such that this "reflecting" is a way of shaping national identity. Priscilla Wald, *Constituting Americans* (Durham, N.C.: Duke University Press, 1995), 106.

78. Melville, *Pierre; or, The Ambiguities*, 254. Melville's tale "Bartleby, the Scrivener" is also about the refusal of the logic of copying.

79. The relation of the daguerreotype to historical memory is one of the central ideas in Hawthorne's novel *The House of the Seven Gables*. On the theme of technological verisimilitude in this novel, see Alan Trachtenberg, "Seeing and Believing: Hawthorne's Reflections on the Daguerreotype," in *The House of the Seven Gables*," *American Literary History* 3 (autumn, 1997). Commenting on how, at the beginning of the 1850s, "cameras could create instant fashions and durable industries," Susan Sontag notes that in in *Pierre* "all forms of portraiture in the business of civilization are compromised; at least, so it appears to Pierre, a paragon of alienated sensibility." Susan Sontag, *On Photography* (New York: Macmillan, 2001), 166–67.

80. Newton Arvin, *Herman Melville* (New York: Grove Press, 2002), 224.

81. Poirier, "Melville's Vanity of Failure," in *Trying It Out in America*, 255.

82. Melville, *Pierre; or, The Ambiguities*, 267.

83. Ibid., 283.

84. Ibid.

85. Ibid., 287.

86. Higgins and Parker, *Reading Melville's* Pierre, 161.

87. Garvin notes that the "ruinous and desolate scenery" of Melville's description is stylistically close to Anne Radcliffe's descriptions of landscape in *The Mysteries of Udolpho*. See Newton Arvin, "Melville and the Gothic Novel," *New England Quarterly* 22, no. 1 (1949): 37.

88. Melville, *Pierre; or, The Ambiguities*, 285.

89. For an interesting discussion of allegory, experience, and emblems in Hawthorne's fiction, see Theo Davis, *Formalism, Experience, and the Making of American Literature* (Cambridge: Cambridge University Press, 2007), 82–92.

90. Melville, *Pierre; or, The Ambiguities*, 341.

91. Ibid., 342.

92. Ibid.

93. On Melville's allusions to Bunyan more generally, see Berkovich, *Rites of Assent*.

94. Roger Pooley, "*The Pilgrim's Progress* and the Allegorical Line," in *Cambridge Companion to Bunyan*, ed. Anne Dunan-Page (Cambridge: Cambridge University Press, 2010), 84.

95. John Bunyan, *The Pilgrim's Progress* (New York: Penguin 1965), 105.

96. Melville, *Pierre; or, The Ambiguities*, 344.

97. Melville, *Pierre; or, The Ambiguities*, 354.

98. Melville, *Moby-Dick*, 184. It should be pointed out that *Moby-Dick* also experiments with the sorts of Brownean impactions that fill *Pierre*, as when Ahab says: "I am madness maddened!" (*Moby-Dick*, 168).

99. "Undoffable" was one of the words George Washington Peck singled out in his review of the novel in the *American Whig* as an "extraordinary...thickly studded...concoction." Branch, *Melville: The Critical Heritage*, 319.

100. Melville, *Pierre; or, The Ambiguities*, 346.

101. Arvin, *Herman Melville*, 227.

102. One of Melville's last efforts at serious composition—the long poem *Clarel*—returns overtly to a thematics of "stone." A journal entry from the trip to Jerusalem that became the basis for the poem runs as follows: "We read a good deal about stones in Scriptures. Monuments & stumps of the memorials are set up of stones; men are

stoned to death; the figurative seed falls in stony places. . . . Judea is one accumulation of stone—Stony mountains & stony plains; stony torrents & stony roads; stony walls & stony fields, stony houses & stony tombs; stony eyes and stony hearts. Before you and behind you are stones. Stones to the right & stones to the left." Melville, *Journals,* January 1857.

103. Duyckinck, "Unsigned Review of *Pierre,*" in *Melville: The Critical Heritage,* 302.

104. Ibid.

105. Ibid.

CHAPTER 4

1. George Santayana, "The Genteel Tradition in American Philosophy," in *The Genteel Tradition in American Philosophy and Character and Opinion in the United States,* ed. James Seaton (New Haven: Yale University Press, 2009), 3–4.

2. Ibid., 4.

3. Ross Posnock, *The Trial of Curiosity* (New York: Oxford University Press, 1991), 193.

4. Ibid., 205.

5. Santayana, "The Genteel Tradition in American Philosophy," in *The Genteel Tradition,* 8–9.

6. Ibid. For more on James's criticisms of Josiah Royce's notion of the "absolute," see Bruce Kuklick, *The History of Philosophy in America* (New York: Oxford University Press, 2001), 150–63.

7. Santayana, "The Genteel Tradition in American Philosophy," in *The Genteel Tradition,* 10.

8. Henry James, *Henry James: A Life in Letters,* ed. Philip Horne (London: Allen Lane, 1999), 425. More recently, John Ashbery has described Henry's late style as an "endless process of elaboration which gives the work . . . a texture of bewildering luxuriance—that of a tropical rain forest of ideas." John Ashbery, *Selected Prose,* ed. Eugene Richie (Ann Arbor: University of Michigan Press, 2004), 13

9. William James, *A Pluralistic Universe* (New York: Longmam, Green, 1909), 235, 271.

10. Henry James, *Literary Criticism: European Writers and Prefaces to the New York Edition,* ed. Leon Edel and Mark Wilson, vol. 2 (New York: Library of America, 1984), 1332.

11. William James, "A World of Pure Experience," in *Writings: 1902–1910* (New York: Library of America, 1987), 1159–82. See also, "The Thing and Its Relations," Appendix A, *A Pluralistic Universe.* The phrase "radical empiricism" first appears in the 1897 preface to *The Will to Believe* in *The Writings of William James: A Comprehensive Edition,* ed. John J. McDermott (Chicago: University of Chicago Press, 1977).

12. Myra Jehlen offers a nuanced account of some of the disagreements between William and Henry around the issue of prose style. Jehlen sees William's impatience with the late style as evidence of his tendency falsely to separate form and content. But in treating both William and Henry as preoccupied with the relation of literary form to "knowledge," Jehlen occludes the fact the neither of them (particularly in 1905–07) were much interested in problems of epistemology. And when Jehlen says that Henry's method of composition was "entirely open to the hints and clues writing turns up . . . not imposing a resolution to the problems that emerged [in composition] but still actively charting [a] path," a process Jehlen says "could be that of a scientist . . . conduct[ing] an experiment," she gives what I think is a perfect description of Henry's compositional method; but, again, that method has nothing to do with epistemology, but of abandoning the problem of squaring inner with outer matter as an intellectualist illusion. Jehlen's emphasis on "experiment," however, directs us to a word both of them *were* deeply concerned with: "experience." See Myra Jehlen, "On How, to Become Knowledge, Cognition Needs Beauty, no. 2: On How Philosophers Tend Not to Recognize This Condition," *Raritan* (Spring 2011): 30, 47–65.

13. Henry James, *The Ambassadors*, ed. S. P. Rosenbaum, 2d ed. (New York: W. W. Norton, 1994).

14. For a thorough exploration of the relation of William's philosophy to Henry's aesthetics, see Ross Posnock, "The Politics of Non-Identity," *boundary 2* 19 (1992): 35; and *The Trial of Curiosity*.

15. William James, *Correspondence of William James*, December 14, 1902, Cambridge Mass. to Villa Montmorency, 18 Avenue des Tilleuls, Paris. Jean Wahl says of this letter that in it James, "s'éloigne des vieilles categories, des vieilles croyances usées, on fait passer des lignes de demarcation par des voies tout à fait nouvelles." *Ver le concret: Études d'histoire de la Philosophie Contemporaine* (Paris: Vrin, 2004), 94.

16. Henri Bergson's first letter back to William James is smudged and broken to the point of illegibility. See Henri Bergson, *Correspondances* (Paris: PUF 2002), 80. All translations from Bergson's letters are my own unless otherwise indicated.

17. William James, *The Complete Correspondance of William James, 12 volumes* (Charlottsville: University of Virginia Press, 2004), 4:679.

18. For an excellent account of British idealism at this time, see Peter Hylton, *Russell, Idealism and the Emergence of Analytic Philosophy* (Oxford: Oxford University Press, 1992). For an account of the relation of British idealism to American philosophy at the time, see Timothy L. S. Sprigge, *James and Bradley: American Truth and British Reality* (Chicago: Open Court, 1993).

19. Bergson's letters from this portion of the correspondence are mostly illegible. From the letter between James's 1905 letter from Cannes and the June 1907 letter, we have three from Bergson. Aside from the usual "Croyez, je vous prie, a mes sentiments les plus dévoués, H. Bergson," there are suggestive but not very conclusive fragments like, "inspire une admiration," "l'idealisme platonicien," which might lead one to infer that Bergson is expressing his "admiration" for James's own (or at least some version of an) overturning of "Platonic idealism." See Bergson, *Correspondances*, 171.

20. *Complete Correspondence of William James*, 5:377.

21. In a 1904 letter to Francois Pillon, James acknowledged the nearly synonymous relations between his radical empiricism, pluralism, and "tychism": "My philosophy is what I call a radical empiricism, a pluralism, a 'tychism,' which represents order as gradually won and always in the making.... It rejects all doctrines of the absolute." *Complete Correspondence of William James*, 2:203.

22. Charles Peirce, "The Law of the Mind," in *Essential Peirce*, ed. Nathan Houser and Christian Kloesel, vol. 1 (Bloomington: Indiana University Press, 1992–1998), 312–33.

23. Santayana, "The Genteel Tradition in American Philosophy," in *The Genteel Tradition*, 16. The influence of Darwinism can also be felt here. For good accounts of how Darwin's discoveries influenced the classical pragmatists, see Philip Wiener, *Evolution and the Founders of Pragmatism* (Cambridge, Mass.: Harvard University Press, 1949); and Joan Richardson, *A Natural History of Pragmatism* (New York: Cambridge University Press, 2007).

24. Bergson, *Correspondences*, 186 (my translation; English in original).

25. James, *Complete Correspondence*, 5:904. In *L'évolution créatrice* Bergson tried to argue a middle way between Larmarkian telos and Darwinian randomness, in which the evolution of organic structures was "qualitative, dynamic and continuous." Henri Bergson, *Creative Evolution* (New York: Barnes and Noble Books, 2005), ix.

26. James, *Complete Correspondence*, 5: 989.

27. Ibid., 5:909.

28. William James, "Bradley or Bergson?," in *Writings: 1902–1910*, 1266.

29. One of the first such comparative studies was that of James's student Horace Meyer Kallen in his 1914 *William James and Henri Bergson: A Study in Contrasting Theories of Life.*

30. Horace Meyer Kallen, *William James and Henri Bergson: A Study in Contrasting Theories of Life* (Chicago: University of Chicago Press, 1914), 10.

31. Bergson, "Introduction" to *Le Pragmatisme*, in *Bergson: Key Writings*, ed. Keith Ansell Pearson (New York: Continuum, 2002), 268.

32. While the notion that the relations between the terms of our experience are real, and so can be experienced, is alluded to peripherally in *The Varieties of Religious Experience* (*Writings: 1902–1910* [New York Library of America, 1987 [1897]]) and, more distantly, in *The Principles of Psychology* (*Writings 1878–1899* [New York Library of America, 1992 [1892]]), it is only after the two essays of 1904 that it becomes the central thesis of what James began to call "radical empiricism." On James's notion that the world is open and always "in the making" David Lapoujade writes: "[G]enerally speaking, William James's philosophy is a philosophy of the way man makes himself in a world that is itself in the making [*en train de se faire*]. David Lapoujade, *William James: Pragmatisme et empirisme* (Paris: PUF, 1997), 9 (my translation).

33. James, *Writings*, 1142.

34. Jean Wahl describes this aspect of radical empiricism, whereby subject/object dualism is replaced with a single "confluence" of experience: "When we have two minds which know the same thing...we are in the midst of an experience of confluence." Jean Wahl, *Les philosophies pluraliste d'Angleterre et d'Amérique* (Paris: Empêcheurs de Penser en Rond, 2005), 176 (my translation). Wahl seems here to mean by "confluence" the way two minds can simultaneously partake of the same piece of experience.

35. These are admittedly simplified descriptions of the substance dualism described in Descartes's *Meditations*, and Kant's argument, in his First Critique, for a metaphysics of experience that could serve as the basis for natural science, or what Kant calls the "theoretical cognition of nature." See Descartes, *Meditations on First Philosophy*, ed. John Cottingham (Cambridge: Cambridge University Press, 1996 [1641]) and Kant, *Critique of Pure Reason*, ed. Paul Guyer and Allen Wood. Cambridge: Cambridge University Press, 1998 [1787].

36. Lapoujade, *William James: Empirisme et pragmatism*, 9 (my translation).

37. James, *Writings*, 1103.

38. Ibid., 1165.

39. Ibid. James's realism about relations intersects with the debate between F. H. Bradley and Bertrand Russell about the role of relations in logic. Bradley denied the existence of relations saying they were ideal and not real, whereas Russell developed his logical atomism from out of the notion of the reality of relations. For more on Bradley and Russell on relations, see Peter Hylton, *Russell, Idealism, and the Emergence of Analytic Philosophy* (Oxford: Oxford University Press, 1992), 45–101. For a good account of the metaphysics of internal and external relations, from Leibniz to Russell, and its relevance to classical pragmatism, see Vincent Descombes, *Les institutions du sens* (Paris: Les Editions de Minuit, 1996), 185–236.

40. Zeno's paradoxes center on the infinite regress that arises when categories of spatial discreteness and temporal continuity are confused. James discusses in detail the way the notion of external relations can be attacked as falling into a Zeno-like paradox in his lecture "Bergson and Intellectualism" in *A Pluralistic Universe*, in *Writings, 1902–1910*, 731–55.

41. James, *Writings,*, 898.

42. Ibid.

43. William James, *The Principles of Psychology*, vol. 2 (New York: Holt, 1890), 148–49. Interestingly, James's discussion of the reality of spatial relations is close to Bergson's discussion of the relation between number and space in his *Essai sur les données immédiates de la conscience*, published in 1889, just one year before the *Principles*. There is no evidence that James had any familiarity with Bergson's *Essai* at the time, though the affinities between them are belatedly borne out in their correspondence, as noted above.

44. Henri Bergson, *Introduction to Metaphysics*, trans. T. E. Hulme (New York: Palgrave Macmillan, 2007), 37 (slightly modified).

45. David Lapoujade identifies James's "pure experience" as a transcendental empiricism (*William James: Empirism et pragmatisme*, 25). While the phrase "transcendental empiricism" of course seems like a contradiction, versions of the idea can be found in thinkers as different as Gilles Deleuze and John McDowell. By transcendental empiricism Deleuze means a literal overturning of Kantian transcendental idealism, which involves rethinking Kantian ideas of reason (which are undetermined but regulative) as "problems" imminent in a transcendentally empirical field. See Gilles Deleuze, *Différence et repetition* (Paris: PUF, 1968), 187–230. For John McDowell, conversely, "transcendental empiricism" names the way perception is itself already conceptually contentful, but is nevertheless also able to yield new empirical particulars. See John McDowell, *Mind and World* (Cambridge, Mass.: Harvard University Press, 1994); and his "Transcendental Empiricism" (unpublished). For more on Bergsonian *durée* as a form of transcendental empiricism, see Gilles Deleuze, *Le bergsonisme* (Paris: PUF, 1966), 29–44.

46. James, *Literary Criticism*, 2:1041. In a recent study of the James brothers, Lapoujade writes that "Le monde des frères James est avant tout un monde de relations." *Fictions du pragmatisme* (Paris: Editions de minuit, coll. Paradoxe, 2008).

47. James, *The Ambassadors*, 130. Leon Edel says Strether tries to "remain open to experience and doesn't require [that] life measure up to the Woollett yardstick." Leon Edel, *Henry James: The Master* (London: R. Hart-Davis, 1972), 77.

48. James, *The Ambassadors*, 90.

49. James himself referred to the character of Maria Gostrey as one of his *ficelles*—a device used to get the reader into a certain connection with Strether, and so a purely relational element in the composition. James borrows the word *ficelle* from the phrase *ficelle du theatre*, which is literally a string or thread.

50. James, *The Ambassadors*, 62–63. Describing another instance of Strether's "pausing" during one of his walks through Paris, Jonathan Levin writes of his "want[ing] to stop his imagination from wandering and indulging itself, but find[ing] himself unable to catch it before it has already gotten itself too far along." Jonthan Levin, *The Poetics of Transition* (Durham, N.C.: Duke University Press, 1999), 126.

51. James, *The Ambassadors*, 63.

52. Ibid.

53. S. P. Rosenbaum reminds us that "French fiction was customarily published in yellow paper-backed editions." James, *The Ambassadors*, 63.

54. As S. P. Rosenbaum points out, the journal Strether edits might be thought of as comparable to *The North American Review*, the periodical in which *The Ambassadors* was initially serialized in 1903. As a piece of fiction, *The Ambassadors* was something of an anomaly in its pages. See S. P. Rosenbaum, "Editions and Revisions," in *The Ambassadors*, 357.

55. James, *The Ambassadors*, 77.

56. Robert Pippin says of the "lemon-coloured volumes" that they remind Strether of "his own optimism...when he collected his own supply during that first trip with his young wife, convinced he could keep some private faith with art and high culture, could arrange his own private redemption in the world of commerce he returned to." Robert Pippin, *Henry James and Modern Moral Life* (Cambridge: Cambridge Univeristy Press, 2001), 154.

57. For more on the lavishness of analogy and metaphor in James's late prose, see Ruth Yeazell, *Language and Knowledge in the Late Novels of Henry James* (Chicago: University of Chicago Press, 1976), 39–49.

58. James, *The Ambassadors*, 118.

59. For a rich discussion of the significance of "light" in *The Ambassadors*, see Richardson, *A Natural History of Pragmatism*, 137–78; and Collin Meissner, *Henry James and the Language of Experience* (New York: Cambridge University Press, 1999), 129–84.

60. James, *The Ambassadors*, 120.

61. Ibid., 121.

62. Posnock, *The Trial of Curiosity*, 225.

63. James, *The Ambassadors*, 123. James claimed this line was the original "germ" for the novel. In a notebook entry for October 31, 1895, James says Jonathan Sturges told him of having overheard William Dean Howells, upon visiting Paris late in life, saying to him, in a brooding, melancholic tone "you are young, you are young—be glad of it and *live*. Live all you can." See "Notebook Entries," in James, *The Ambassadors*, 373–77.

64. My wording here is a partial allusion to Keats well-known formulation of "negative capability," as being "capable of being in uncertainties, Mysteries, doubts without any irritable reaching after fact & reason." John Keats, Letter to George and Tom Keats, December 21, 1817, in *Complete Poems and Selected Letters of John Keats*, ed. Edward Hirsch (New York: Modern Library Classics, 2001), 492.

65. James, *The Ambassadors*, 132.

66. Ibid., 130

67. Ibid., 278–79.

68. Ibid., 300.

69. Pippin, *Henry James and Modern Moral Life*, 147–70. W. E. B. Du Bois also spoke, in *The Souls of Black Folk*, of "double consciousness." For Du Bois the term is used to describe a split in consciousness such that the subject must simultaneously live in both their own sense, and the social fantasy of, their personal identity. Du Bois describes this as a "peculiar sensation...of always looking at one's self through the eyes of others, of measuring one's soul by the tape of a world that looks on in amused contempt and pity." W. E. B. Du Bois, *The Souls of Black Folk* (New York: Library of America, 1996), 3–4. Du Bois was William James's student at Harvard in the late 1880s, so it is not surprising that his description of "double consciousness" has some affinity with James's critique of "intellectualism"; that is, as reducing the lived continuity of experience to the different "labeling tape[s] of the world." For more on Du Boisian "double consciousness" and cosmopolitanism, see Ross Posnock, "The Dream of Deracination," *American Literary History* 12 no. 4 (winter 2000): 810–15.

70. Ibid., 800.

71. Ibid., 816n3.

72. Gregg Crane, *Race, Citizenship and Law in American Literature* (New York: Cambridge University Press, 2002), 89–90. Much of the recent scholarship on cosmopolitanism confirms Crane's Kantian construal, centered on the tension between conceptual understanding and the arrival of new particular for which universals are yet to be found. Anthony Appiah has offered a formula for this idea of "cosmopolitanism": "universalism plus difference." Kwame Anthony Appiah, *Cosmopolitanism: Ethics in a World of Strangers* (New York: W. W. Norton: 2006), 151. Bruce Robbins thinks cosmopolitanism should be "understood as a fundamental devotion to the interests of humanity as a whole [and it] often seem[s] to claim universality by virtue of its independence, its detachment from the bonds, commitments, and affiliations that constrain ordinary nation-bound lives." Bruce Robbins, introduction to *Cosmopolitics*, ed. Pheng Cheah and Bruce Robbins (Minneapolis: University of Minnesota Press, 1998), 5. Along these lines, David Hollinger writes that "cosmopolitanism shares with all varieties of universalism a profound suspicion of enclosures [and] urges each individual and collective unit to absorb as much varied experience as it can, while retaining its capacity to advance its aims effectively." David Hollinger, *Postethnic America* (New York: Basic Books, 1995), 23. More recently, Branka Arsić highlights the

way Crane's description treats cosmopolitanism, less as some form of elitism, and more as a "pragmatics of processual thinking allowing for change and the fragility of concepts." Branka Arsić, *On Leaving* (Cambridge, Mass.: Harvard University Press, 2010), 253.

73. Hannah Arendt, *Lectures on Kant's Political Philosophy*, ed. Ronald Beiner (Chicago: University of Chicago Press, 1992).

74. Immanuel Kant, *Critique of the Power of Judgment*, Introduction §IV, ed. Paul Guyer (Cambridge: Cambridge University Press, 2000).

75. Kant, *Critique of the Power of Judgment*, Introduction §IV.

76. Arendt, *Lectures of Kant's Political Philosophy*, 76.

77. Ibid. The idea of "purposiveness" is central to Kant's Third Critique, underlying his argument about what he calls the "technics of nature." For an account of how a notion of the purposive telos of nature informs Kant's *Critique of the Power of Judgment*, see Ernst Cassirer, *Kant's Life and Thought*, trans. James Haden (New Haven: Yale Univeristy Press, 1981), 271–360. For more on Arendt's appeal to Kant's "reflecting" judgments as the basis for the "enlarged mentality" of the world citizen, see Seyla Benhabib, *The Reluctant Modernism of Hannah Arendt* (London: Rowman & Littlefield, 1996), 188–91.

78. Arendt, *Lectures of Kant's Political Philosophy*, 76. Arendt also discusses in this lecture the role of exemplarity in Kant's aesthetics, but here I want to stick to the role of the regulative ideals of *sensus communis* and "purposiveness" for the making of reflecting judgments.

79. Paul Guyer, "Editor's Introduction," *Critique of Judgment*, xxii (my emphasis).

80. Maurizio Passerin D'Entrèves, "Arendt's Theory of Judgment," in *Cambridge Companion to Hannah Arendt*, ed. Dana Villa (New York: Cambridge University Press, 2000), 250.

81. Ernst Cassirer, *Kant's Life and Thought*, trans. James Haden (New Haven: Yale University Press, 1981), 307.

82. James, *Literary Criticism*, 2:1310.

83. Beatrice Longuenesse, *Kant and the Capacity to Judge*, trans. Charles T. Wolfe (Princeton: Princeton University Press, 1998), 163. Longuenesse is concerned to show that reflective judgments are not confined to the Third Critique, but in fact make the determinative judgments, which are the focus of the First Critique, possible. See her *Kant and the Capacity to Judge*, 164.

84. James, *The Ambassadors*, 302–3.

85. Ibid., 303.

86. Ibid., 305.

87. Ibid., 310.

88. Ibid. In the preface he added to *The Ambassadors*, James called this process a "drama of discrimination." James, *Literary Criticism*, 2:1309.

89. James, *The Ambassadors*, 310.

90. Ibid., 18.

91. Pippin, *Henry James and Modern Moral Life*, 160.

92. James, *The Ambassadors*, 312.

93. Ibid.

94. Ibid.

95. Ibid., 125.

96. We are reminded here of Melville's imagining a similar "cosmopolitan" tension when Ishmael, upon deciding whether or not he ought to share a bed with Queequeg at the Spouter Inn, says that it is "better to sleep with a sober cannibal than a drunken Christian" (Herman Melville, *Moby-Dick, Or The Whale, The Northwestern-Newberry Edition*, ed. Harrison Hayford, Hershel Parker, G. Thomas Tanselle (Evanston, Ill.: Northwestern University Press, 1988), 24.

97. James, *The Ambassadors*, 245.

98. Ibid., 247.

99. Ibid.
100. Ibid., 259
101. Ibid.
102. Ibid., 301.
103. Ibid.
104. Ibid., 334.
105. Sounding a little like Santayana, Leon Edel says that in *The Ambassadors* James "dissects America and Europe and re-imagines his international myth . . . the ex-ambassador learns how to relax his moral and intellectual bondage. He will return to Woollett with a recognition that if Europe is amoral (by Woollett standards) it offers him beautiful illusions of freedom. He can live by his illusions—if he remains open to experience and doesn't require life to measure up to the Woollett yardstick." Leon Edel, *Henry James: A Life* (New York: Harper & Row, 1985), 536. All of this Edel says is indissociable from the "resourceful experiments" of the late style, such that *The Ambassadors'* complex style was fashioned from "mobile angles of vision" and that the novel is one of the most overtly "composed" and as such "spoke to the central myth of James's life"—that of the choice to live either in Europe or the United States. Edel, *Henry James: A Life*, 537.

CHAPTER 5

1. William James, "Address at the Centenary of Ralph Waldo Emerson, May 25, 1903," in *Writings, 1902–1910* (New York: Library of America, 1987), 1120.
2. Ibid., 1120.
3. Henry James, *Literary Criticism: European Writers, Prefaces*, ed. Leon Edel and Mark Wilson, vol. 2 (New York: Library of America, 1984), 1332.
4. Ibid., 2:1332.

INDEX

Cascardi, Anthony, 125n17

Cassin, Barbara, 126n37

Cassirer, Ernst, 167n77

Cavell, Stanley, 3–8, 10–14, 32, 39, 124n8,
    124n13, 125nn17–18, 125n22,
    126n35, 127n42, 130nn57–59,
    131n72, 141n107, 151n64

Chalmers, David, 140n95

chess
    as criterion for thinking, 43–45, 46, 47,
        48–49, 51, 54, 55, 64, 143n3
    as played by a machine, 2, 15, 42–45,
        51, 61, 62–64, 93, 121, 143nn2–3,
        146nn12–13
    as rule-bound, 49, 62–64

Chorley, Henry Fothergill, 155n13

Christensen, Jerome, 134n17

Clark, James Freeman, 136n43

Cohen, Thomas, 151n71

Coleridge, Samuel Taylor, 17–22, 25, 29,
    31, 133nn14–15, 134n17, 134n19,
    134n22, 134nn24–26, 156n20

compatibilism, 15, 16, 33–36, 37, 38, 39,
    120–21, 140n95, 141n106

composition
    as algorithm, 15, 62–63, 64, 150n50,
        153n89
    as experience, 1–2, 7, 13, 23, 24, 26, 27,
        29, 31, 38, 124n5
    as experiment, 7–8, 10–13, 15, 22–23,
        25, 63–64, 70, 124n5, 126n35,
        127n43, 153n89
    as "history of an effect of experience"
        (James), 1–2, 14, 92–93, 129n53
    as justification, 11, 54, 130n57
    as method, 6–7, 14, 15, 25, 27, 29, 32, 33,
        39, 127n43, 138n67, 142nn118–19,
        162n12
    as revision, 1, 13, 92–93, 122, 135n29
    as stepwise, 6, 20, 22, 26, 59–63,
        142n122, 153n89
    as succession, 6

Conant, James, 132n75, 148n28

Constantinesco, Thomas, 138n74

Cooke, Philip Pendleton, 143n4

Copeland, Jack, 148n29

cosmopolitanism, 16, 94–95, 110–16, 119,
    121–22, 166n69, 166n72, 167n96

Cousin, Victor, 28

Crane, Gregg, 110, 112, 166n72

cryptography, 54, 122, 149n37

Curley, Edwin, 138n67

Cuvier, Baron (Georges), 2–3, 15, 21–22,
    29, 31, 53, 54, 93, 121, 134n26,
    150n62, 158n33

Darwin, Charles, 9, 127n44, 129n53,
    134n26, 163n23, 163n25

Davis, Martin, 145n10

Davis, Theo, 132n73, 161n89

Day, William, 125n18

Deep Blue, 146n13

Defosse, Marcel (Denis Marion), 145n11

Delbanco, Andrew, 158n36

Deledalle, Gerard, 125n28

Deleuze, Gilles, 165n45

de Man, Paul, 156n20, 158n43

Deming, Richard, 124n5, 124n8

Dennett, Daniel, 144n6

De Quincey, Thomas, 69, 70, 84, 157nn30–
    31

Descartes, Rene, 93, 100, 164n35

Descombes, Vincent, 164n39

determinism, 33–34, 40, 46, 47, 48, 49,
    64, 140n95, 141n106, 145n11,
    148nn29–30

Dewey, John, 2, 6–9, 10, 13–14, 125n28,
    126n31, 126n37, 127nn41–44,
    128n48, 129n53, 132n73

Dickinson, Emily, 11, 124n5

Doyle, Sir Conan, 143n4

Dreyfus, Hubert, 144n6

Du Bois, W. E. B., 166n69

Duquette, Elizabeth, 158n45

Duyckinck, Evert, 3, 15, 65–69, 70, 71, 73,
    74, 77, 78, 79, 80, 81, 83, 84, 87, 89,
    93, 121, 154nn3–4, 155nn11–12,
    155n16, 157n29, 157n31, 159n53,
    160n73, 160nn76–77

Duyckinck, George, 80, 160n73

Dyson, George, 148n29

Eco, Umberto, 143n4, 148n33

Edel, Leon, 165n47, 168n105

Edwards, Jonathan, 18, 131n70

Eldridge, Richard, 125n18

Eliot, T. S., 152n81

Emerson, Edward Waldo, 21, 138n79

Emerson, Ralph Waldo
    "Address to the Citizens of Concord on
        the Fugitive Slave Law," 141n115
    "The American Scholar," 25, 31, 136n44